China-ASEAN Tourism Education and
Talent Cultivation Report 2019

中国—东盟
旅游教育与人才培养研究报告
2019

徐红罡　张朝枝　高　俊 ◎ 编

中山大学出版社
·广州·

版权所有　翻印必究

图书在版编目（CIP）数据

中国—东盟旅游教育与人才培养研究报告.2019：中文、英文/徐红罡，张朝枝，高俊编.—广州：中山大学出版社，2022.12
ISBN 978-7-306-07694-6

Ⅰ.①中… Ⅱ.①徐… ②张… ③高… Ⅲ.①高等教育—旅游教育—国际合作—人才培养—研究报告—中国、东南亚国家联盟-2019-汉、英 Ⅳ.①F590

中国版本图书馆 CIP 数据核字（2022）第 254536 号

ZHONGGUO – DONGMENG LÜYOU YU RENCAI PEIYANG YANJIU BAOGAO 2019

出版人：王天琪
策划编辑：张　蕊
责任编辑：张　蕊
封面设计：曾　斌
责任校对：邱紫研
责任技编：靳晓虹
出版发行：中山大学出版社
电　　话：编辑部 020-84110283，84113349，84111997，84110779，84110776
　　　　　发行部 020-84111998，84111981，84111160
地　　址：广州市新港西路135号
邮　　编：510275　　传　真：020-84036565
网　　址：http://www.zsup.com.cn　E-mail：zdcbs@mail.sysu.edu.cn
印 刷 者：广州方迪数字印刷有限公司
规　　格：787mm×1092mm　1/16　17印张　315千字
版次印次：2022年12月第1版　2022年12月第1次印刷
定　　价：52.00元

如发现本书因印装质量影响阅读，请与出版社发行部联系调换

中国与东盟旅游教育与研究（序）

中国与东南亚国家联盟（简称东盟）一直保持着友好关系。中国与东盟在1991年正式开启对话，2003年建立战略伙伴关系。中国与东盟在政治、经济、文化以及国际多边舞台上进行了密切的合作，取得了令人瞩目的成就。2018年，中国—东盟共同发表了《中国—东盟战略伙伴关系2030年愿景》，旅游和高等教育都是其中的重点：在经济合作领域提出了建立正式的高级别合作机制，加强、深化和拓展双方旅游合作；在社会文化合作领域提出了加强教育创新和学术交流。

教育一直是中国与东盟的合作重点，迄今为止出台了多个促进合作交流的政策，也建立起多层次的合作机制。中国与东盟组织制定了多个合作政策，例如，《中国—东盟全面经济合作框架协议》（2002年）、《中国—东盟面向和平与繁荣的战略伙伴关系联合宣言》（2003年）、《中华人民共和国政府与东南亚国家联盟成员国政府文化合作谅解备忘录》（2005年）、《落实中国—东盟面向和平与繁荣的战略伙伴关系联合宣言的行动计划（2016—2020）》（2016年）等，这些合作协议涉及人力资源开发、相互派遣留学生、开设学校或教育培训机构等高等教育合作政策。中国也分别与东盟各国签署了相关的教育合作协议。例如，与马来西亚、老挝、文莱、柬埔寨、泰国等国签署了教育交流与合作协议，对双方教育合作事宜进行了规约；与泰国等国签署了学历和学位互认协议，制定了招收外籍留学生及跨境学生奖学金的政策。

与此同时，中国与东盟也搭建了教育合作与沟通的相关机制。一是举办年度领导人会议机制，与高等教育直接相关的人力资源开发是"10+1"[①]确定的五大重点合作领域之一。二是召集直接涉及教育领域的年度部长级会议机制。三是召开工作层对话会议机制，主要涉及中国—东盟高官磋商、中国—东盟联合合作委员会、中国—东盟科技联委会等五大平行对话合作机制。

中国和东盟国家的旅游资源丰富，旅游产品互补性强，空间距离短，互为重要的客源地和旅游目的地。中国是东盟第一大旅游客源国，2018年我国的主要客源市场前17位的国家中，7个为东盟国家。与此同时，中国与东盟国家搭建了旅游"10+1旅游部长会议"对话机制，未来关于旅游的交流的空间

[①] "10+1"指东盟10国与中国领导人举行的会议。

会更广、更深。

中国和东盟各国在旅游教育和研究上也离不开彼此。中国和东盟各国面临的主要问题依然是可持续发展问题，旅游是可持续发展的重要途径。中国和东盟各国在利用旅游促进可持续发展方面积累了许多宝贵的经验。旅游业是中国和大部分东盟国家重要的支柱产业，也是一些国家外汇收入的主要来源；旅游业是解决就业的重要渠道；旅游业在消减贫困、促进乡村发展方面起着重要的作用；旅游业也是中国、东盟各国文化遗产保护和利用的重要手段。但是，旅游业在中国和东盟各国可持续发展中的作用还没有得到充分的发挥，还有许多相似的难题，中国和东盟各国共同研究可以加快找到解决问题的对策；同时，各国旅游业的发展阶段不同，相互交流可以帮助后续发展的国家和地区少走弯路。

虽然中国和东盟关于旅游业的交流量较大，但是对跨境旅游合作人才供给与研究的交流相对较少。虽然东盟各国都较为重视旅游高等教育，中国与东盟均有一批业务能力强、综合素质高的旅游教育和研究人才，但是，中国与东盟国家在跨境旅游专业人才供求和研究积累方面存在信息不对称的问题。中国—东盟旅游教育专业结构、研究与跨境旅游产业发展相脱节，难以满足跨境旅游合作发展的需要。双方应加大人才交流合作力度，相互取长补短，为旅游可持续发展提供更多的人才供给和研究成果。

2019年，在中山大学"一带一路"研究院的资助下，中山大学旅游学院承办了中国—东盟旅游研究与人才培养国际会议，中国及泰国、新加坡、菲律宾、越南、印度尼西亚、柬埔寨、老挝、缅甸等东盟8个国家16所高校的专家学者们参加了会议并发言。本次会议达成了中国—东盟旅游研究与教育合作的共识，中国与东盟高校间的合作将会朝着深入化、密切化、常态化的方向发展。会后，本书编者将13份演讲稿整理成文，汇集成书，希望更多的国内外学者参与到中国—东盟人才培养和研究网络中。

本书的出版，感谢谢书悦、肖学宏、曹荣培、钟小凤、杨雪珂等在翻译和转录中的付出。

徐红罡
2020年5月

Tourism Education and Research in China and ASEAN (Preface)

China and Association of Southeast Asian Nations (ASEAN) have always maintained friendly relations. In 1991, China and ASEAN formally established an official relationship and further established a strategic partnership in 2003. China and ASEAN have carried out close cooperation in political, economic, cultural and international multilateral arenas, and have made remarkable achievements. In 2018, China-ASEAN jointly published the 'China-ASEAN Strategic Partnership Vision 2030', in which both tourism and higher education are the focus. In the field of economic cooperation, it is proposed to establish a formal high-level cooperation mechanism to strengthen, deepen and expand the tourism cooperation between the two sides; in the field of social and cultural cooperation, it is proposed to strengthen educational innovation and academic exchanges.

Education has always been the focus of cooperation between China and ASEAN. To date, several policies have been issued to promote cooperation and exchanges, and a multi-level cooperation mechanism has also been established. China and ASEAN have formulated several special education cooperation policies. For instance, 'Framework Agreement on Comprehensive Economic Cooperation between the People's Republic of China and the Association of Southeast Asian Nations' (2002), 'Joint Declaration on Strategic Partnership for Peace and Prosperity between China and ASEAN' (2003), 'Memorandum of Understanding between the Government of China and the Association of Southeast Asian Nations on Cultural Cooperation' (2005), 'Plan of Action to Implement the Joint Declaration on China-ASEAN Strategic Partnership for Peace and Prosperity (2016 – 2020)' (2016), etc. These cooperation agreements all involve human resources development, mutual sending of foreign students, the establishment of schools or educational training institutions and other higher education cooperation policies. China has also issued relevant educational cooperation agreements with ASEAN countries. For example, China has signed educational exchange and cooperation agreements with Malaysia, Laos, Brunei, Cambodia, Thailand, etc., and regulated the educational cooperation between the two sides. China has also carried out mutual recognition policies for academic qualifications and degrees with Thailand and other countries, formulated policies for recruiting foreign students, and established a scholarship policy for cross-border students.

At the same time, China and ASEAN have also established relevant mechanisms for educational cooperation and communication. Firstly, hold an annual leader meeting mechanism, as human resource development related to higher education is one of the five key cooperation areas identified by '10 + 1'. Secondly, convene an annual ministerial meeting mechanism related to education. Thirdly, hold a working meeting dialogue mechanism. It mainly involves China-ASEAN Senior Officials' Consultation, China-ASEAN Joint Cooperation Committee, China-ASEAN Science and Technology Joint Committee, etc.

China and ASEAN have rich tourism resources, strong complementarity of tourism products, and short spacial distance. China-ASEAN countries are important tourist destinations for each other. China is the largest source market for ASEAN countries. According to the Ministry of Culture and Tourism in China, among the top 17 source markets, seven are ASEAN countries in 2018. At the same time, China and ASEAN countries have established a '10 + 1 Tourism Ministers Meeting' dialogue mechanism. The space for tourism exchange will be wider and deeper in the future.

China and ASEAN countries are also inseparable from each other in tourism education and research. The main problem facing China and ASEAN countries is still the issue of sustainable development. Tourism is an important way for sustainable development. China and ASEAN countries have also accumulated many valuable experiences. Tourism is an important pillar industry for China and most ASEAN countries, and it is also the main source of foreign exchange income in some countries. Tourism is an important channel to solve employment problems and plays an important role in poverty reduction and rural development. It is also an important means for the protection and utilization of cultural heritage in China and ASEAN countries. However, the role of tourism in sustainable development has not yet been fully exerted, and there are many similar problems. Joint research can speed up finding solutions. Furthermore, the development stages of tourism in different countries are different. With more frequent communication, countries and regions that follow up can avoid detours.

Despite the large amount of tourism exchanges between China and ASEAN, cross-border tourism cooperation, talent supply and research cannot meet the demand. Currently, China and ASEAN countries have incomplete and asymmetric information on the supply and demand of cross-border tourism professionals. The professional structure of China-ASEAN tourism education is divorced from the development of the cross-border tourism industry, and it is difficult to meet the needs of cross-border tourism cooperation and development.

ASEAN countries all pay attention to tourism higher education. Both China and ASEAN have a group of tourism management talents with strong abilities and high comprehensive qualities. Both sides should strengthen the exchange and cooperation of talents, learn from each other's strengths, and provide more talents and research outputs for the sustainable development of tourism.

In 2019, funded by the Belt and Road Research Institute of Sun Yat-sen University, the School of Tourism of Sun Yat-sen University undertook the China-ASEAN Tourism Research and Talent Training International Conference. Experts and scholars from 16 colleges and universities in China and eight ASEAN countries including Thailand, Singapore, the Philippines, Vietnam, Indonesia, Cambodia, Laos and Myanmar participated in the meeting and made speeches. This meeting reached a consensus on China-ASEAN tourism research and education cooperation. The cooperation between China and ASEAN universities will develop in an in-depth, intensified, and normalized direction. After the meeting, the 13 authors of this book rewrite their speeches into articles, hoping that more domestic and foreign scholars would participate in the China-ASEAN talent training and research network.

Special thanks are given to Xie Shuyue, Xiao Xuehong, Cao Rongpei, Zhong Xiaofeng, Yang Xueke, et al. in their translation and transcription work.

Xu Honggang
May 2020

目 录

批判性旅游研究及其对亚洲旅游教学、学习和研究的启示 …………… 1
Critical Tourism Studies and Implications for Teaching,
    Learning and Research in Asia ……………………………………… 7

中国旅游教育 …………………………………………………………………… 15
Tourism Education in China ………………………………………………… 23

马来西亚旅游教育：基于个人的反思 ………………………………………… 35
Tourism Education in Malaysia: A Personal Reflection ………………… 42

缅甸旅游教育 …………………………………………………………………… 53
Tourism Education in Myanmar …………………………………………… 56

遗产旅游：越南近期研究和教育回顾 ………………………………………… 60
Heritage Tourism: A Review of Recent Research and
    Education in Vietnam ……………………………………………………… 68

菲律宾旅游和酒店教育：挑战与机遇 ………………………………………… 81
The Philippine Tourism and Hospitality Management
    Education: Challenges and Opportunities …………………………… 88

菲律宾旅游和酒店教育：基于能力的培养模式 ……………………………… 97
Tourism and Hospitality Education in the Philippines:
    A Competency-Based Approach ………………………………………… 110

泰国私立大学旅游和酒店教育 ………………………………………………… 129

Hospitality and Tourism Education from a Private
　　University in Thailand ……………………………………………… 133

泰国清迈大学旅游研究……………………………………………………… 138
Chiang Mai University Tourism Research ……………………………… 155

泰国旅游教育的单一化发展………………………………………………… 177
The Unvaried Growth of Tourism Education in Thailand …………… 184

旅游研究转变及其对泰国旅游教育的影响………………………………… 194
Dynamic Movements of Tourism Research and Its Impacts
　　to Tourism Education in Thailand ………………………………… 199

手工艺对旅游扶贫的直接和间接影响：对越南承天顺化省案例的研究…… 206
Pro-poor Direct and Indirect Impacts of Handicraft-Based
　　Tourism：The Case of Thua Thien Hue Province, Vietnam ……… 219

印度尼西亚巴厘岛旅游专业人才培养……………………………………… 238
Preparing Scientific-Based Professionals in Tourism for Bali Indonesia
　　………………………………………………………………………… 241

粤港澳暨东盟旅游研究与教育论坛宣言…………………………………… 246
Declaration of the Tourism Research and Education Forum of
　　Guangdong-Hong Kong-Macau and ASEAN ……………………… 247

批判性旅游研究及其对亚洲旅游教学、学习和研究的启示

T. C. Chang　新加坡国立大学地理学系

1　介绍

本文将聚焦批判性旅游研究（critical tourism studies，CTS）及其对亚洲旅游教学、学习和研究的启示。批判性旅游研究可以被定义为聚焦批判性方法、视角和目标的旅游研究；该研究还特别关注批判性旅游研究对批判性教育学（研究教学实践的一个学科）的启发。随着越来越多的高等院校将旅游列为一门学科（尤其是在亚洲），重视批判性的教学并讨论如何以批判性的视角进行教育、学习和研究是极为重要的。本文涵盖三个部分：首先，我将简要地解释何为批判性旅游研究以及怎样理解其中的"批判"一词；接着我将讨论批判性旅游研究对旅游教学、学习和研究三个方面的启示；在结尾部分，考虑到亚洲批判性旅游研究的未来，我将概述一些批判性旅游教学面临的挑战。

2　何为批判性旅游研究

在批判性旅游研究这个术语被广泛运用之前，对批判性研究的最基本理解是"仔细观察某些事物，通过调查发现错误"。最早的批判性旅游研究来源于20世纪80年代非政府组织（non-governmental organizations，NGOs）对目的地社区发展经历的研究，其强调旅游业对当地社区产生的负面影响（Higgins-Desbiolles，Whyte，2013）。一些非政府组织，例如，夏威夷普世联盟（Hawaii Ecumenical Coalition）、旅游普世联盟（Ecumenical Coalition on Tourism，总部位于曼谷）和EQUATIONS（位于印度），出版了一些教材而非学术研究报告。例如，夏威夷普世联盟的《岛民眼中的太平洋旅游业》（*Pacific Tourism as Islanders See It*，1980），该书立足于"当地社区的视角和发展经历，而非外部客位视角"（Higgins-Desbiolles，Whyte，2013）。因此，批判性视角的根源在于"行动主义"和社区，源于"受到各种形式的旅游活动负面影响的社区居民和试图代表他们的非政府组织"（Higgins-Desbiolles，Whyte，2013）。

除了关注对社会有批判性价值的话题、审慎地调查和寻找错误，近来旅游业研究者采用批判性视角试图挑战产生于西方的理论，追问旅游知识源于何处以及如何产生（即对旅游认识论的关注）。20世纪90年代后期，在东欧举办的两年一度的会议认为，旅游研究应倡导以人本主义价值为导向的研究视角。正是由于认识到"本土知识的力量"（Pritchard，Morgan，and Ateljevic，2011），批判性旅游研究力求"在研究者和旅游利益相关者之间保持公正的关系"，并且通过参与式的研究方法使研究人员更具有反思性和文化敏感性（Higgins-Desbiolles and Whyte，2014）。2005年于杜布罗夫尼克举办的第一届批判性旅游会议以及发表于2007年的文章中，联合举办方与编辑Ateljevic、Pritchard和Morgan（2007）提出，批判性旅游研究的目标是"挑战旅游研究中的主导话语体系"。这种主导话语体系建立在"基于男性传统的西方思想"之上。

简而言之，批判性旅游研究是对"权力"的批评——谁拥有权力，如何使用权力以及如何争取权力。这里的权力既指"现实"世界的政府（政治）和商业（经济学），同时也包括出版和知识生产的"研究"领域（学术界）。在这两种情况下，批判性旅游研究的作用都是探究谁在旅游业发展中行使了权力。例如，是国企还是跨国公司，是当地社区还是非政府组织？谁在创造旅游知识？是发达国家的作家和出版机构创造的吗？那与发展中国家相关的旅游知识又是由谁创造和出版的呢？因此，批判性旅游研究力图"揭示谁的利益被满足了、权力在被谁运用以及意识形态对研究情境和研究本身的影响"（Tribe，2007）。关注旅游中的关键问题，并探究批判性旅游研究如何启发和影响我们在授课、学习和研究中的实践。

3 批判性旅游研究对旅游教学、学习和研究的启示

在考虑批判性旅游研究对教育领域的启示时，我们必须思考"批判性旅游教学法"意味着什么。这种教学法是指批判地进行旅游教学、旅游学习和旅游研究的方法和实践。这里强调三种具体的教学方式：支架式教学、体验式学习和合作研究。

3.1 支架式教学

在教学方面，"支架"是指为学生提供支持和帮助，使学生达到原本难以达到的水平。在讨论"支架式教学"（或者说教学中的支架）时，我认为应重视不同旅游教育层次的旅游课程设计和教学方法。索菲尔德（Sofield，2000）

提出的"旅游研究的四个平台"应用于教学时很有用,这四个平台是支持、警示、适应和基于知识。

索菲尔德(Sofield,2000)解释,第一,"支持"是指研究应当强调和支持旅游业的经济和社会文化价值。在教学方面,尤其是对处于低年级水平的学生(即本科一年级或二年级的学生),需要强调旅游业的积极影响以及旅游业发展如何使当地居民获得收益。第二,"警示"是指预警旅游业发展会带来的消极影响。在对低年级的学生进行教学时,不仅要强调旅游业的积极影响与益处,还应帮助学生意识到旅游业可能带来的消极影响。正确地理解正面和负面影响能让学习者对当代社会旅游业有更为整体的认识。第三,"适应"是指学习如何根据当地环境和需求对旅游业进行调整和改进。这是向较高年级的学生传授旅游发展过程中的旅游可持续性和赋权问题,让学生认识到并不存在对所有旅游目的地都适用的唯一的"旅游解决方案"或者发展路径,因此保持地理上的敏感性并使旅游发展适应当地环境和社会是十分必要的。第四,"基于知识"是指研究和传授旅游知识。这里特别强调的是旅游认识论(了解旅游知识在何处产生和如何被建构,以及旅游中知识产生和传播过程中的政治关系)。因此,较高年级的学生在教学中应该了解旅游认识论和旅游知识生产的政治。正如 Teo(2009)所说,在亚洲旅游的情境中(不论是在研究还是教学中),都应该更注重"谁"生产知识以及"如何"生产知识,而不是只关注知识"是什么"的问题。对于亚洲的学生,我们需要明确辨别在旅游理论中的"殖民"传统或者说西方主导的传统路径,并进一步使旅游研究向情境化或者更具亚洲特色的路径发展。这一转变对教学工作者如何实现具有自身特色的课程设计和教学目标,以及学术研究者如何进行研究和发表成果具有很重要的现实意义。

3.2 体验式学习

体验式学习方法是让学生获得工作经验并促使他们在工作反思中变得具有批判精神。书本知识通常是在课堂上习得的,工作经验则给学生提供了接触真实世界的机会。但是,必须引导学生对他们的工作经验进行批判性的思考,以对在课堂上学习的知识和学术界现有的知识进行补充(在某些情况下,也需要反驳)。

Fullager 和 Wilson(2012)强调了利用学生的个人经验来学习有关旅游管理概念的重要性。他们重点介绍了一个大学生在香港的酒店实习并利用工作经验建构了可能在课堂上未曾讲授的旅游领导力模型的案例。与其向亚洲学生讲解西方领导力的概念,不如让学生自己解构他们对领导力的假设,并根据个人的、基层的经验重新建构模型。要鼓励学生们分享自己的实践经验,尤其是他们观察到的"日常生活中的权力关系"以及旅游工作场所有效和低效的领导力的事例(Fullagar and Wilson,2012)。采用基于个人经验而不是从其他地方引入概念的、具有批判性反思特质的教学方法,对于教育者和学习者双方都是有益的。

越来越多的人强调,需要从以往职业化或技能化的实习转向能让学生习得和理解的"软技能"实践。这种软实力和无形的技能包括创造力、领导力、同理心、责任感和沟通能力(Liu and Schänzel,2019)。亚洲的旅游教育必须着眼于帮助学生掌握这些在颠覆性经济环境和"VUCA"[①] 世界中极为重要的技能。

新加坡国立大学通过学校、学院、系三个层级给学生提供实习机会。学校一级创建了一个人才链接(Talent Connect)门户网站(请参阅:https://nus-csm.symplicity.com/)来帮助学生寻找实习机会。由于这个门户网站是面向全校学生的,因而尽管每年有大量的实习机会,但每个岗位的竞争非常激烈。在学院一级,不同的学院会专门根据该院学生的需求提供实习岗位。例如,在人文与社会科学学院(Faculty of Arts & Social Sciences,FASS),学生们可以申请参加与他们的主修专业(如地理学、经济学和社会学)相关的实习。自2019年8月起,人文与社会科学学院还启动了一项叫作 FASS 2.0 的新认证。这个项目规定,如果学生有两次实习经历并修满三门相关课程,就可以获得相关行业的证明。该认证体系旨在帮助学生为求职做更充分的准备,以更好地适应行业需求。(请参阅:https://www.fass.nus.edu.sg)系一级会为学生提供针对其专业训练和学科知识的实习列表。例如,地理系就提供了在博物馆、圣淘沙(Sentosa,新加坡的一个度假旅游岛)、规划机构、环境类非政府组织的实习机会。不管通过何种方式取得实习机会,重要的是学生们不只获得了实践经验,还能习得可以伴随他们一生的重要技能。之前提到的软实力、批判性思维与反思能力对于任何一个称职和自省的员工都是必不可少的。大学的课程设置如何让学生具备这些重要技能还需要进一步的研究。

3.3 合作研究

21世纪以来,由西方导师和他们的亚裔学生合作完成的旅游研究方面的出版物数量不断增加(Huang,van der Veen,and Zhang,2014)。随着越来越

[①] VUCA 指 volatile(不稳定的)、unpredictable(不可预测的)、complex(复杂的)、ambiguous(不明确的)。

多的亚洲学生攻读旅游相关专业研究生，批判性旅游教学法也同样在这种导师—学生的合作中显现。在中国旅游教育环境中，Huang 等（2014）注意到亚洲与西方合作的文章不断发表。这里着重介绍两种与教学法有关的合作关系。第一种是"中国学生和西方导师的二元关系"，其中，共同学习和合作产出知识形成了"跨文化语境下的对话与阐释"（Huang, van der Veen, and Zhang, 2014）。第二种则是中国学生在西方大学接受学术训练，然后带着后实证主义、民族志研究方法以及对社会热点的关心回到祖国。如果在西方世界获得的方法和经验能结合当地的教育需求和社会现实，那么第二种关系则尤其有益。

总而言之，要使亚洲旅游研究具有批判性，就需要批判性的教学方法。这种教学方法源自对旅游业的问题与可能的思辨性的教授（教学内容），也同样来源于知识创造与传播的政治研究（思想争鸣）。批判性教学法不应该局限于课堂中，很多学习机会来源课堂之外的活动和实践，将之与反思个人经历相结合才是更好的习得知识的途径。批判性的教学法也不应仅仅局限于本科生，因为通过合作共同创造知识的方式同样适用于研究生，其可使学生和导师双方都受益。

4 批判性旅游教学法在亚洲面临的挑战

让我们反思一下在亚洲推广批判性旅游研究所面临的一些内在挑战。由于批判性旅游研究需要质疑权威和现状，要连根拔起某些根深蒂固的地位必然会遇到困难。正如 Pritchard 和 Morgan（2007）所说，要创造"更适宜的旅游知识世界"和新的知识，"我们必须学习非洲、亚洲以及世界各地的原住民的各种日常的知识传统"。整合来自亚洲的见解可以使人们对旅游现象和影响有更深刻的理解，但是直到更多的亚洲研究者以批判性转向的视角发声和写作，并且"其他"研究者能接受和认可亚洲研究者的观点作为主流（相对于边缘）观点之前，这个目标将很难实现。

批判性旅游研究旨在解构权力并引发社会改变。亚洲的"行动主义"研究可能被视为一种形式的批判性话语。在大多数亚洲国家被定义为"发展中国家"的情况下，亚洲旅游研究能为识别旅游业中的弊端、展现旅游业主体的社会关怀和责任等做出重大贡献。凭借大量的有道德和负责任的旅游实践以及倡导地方社区权利和社会变革（UNWTO, 2011），亚洲旅游研究能够帮助记录、批判和实现批判性学术思潮的目标。当然，这需要确保亚洲旅游研究能够推进赋权，回应"谁创造了知识"以及"如何创造知识"等问题。目前，对于非批判性的经验议题（回答"是什么"的知识）已经有了丰富的研究成果。研究人员在何种程度上准备好了抛弃一般化的研究，转向以更批判的、基于知识的方式进行研究是一个很难提出或回答的问题。

旅游的世界永远是由规划师、从业者和市场营销者来创造、改变以及再造的。在学术领域，我们也许还可以加上研究者和教育者，因为他们同样是"创造和改变"旅游知识世界，将其变成文章或话语的人。进入21世纪以来，学者们开始更多地对抗"以欧洲为中心的世界观"和设计新的"从不同的多个立场的阐释"（Hollinshead，2007）。改变主流观点并用新的视角重塑它是亚洲批判性旅游研究者们力图实现的。但是，目前的改变并不一定要抛弃过去的研究成果，而是通过修正传承下来的概念和视角来重塑它。只有接纳关于人、地方和"（旧有的）他者"观点，才可能创造一个后殖民、后工业、后西方的旅游世界。

Critical Tourism Studies and Implications for Teaching, Learning and Research in Asia

T. C. Chang, Department of Geography, National University of Singapore

1 Introduction

This presentation will focus on critical tourism studies (CTS) and its implications for teaching, learning and research in Asia. CTS may be defined as the field of tourism research specially focused on critical methods, perspectives, goals. Of particular concern in this presentation is CTS's implications for critical pedagogy which is the practice of teaching and learning as an academic subject. As more schools and universities cover tourism as a discipline (particularly in Asia), it is important to highlight critical pedagogical concerns and discuss how we should be teaching, learning and researching in a critical manner. This presentation covers three sections. First of all, I will explain briefly what CTS entails and what it means to be 'critical'. This is followed by discussing the three-fold implications of CTS for teaching, learning and Research. In the Conclusion, some of the challenges in critical tourism pedagogy are outlined as we consider the future of CTS in Asia.

2 What is Critical Tourism Studies?

Before the term CTS came into popular usage in the 2000s, the most fundamental understanding of critical research was to scrutinise something carefully and to uncover faults through enquiry. The earliest critical tourism research emerged from Non-Government Organisations (NGOs) in the 1980s voicing the experiences of local communities and critiquing tourism's impacts on them (Higgins-Desbiolles and Whyte, 2014). NGOs like Hawai'i Ecumenical Coalition, the Ecumenical Coalition on Tourism (based in Bangkok) and EQUATIONS (India) produced educational materials rather than academic research, an example being the Hawaii Ecumenical Coalition's *Pacific Tourism as Islanders See It* (1980) which focused on the 'experiences and viewpoint from the inside looking out rather than the other way around' (Higgins-Desbiolles and Whyte, 2014). The roots of critical perspectives are therefore 'activistic' and community-based, emerging from 'people who have been harmed by various forms of tourism and the NGOs that have sought to represent them' (Higgins-Desbiolles and Whyte, 2014).

Beyond the examining topics of critical value to society and scrutinising facts and looking for faults, more recent understandings of critical approaches focus on tourism studies that challenge theoretical approaches from West, asking where/how tourism knowledge is derived (i. e. concerns about tourism epistemologies). In the late 1990s, a series of biennial conferences in Eastern Europe and publications saw tourism studies aspiring to values-led, humanist research approaches. Recognising the 'power of sacred and indigenous knowledge' (Pritchard, Morgan and Ateljevic, 2011), critical research strove for 'just relations between researchers and tourism stakeholders' and participatory methodologies as a way for the researcher to be more reflexive and culturally sensitive (Higgins-Desbiolles and Whyte, 2014). At the first Critical Tourism conference in Dubrovnik in 2005 and in its subsequent publication in 2007, co-organisers/editors Ateljevic, Pritchard and Morgan (2007) expressed CTS' goal to 'challenge the field's dominant discourse' which has traditionally been founded on 'masculine tradition of western thought'.

In brief, CTS is basically a critique on 'power'—who has it, how is it used, and how to reclaim it. Power here refers to both the 'real' world of government (politics) and commerce (economics), as well as within the 'research' realm of publication and knowledge creation (academia). In both instances, CTS' role is to ask questions on who wields the power in tourism development (e. g. is it the state or transnational corporations, or is it the local community or non-government organisations?) and also tourism knowledge creation (e. g. is it writers and publication outlets in the Global North? What about researchers and publications in the Global South, especially as it pertains to tourism knowledge in the developing world?). The goal of critical tourism perspectives thus seeks to 'expose whose interest are served and the exercise of power and the influence of ideology in the research situation and the research itself' (Tribe, 2007). Asking critical questions on tourism and in this particular case, probing how CTS implicates and impinges on pedagogical practices in teaching and learning.

3 CTS' Implications for Teaching, Learning and Researching Tourism

In thinking through the implications of CTS in the education realm, we must consider what is meant by 'Critical Tourism Pedagogy'. Such a pedagogy refers to the method and practice of teaching, learning, researching critically about tourism. Three specific points are highlighted: (a) scaffolded teaching, (b) experiential learning, and (c) collaborative research.

3.1 Scaffolded Teaching

In the realm of teaching and learning, 'scaffold' refers to the concept of providing support or assistance in order to get students to a higher level which they otherwise cannot reach without some kind of help. In talking about 'scaffolded teaching' (or scaffolding in teaching), I highlight the value of tourism curriculum planning and teaching at different levels of an undergraduate education. Sofield's (2000) four 'Platforms of Tourism Research' are useful here when applied to teaching. He asserts that the four platform are: advocacy, cautionary, adaptancy, and knowledge-base.

By 'advocacy', Sofield (2000) explains that research should advocate for tourism's economic and social-cultural value. In the area of teaching, likewise it is important particularly at a lower-level (i.e. first or second year undergraduate) to advocate on tourism's positive impacts and how mindful tourism development can benefit people and place. Secondly, the 'cautionary' platform warns of tourism's negative consequences. In teaching tourism at the lower-level, it is important to not only emphasise the positives/benefits, but also to help students be more aware of its harmful outcomes. Understanding both the good and the bad allows learners to be holistic in their acknowledgement of tourism in contemporary society. Thirdly, 'adaptancy' refers to understanding how tourism may be adapted/modified to cater to local contexts and needs. At a higher-level of learning, this translates into teaching students about sustainability and empowerment issues in tourism development. There is no one 'tourism-solution' or development pathway for all destinations; it is thus necessary to be geographically sensitive and to adapt tourism to local environments and societies, and not the other way around.

Finally, the 'knowledge-based' platform refers to researching on and teaching about tourism knowledge. In particular, the emphasis here is on tourism epistemologies—understanding how and where tourism knowledge is constructed, and the politics of tourism knowledge creation and dissemination. At the highest-level of teaching and learning, therefore, students should be exposed to the epistemologies and politics of tourism knowledge. As Teo (2009) argues in the Asian tourism context, more attention (both in research and teaching) should be focused on 'who' and 'how' knowledge (e.g. who is creating tourism knowledge and how are they doing so), and not just on 'what' knowledge which focuses on content and empirical data. Particularly for Asian students, we need to acknowledge the tradition of 'colonial'/Western-led approaches in tourism conceptualisation, and move towards a more 'contextual'/Asia-specific approach. Such a move has very real implications for how we academic/faculty members approach our curriculum design and teaching goals, and also our research and publication process.

3.2 Experiential Learning

A critical approach to learning is getting students to gain work experience and to be critical in their work reflections. While 'book knowledge' is often acquired in the classroom, working experiences afford students real-world exposure. At the same time, however, students must also be guided to think critically about their work experiences and to co-construct knowledge that will supplement (and in some cases, refute) knowledge acquired in the classroom and extant knowledge from academia.

Fullager and Wilson (2012) have highlighted the importance of using students' personal experiences to learn more about concepts in tourism management. They highlight a case of university students interning in Hong Kong's hotels and using their work experiences to co-construct tourism leadership models that may or may not have been taught in the classroom. Instead of 'preaching' Western concepts of leadership to Asian students, a good starting point is for students to deconstruct their assumptions of leadership, and to re-construct models based on personal, grassroots experiences. Students are encouraged to share reflexively about their practicum particularly their observations of 'everyday dynamics of power' as well as effective and ineffective leadership in the tourism workplace (Fullagar and Wilson, 2012). Pedagogy employing a 'critically reflective approach' based on personal experience rather than one that exports concepts from elsewhere is rewarding for both educators and learners (Fullagar and Wilson, 2012).

Increasingly the need to move from vocational or functional internships to experiences that allow students to acquire/understand 'soft skills' has also been emphasised. Such soft-skills and intangibles include creativity, leadership, empathy, responsibility and communication (Liu and Schanzel, 2019). Tourism education in Asia must begin to look towards helping students pick up such skills that will be critical in a disruptive economy and a 'VUCA' world (volatile, unpredictable, complex, ambiguous).

At the National University of Singapore (NUS), individual departments offer students internships through three approaches—at the university, faculty, and department levels. At the university level, a Talent Connect portal (see: https://nus-csm.symplicity.com/) has been created for students to look for internship opportunities. As this portal is university-wide, a large number of internships are available each year but competition for each job-opening is also extremely stiff. At the faculty level, different schools offer their own internships that are specific to the needs/requirements of their students. At the Faculty of Arts and Social Sciences (FASS at NUS), for example, students can sign up for internships that are relevant to their major disciplines such as geography, economics and sociology. Since August 2019, the FASS has also started a new certification called FASS 2.0 in which students are expected to take on two internships as well as three modules in order to be certified in a particular 'industry track'. It is hoped this certification makes them more career-ready and industry-relevant.

Finally at the department level, different departments will offer a more curated list of internships specific to their majors' training and disciplinary knowledge. At the Geography Department for example, internships at museums, Sentosa (a tourist resort island), planning agencies and environmental NGOs have been made available in the past. Regardless of the approach/level through which internships are accessed, it is essential that students not only acquire practical work-place skills but also critical skills that will last them a life time. The soft-skills noted above as well as critical thinking and reflexivity are essential to any competent and self-aware worker. How and whether universities and programmes are equipping students with these important critical skills needs to be further researched.

3.3 Collaborative Research

Particularly since the 2000s, the increasing number of publications by Western-supervisors and their former Asian-students has been noted (Huang, van der Veen and Zhang, 2014). With more Asians pursuing graduate studies since the 2000s, critical tourism pedagogy can also manifest in student-supervisor collaborations. In the Chinese tourism context, Huang et al. (2014) note an increasing pace in Asian-Western collaborative publications. Two pedagogically inclined relationships are highlighted here, the first being the 'Chinese student – Western supervisor dyadic' in which co-learning and knowledge co-production lead to 'cross-cultural dialogues and interpretations' (Huang, van der Veen and Zhang, 2014). The second concerns Chinese students being trained in Western universities and returning to their homeland with post-positivist, ethnographic approaches and social agendas. The latter is particularly healthy if the methods and experiences acquired in the West are shared in an Asian environment that contextualizes the local educational needs and societal realities.

In summary, for Asian tourism studies to be critical, what is needed is a pedagogy born from mindful teaching about the possibilities and problems of tourism (taught content), but also the politics of knowledge creation and dissemination (thought contest). Critical pedagogy should not be confined to the classroom, and learning opportunities come from doing/being outside the classroom, and knowledge is best acquired through reflexive personal experiences. Neither should critical pedagogy be limited to undergraduates as knowledge co-production can also occur at the graduate level, benefiting both students and supervisors.

4　Challenges in Critical Tourism Pedagogy in Asia

In concluding this presentation on CTS and its pedagogical implications, let me reflect on some inherent challenges in our CTS endeavour in and for Asia. Firstly as CTS is about questioning establishment and status-quo, there are bound to be difficulties in uprooting entrenched positions. As Pritchard and Morgan (2007) aver, to 'decent [er] tourism's intellectual universe' and create new knowledge, 'we must be willing to learn from every knowledge tradition, from Africa, Asia and from indigenous peoples around the world'. Incorporating insights from Asia can make for a more robust understanding of tourism phenomena and impacts, but until more Asian researchers speak/write with a critical bent, and 'Other' researchers are able to accept/endorse their views as mainstream (as opposed to marginal), this goal will remain largely unfulfilled.

CTS is about deconstructing power and engendering social change. Asian research that is 'activistic' may be regarded as a form of critical discourse. With much of Asia designated as 'developing', Asian research can contribute critically to spotlighting areas of abuse and identifying grounds for care and responsibility. With ample empirics on ethical and responsible tourism along with a groundswell of pro-local rights and social change (e.g. UNWTO, 2011), Asian research can help to document, critique and realise the outcomes to which critical scholarship is intended. The goal, however, is to ensure that Asian tourism research serves an agenda of empowerment answering 'Who' and 'How' questions. As it stands, there is already ample research on non-critical empirical issues ('What' knowledge). How prepared are researchers in jettisoning general research for more critical, knowledge-based enquiry is a question that is not easy to ask or to answer.

The tourism world is perpetually made/un-made/re-made by planners, practitioners and marketers. In the academic arena, we might also add that researchers and teachers also 'make/un-make' the tourism knowledge world the written text or spoken word. Since the turn of millennium, writers have become particularly practiced at contesting 'Eurocentric worldmaking gazes' and devising new 'interpretations from various/significant multiple standpoints' (Hollinshead, 2007). This task of un-making dominant viewpoints and re-making them with fresh perspectives is what CTS in Asia aspires to. The task at hand, however, is not necessarily to un-make by discarding past works but to re-make through refining inherited concepts and perspectives. Only by embracing '(previously-) Other' ideas of people, places and pasts is it possible to envision a post-colonial, post-industrial, post-Occidental tourism world (Hollinshead, 2007).

References

[1] ATELJEVIC I, MORGAN N, RITCHARD A. Editor's introduction: Promoting an academy of hope in tourism enquiry [M] //The critical turn in tourism studies. Innovative research methodologies. Oxford: Elsevier, 2007.

[2] FULLAGAR S, WILSON E. Critical pedagogies: A reflexive approach to knowledge creation in tourism and hospitality studies [J]. Journal of hospitality and tourism management, 2012, 19 (1): 1-6.

[3] HIGGINS-DESBIOLLES F, WHYTE K P. No high hopes for hopeful tourism: A critical comment [J]. Annals of tourism research, 2013, (40): 428-433.

[4] HOLLINSHEAD K. 'Worldmaking' and the transformation of place and culture: The enlargement of Meethan's analysis of tourism and global change [M] //The critical turn in tourism studies. New York: Routledge, 2007.

[5] HUANG S, Van der VEEN R, ZHANG G. New era of China tourism research [J]. Journal of travel research, 2014 (10): 379-387.

[6] LIU C, SCHÄNZEL H. Introduction to tourism education and Asia [M] //Tourism education and Asia. Singapore: Springer, 2019.

[7] PRITCHARD A, MORGAN N. De-centring tourism's intellectual universe, or traversing the dialogue between change and tradition [M] //The critical turn in tourism studies. New York: Routledge, 2007.

[8] PRITCHARD A, MORGAN N, ATELJEVIC I. Hopeful tourism: A new transformative perspective [J]. Annals of tourism research, 2011, 38 (3): 941-963.

[9] SOFIELD T H. Rethinking and reconceptualizing social and cultural issues in Southeast and South Asian tourism development [M]. New York: Routledge, 2000.

[10] TEO P. Knowledge order in Asia [M] //Asia on tour. New York: Routledge, 2008.

[11] TRIBE J. Critical tourism: Rules and resistance [M] //The critical turn in tourism studies. New York: Routledge, 2007.

[12] UNWTO. Report of the seminar on tourism ethics for Asia and the Pacific: Responsible tourism and its socio-economic impact on local communities [R]. Bali: UNWTO, 2011.

中国旅游教育

罗秋菊　中山大学旅游学院

1　引言

根据国务院发布的《"十三五"旅游业发展规划》，旅游已经基本成为中国战略性支柱产业。2019年，中国国内旅游人数60.06亿人次，入出境旅游总人数3亿人次，全年实现旅游总收入6.63万亿元，旅游业对GDP的综合贡献为10.94万亿元，相当于GDP总量的11.05%。旅游直接就业2825万人，旅游直接和间接就业7987万人，占全国总就业人口的10.31%。在全行业持续、蓬勃发展的背景下，旅游业的产业结构也正由劳动密集型逐步向劳动、知识双密集型转变，产业结构的转型为旅游教育及人才培养工作提出了更高的要求。

旅游教育为中国旅游业造就了一大批优秀人才，为旅游业发展提供了强大的人才保障和智力支持，是全面提升旅游产业素质和发展水平的前提条件。本文将介绍中国旅游教育的发展现状和发展历程，并通过分析中山大学旅游教育案例，总结高水平旅游教育模式的特点，为中国旅游教育提供借鉴。

2　中国旅游教育概况

2.1　现状

根据文化和旅游部人事司发布的《2017年全国旅游教育培训统计》数据，从教育层次来看，中国旅游教育包括学历教育（涵盖高等教育和职业教育）与岗位教育（培训），形成了涵盖博士、硕士（学术型硕士、专业型硕士）、本科、高职和中职的完备学历教育体系，构成了覆盖旅游、休闲、酒店、会展的完善学科体系。

从旅游院校数量来看，2017年旅游相关专业（方向）博士培养单位（不包含港澳台地区，下同）共有54家，具有旅游管理专业（或相关方向）硕士招生资质的高校有143所，开设旅游管理类本科专业（主要包括旅游管理、酒店管理和会展经济与管理3个专业）的普通高等院校有608所，开设旅游管理类高职专业（主要包括旅游管理、导游、旅行社经营管理、景区开发与管理、酒店管理、休闲服务与管理、会展策划与管理7个专业）的普通高等院校有1086所，开设旅游相关专业（主要包括高星级饭店运营与管理、旅游服务与管理、旅游外语、导游服务、会展服务与管理5个专业）的中等职业学校有947所。

从招生人数来看，2017年全国旅游相关专业（方向）博士研究生招生336人、硕士研究生招生2832人，旅游管理类本科专业共招生5.9万人，旅游管理类高职专业共招生11.3万人，旅游类中职专业共招生10.2万人。

无论是从院校数量还是招生人数来看，中国旅游教育层次基本呈现金字塔结构，旅游人才教育以高职和中职教育为主，本科、硕士和博士培养的数量、比例偏低。（如图1所示）

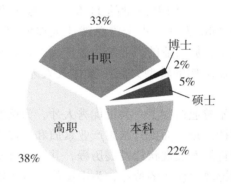

图1　2017年开展旅游教育院校数量层次结构

2.2　发展历程

自中华人民共和国成立以来，经过70余年的发展，中国旅游教育实现了从无到有、从小到大、从弱到强的转变。根据中国旅游教育的发展状况，大致划分为4个阶段，即初始阶段、发展阶段、规模扩张阶段、内涵式发展阶段。

2.2.1　初始阶段（中华人民共和国成立至1977年）

中华人民共和国成立至1977年，中国旅游业处在起步阶段，旅游教育主要是对在职人员的培训。在这一阶段，旅游培训的主要对象为一线接待人员，包括翻译、导游、宾馆服务员和司机。该阶段的旅游教育呈现培训规模较小、培训类型单一、培训形式单调的特点。

2.2.2 发展阶段（1978年至1997年年底）

1978年以后，中国旅游业由外事接待型向经济效益型转变，旅游接待人次和旅游外汇收入大幅度增长，推动了中国旅游教育的快速发展。1978年3月5日，中共中央批转外交部党组《关于发展旅游事业的请示报告》（即中发〔1978〕8号文件），不仅提出了旅游管理体制改革要求，还提出了旅游院校建设的具体意见。

在中等职业和高等职业教育层面，1978年中国第一所旅游中等专业学校——南京旅游学校成立，1979年第一所旅游大专学校——上海旅行游览专科学校成立（2003年划归上海师范大学管理）；在本科层面，从1980年起国家旅游局（现为文化和旅游部）先后与南开大学、杭州大学（后并入浙江大学）、西北大学、中山大学联合开办了旅游系或旅游专业；在硕士层面，1983年南开经济研究所鲍觉民、何自强开始招收旅游地理方向的硕士研究生，杭州大学也于1984年开始正式招收旅游方向硕士研究生；在博士层面，1989年楚义芳从南开大学毕业，成为第一位旅游地理专业博士毕业生。

在学科建设上，1987年12月，国家教委颁布《普通高等学校社会科学本科专业目录》（〔87〕教高一字022号），将原有的98个经济管理学专业减少至48个，将原有的旅游经济、旅游经济管理、旅游管理专业统一称为旅游经济专业。

此阶段旅游教育呈现快速发展趋势。主要表现为：旅游学历教育从无到有地快速发展；教育层次基本完善，学科体系基本形成；培养了一大批旅游业务骨干，成为未来推动旅游业发展的重要力量。

2.2.3 规模扩张阶段（1998年至2009年）

1998年，中央经济工作会议将旅游业定位为"国民经济新的增长点"，确立了旅游业的经济产业地位，全国兴起了"旅游热"。1998年，教育部颁布新的《普通高等学校本科专业目录》（教高〔1998〕8号），调整本科学科专业目录，在管理学门类工商管理一级学科下设旅游管理二级学科。蓬勃发展的旅游产业和国家政策吸引了大量院校兴办旅游专业。1999年，全国旅游管理专业开始扩招。2003年，云南大学和陕西师范大学正式设立旅游管理博士学位点。2004年，中山大学开办旅游学院，旅游学科的地位进一步提升。

在这一阶段，旅游教育呈现整体规模扩张、培养层次提升的特点。主要表现为：旅游高等教育逐渐形成完善的博士、硕士、本科、高职和中职教育层次的金字塔培养体系；旅游院校数量及在校学生数量快速增加，旅游高等院校的数量及在校学生人数超过了中等职业院校，旅游教育层次显著提升。

2.2.4 内涵式发展阶段（2009年年底至今）

2009年10月，国务院颁发41号文件，将旅游业定位为"战略性支柱产业"，强调和提升了旅游产业的重要地位。《中国旅游业"十二五"人才规划（2011—2015年）》的颁布实施，确立了"旅游人才在旅游业发展中优先发展的战略地位"，指明了"发展方式由关注劳动力及资本投入为主向质量效益提高型为主转变"的方向，确立了"加大旅游人才开发力度，努力形成旅游人才竞争的比较优势，培养造就一支规模宏大、素质优良、结构合理，与旅游业发展相匹配的旅游人才队伍"的目标。2010年，国务院学位委员会批准设置旅游管理硕士专业学位（MTA）。在学科建设上，根据教育部发布的《2014年高考普通高等学校本科专业目录》，"旅游管理"升格为专业类。但在国务院学位办的专业目录中，"旅游管理"仍然是"工商管理"下设的二级学科。

本阶段的内涵式发展体现在：旅游产业地位提升，对旅游教育的重视程度和要求也随之提高；旅游教育机构数量仍在增加，但在校人数规模开始显著缩小，人才集约化培养，更加注重人才素质的提升。

3 中山大学旅游学院

3.1 概况

在整合中山大学旅游教育和研究有关力量的基础上，中山大学旅游学院（下称"中大旅院"）于2004年11月正式成立。根据2020年软科世界一流学科排名，中山大学在旅游休闲管理学科榜单中位列全球第四，形成了涵盖本科、硕士（包含学术型硕士和专业型硕士）、博士的完整办学层次，并设有博士后流动站。学院下设旅游管理（含酒店管理方向）、会展经济与管理两个本科专业；与国际名校合作开展2+2、3+1本科生国际联合培养项目，以及3+2、4+1、3+1+1本硕衔接项目[①]；开设了旅游管理专业本科生整建制留学生班。

总而言之，中大旅院师生规模较大，现有专任教师34人、博士后和专职研究人员29人、在校学生1303人（含本科、硕士、博士）；师资结构呈现多

---

① 2+2（在中山大学修读2年本科课程，海外名校修读2年本科课程）；3+1（在中山大学修读3年本科课程，海外名校修读1年本科课程）；3+2（在中山大学修读3年本科课程，海外名校修读2年本科课程）；4+1（在中山大学修读4年本科课程，海外名校修读1年本科课程）；3+1+1（在中山大学修读3年本科课程，海外名校修读1年本科课程及1年硕士课程）。

元化、年轻化、国际化特征，专任教师均有博士学位，教授占比21.4%，副教授占比58.8%，35岁以下占比48%，境外专职教师占比21%；人才培养初具规模，已培养本科毕业生3025人、硕士及博士毕业生308人；科学研究质与量并重，2019年度，学院共获11项国家自然科学基金立项资助项目、5项国家社科基金项目和2项教育部人文社科基金项目的资助。

中大旅院秉承"以学术研究为基础、以产业需求为导向"的高标准、国际化办学理念，以跨学科培养、研究型教学、国际化办学为宗旨，致力于为社会培养一批复合型、应用型和国际化的高层次旅游管理人才和旅游研究人才。

经过多年深耕与动态调整，中大旅院形成了教学、科研、社会服务三位一体的旅游教育模式，发展出四大本科专业建设路径。

3.2 课程体系

中大旅院的人才培养课程体系可划分为校级培养、院级培养、系级培养3个层次。校级培养课程以大类通识课为主，包括语言、体育、思政类课程，涵盖中国文明、人文基础、全球视野、科技经济社会等模块；院级培养课程以专业基础课、专业核心课为主，分为数学与统计、地理学、管理学三大板块，体现出跨学科培养特点；系级培养课程以专业选修课、跨专业选修课、专业实践为主，划分为旅游规划与目的地管理、旅游可持续发展、新技术与新方法模块，突出了人才培养的研究性和应用性。

此外，院级培养中的"旅游地理学"课程更是成了面向三级认证的改革范例，既要求学生牢固掌握旅游地理学的关键概念和核心理论，了解旅游地理学的研究和解释方法，也以小组合作的形式初步培养学生的分析和开发决策能力、团队协作能力。

3.3 专业建设路径

3.3.1 路径一：开设特色班，增加专业吸引力

特色班的开设注重与国际名校合作，开展联合培养。学院专业设置包含旅游管理与规划、会展经济与管理、酒店与俱乐部管理三大传统方向，以及国际旅游（与翻译学院合办）特色方向。国际联合办学方面，学院项目包含澳大利亚昆士兰大学2+2联合培养（会展经济与管理）和法国昂热大学3+1联合培养（旅游管理）。特色班的设立不仅增加专业吸引力，同时也有助于培养出更多基本功扎实、具有开阔眼界与博大胸怀的旅游领域人才。

以中山大学—昆士兰大学2+2项目为例，该项目学生前两年在中大旅院学习，后两年在昆士兰大学商学院学习，获两校学位证书及中山大学毕业证

书；项目每年招生约 40 人，截至 2017 年已毕业 300 人左右；大部分毕业生选择境外深造，并且得到了昆士兰大学的好评。

3.3.2 路径二：设置多层次的实践教学体系

中大旅院的旅游教育不只局限于课堂教学，也注重在多层次实践中实现对学生的引导，在科研实习和课程实习中使学生实现从知识到能力的转变。不同层次的实习经历，使学生完成从对行业有一定的认识到深入了解的转变，最终实现对学生行业管理能力的锻炼。

深入行业和目的地，是中大旅院实践教学体系的核心。学院正在主持或已主持社会咨询项目 310 余项，包括 4 项跨省规划项目、2 项省级规划项目、60 多项国家级重点旅游城市和旅游景区的规划项目等。学院与旅游企业及目的地，如长隆集团、东部华侨城、广之旅等企业，广西阳朔、湖南张家界、新疆喀纳斯、广东开平碉楼与村落等，展开了多方合作，建立了教学与科研实习基地。其中，"阿者科计划"更是作为典型项目得到了教育部的赞扬。

除此之外，学院和联合国世界旅游组织旅游可持续发展观测点管理与监测中心（UNWTO–MCSTO）建立了合作关系，定期在广西阳朔、安徽黄山、湖南张家界、新疆喀纳斯、四川成都、河南开封、云南西双版纳、江苏常熟、广东开平九地开展实习并形成调研报告，积极为当地旅游发展建言献策，把旅游知识回馈于社会现实，推动旅游可持续发展。

依托行业合作资源，学生拥有了解行业运营、结合知识与实践的机会。以旅游管理专业为例，见习实习设置在第一学年，学院统一安排学生前往知名酒店、开平碉楼世界遗产地、广交会展馆等地参观学习，加深学生对旅游行业的认知。第一次专业实习为旅游基层企业实习，学生可以亲身体验旅游基层企业工作，如 2017 级本科生在第一学年暑期前往珠海长隆度假区进行了为期 40 天的景区基层实习；第二次专业实习更加注重提升学生的科研能力，在实践中去发现和探索旅游发展中的实际问题，如 2017 级本科生在第二学年暑期前往元阳梯田景区进行了为期 6 天的专业实习，要求运用已学的专业知识实地调研，分析元阳旅游发展的现状和存在的问题。

3.3.3 路径三：深耕本土与全面国际化相结合的培养模式

根植本土强调深入了解本土化案例、本土化制度和环境解读；全面国际化突出培养国际化思维、开展国际化研究，实现本土化与国际化紧密结合。

在本土化方面，中大旅院深耕本土，立足理论与中国实践，学院教师长期跟踪国内的典型案例（如阳朔、西递宏村等旅游监测地）并反哺于教学，带领众多学生调研，引导他们从实践中寻找和提炼学术问题。

国际化培养模式体现在引入国际理念、联合办学、组织海外交换生及实习、师资队伍国际化四个方面。引入国际理念方面，学院 2010 年、2015 年获联合国世界旅游组织旅游教育质量认证（UNWTO TedQual），属于目前 UNWTO TedQual 给予的最高认证等级。联合办学方面，截至 2017 年 12 月，学院已与 22 个国家和地区的 47 所高校在合作办学、学生交流、科研合作、教师互访等方面建立及开展了合作。此外，学生派出交换及海外实习人数持续稳定，教职工出访交流频繁，学院的国际化水平不断提升，并促进了师资队伍的国际化。

为了让学生更好地参与全球化的旅游产业，学院与全球多所学校有深入的和多元化的交流与合作，目前正与 22 个国家和地区的 35 所高校进行合作，包括与昆士兰大学、昂热大学的双学位项目，与萨里大学、天普大学、伊利诺伊大学厄巴纳 – 香槟分校的本硕项目，与利兹贝克特大学等海外高校合作的交换与海外实践项目。

整体而言，学生派出交换及海外实习规模持续稳定，学生出国留学人数呈稳步增长趋势，境外来访交流人员数量大、批次多，举办的国际会议影响力大，学院教职工出访交流频繁，彰显了中大旅院的国际化办学宗旨。

3.3.4 路径四：科教融合，注重质量

在科研、教学融合方面，学院实现了"三个融入"。其一，将丰富的科研活动与扎实的科研成果融入教学，寓研于教、以研促教、教研融合、教研转化；其二，将一流业界资源与实践机会融入人才培养体系，充分利用与一流旅游地和旅游企业的多方合作机会；其三，学界名师与业界精英融入人才培养过程，著名教授、业界精英、优秀校友进课堂。教师通过带领学生参加各种科研活动，深入旅游企业、旅游地进行调查研究，开展多种形式的课外活动与讲座，帮助学生提升科研素养的同时增强实践能力，让学生对专业有更深刻的理解。

除了科教融合，学院也注重教学质量的提升。例如，学院对研究方法类课程做全面更新和打通设计，充分考虑从本科到硕士研究生、博士研究生在研究方法学习方面的渐进提升需要，面向低年级本科生开展基础课程（研究方法入门、统计分析与应用基础），面向高年级本科生和硕士研究生设置中级课程，涵盖量化研究板块、质的研究板块和学术素养板块。又如，学院建立了面向本科生的科研激励机制，鼓励本科生申报和参与各类科研项目，锻炼学生的综合能力。本科生参加科研项目成为传统，近几年学院学生参与校级以上科研立项 99 项，学生的学习、实践与导师的科研融为一体。

3.4 小结

中山大学旅游学院在多年的旅游教育实践中不断改进，目前形成了教学、科研和社会服务三位一体的旅游教育模式，通过四大专业建设路径将三者有机结合，充分利用学校和社会资源，合理安排课程学习与社会实践，使人才培养方案、教学内容和实践环节更加贴近社会发展的需求，促进了学生社会实践能力、研究能力和整体素质的提高，达到培养高素质人才的目的。学院不少学生在毕业后选择深造或主动承担社会责任，成为旅游业的新兴发展力量。

4 结论

中国旅游教育经历了70多年的发展，进入内涵式培养阶段，但是仍然存在不少问题。一是在人才培养上，旅游学科地位有所提升但仍不高，这造成了师资不强、资金投入少、旅游教材体系不够完善等问题；另一重大问题是旅游服务行业入门门槛低，早期人口红利导致旅游服务业供给过剩、工资过低，旅游行业对于毕业生缺乏吸引力，许多旅游优质人才流失。随着旅游业成为国民支柱产业，旅游教育发展的问题应该得到更多的重视。通过对中山大学旅游学院案例的介绍和分析，希望为中国旅游教育的人才培养问题提供经验借鉴和解决方向。

Tourism Education in China

Luo Qiuju, Sun Yat-Sen University

1 Introduction

According to the 13th Five-Year Plan for Tourism Development, tourism has become one of China's strategic pillar industries. In 2019, China had 6.006 billion domestic tourists and 300 million inbound tourist visits. Tourism yielded a gross income of 6.63 trillion *yuan*, made a comprehensive contribution of 10.94 trillion *yuan* (11.05% of the GDP) and directly provided 28.25 million jobs. When combined with jobs indirectly created by tourism, this figure of 28.25 million increases to 79.87 million, accounting for 10.31% of the nation's workforce[1]. Under this circumstances of rapid growth, the structure of tourism is turning from labor-intensive to labor-and-knowledge intensive. Such transformation urges higher standard for tourism education and personnel training.

Tourism education has provided the industry with many talents and a solid back-up of human resources and knowledge. Such education is the prerequisite for the comprehensive improvement of the quality and development of tourism. This report introduces the current conditions and development phases of China's tourism education. In hope of providing a solid understanding of China's tourism education, the report also sums up the traits of high-level tourism education by analyzing the tourism education provided by School of Tourism Management, Sun Yat-Sen University.

2 General Conditions of China's Tourism Education

2.1 Current Conditions

In terms of education, students in China can begin studying tourism at either

---

[1] Data source: China Tourism Academy, Basic Situation of Tourism Market in 2019.

undergraduate degree level (including higher education and vocational education) or as on-job education (training). As a subject at university, tourism studies can now be found at all levels of higher education including PhD, master's degrees (course-based masters and research-based masters), bachelor's degrees, higher vocational education, and medium vocational education. Indeed, a complete disciplinary system has formed covering tourism, recreation, hotel service, and exhibition.

In 2017, in terms of the number of higher education institutes that provided tourism education (or education in related disciplines), there were 54 institutes (not including schools in Hong Kong, Macao, or Taiwan) providing PhD education and 143 institutes providing Master's level education. There were 608 universities that provided bachelor education in tourism (mainly tourism management, hotel management, and exhibition economics and management). One thousand and eighty-six institutes provided tourism management vocational education (mainly tourism management, tour guiding, travel agency operation and management, hotel management, recreational service and management, and exhibition planning and management). Nine hundred and forty-seven medium vocational schools also provided tourism-related education (mainly star hotel operation and management, tourism service and management, foreign languages for tourism, tour guiding service, and exhibition service and management)[①].

Also in 2017, in terms of the number of students of tourism majors (or majors in related disciplines) enrolled, there were 336 PhD-to-be students, 832 master-to-be students, and 59,000 bachelor-to-be students; there were also 113,000 students studying for higher vocational education and another 102,000 for medium vocational education[②].

Whether seen from the perspective of the number of schools or of students, China's tourism education is a pyramid, with higher and medium vocational education being the foundation, as well as bachelor and master and PhD education being the tip with a relatively low number and proportion. (See Figure 1)

---

① Ministry of Culture and Tourism, Statistics of China's Tourism Education and Training in 2017.
② Ministry of Culture and Tourism, Statistics of China's Tourism Education and Training in 2017.

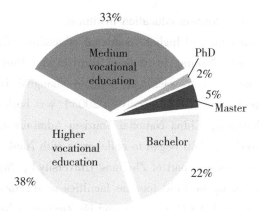

Figure 1 Pie chart of institutes with tourism education in 2017

2.2 Development Phases

Over the past seven decades since the foundation of the People's Republic of China, tourism education in China, starting from scratch, has grown from small to large, from weak to strong. According to the conditions of its development, it can be categorized into four phases: preliminary phase, developing phase, scale expansion phase, and connotative development phase.

2.2.1 Preliminary Phase (from the foundation of the PRC to 1977)

From the foundation of the PRC to 1977, China's tourist industry remained in its infancy and the only form of 'tourism education' came from on-the-job training. Those who received training in the tourism industry were mainly front-line employers including interpreters and translators, tour guides, hotel waiters and waitresses, and drivers. Tourism training in this phase was of very limited size, scale and extent.

2.2.2 Developing Phase (from 1978 to the end of 1997)

After 1978, China's tourism industry turned from a diplomatic-reception-oriented approach to a more economic-performance-oriented approach. China received many more tourists and much greater foreign exchange revenue, which in turn boosted China's rapid tourism education development. On March 5th, 1978, the Central Committee of Communist Party of China processed the Request from the Party Committee of the Foreign Ministry to Develop Tourism (code [1978] 8). The request suggested that the tourism management system be reformed, and made concrete suggestions about building tourism education institutes.

With regard to medium and higher vocational education, China's first medium tourism vocational school—Nanjing Institute of Tourism and Hospitality was built in 1978. The first higher tourism vocational school—Shanghai Institute of Tourism (became part of Shanghai Normal University in 2003) was built in 1979. With respect to bachelor education, China National Tourism Administration (now Ministry of Culture and Tourism) in 1980 began to collaborate with Nankai University, Hangzhou University (later became part of Zhejiang University), Northwest University, and Sun Yat-Sen University to build tourism faculties or disciplines. In regards to Master level education, in 1983 Bao Juemin and He Ziqiang in Nankai Institute of Economics started to offer a master of education in tourism and geology. In 1984 Hangzhou University also officially started to enroll master students. With respect to PhD education, in 1989 Chu Yifang in Nankai University graduated as the first PhD in tourism and geology.

In terms of discipline construction, in December 1987 the State Education Commission issued the Catalog of Social Science Disciplines in Bachelor Education in Higher Education Institutes (code [87] 022). In this catalog, the original 98 economic management disciplines were reduced to 48. The original disciplines of tourism economics, tourism economic management, and tourism management were merged into one discipline—tourism economics.

In this phase of development, tourism education was developing fast. Degree education was developing rapidly starting from scratch; there was a complete set of different levels of education and a disciplinary system had taken shape; in terms of personnel training, there was huge recruitment drive for graduates with tourism-based degrees in this period, many of which would become the leaders and the core driving force of tourism development in China.

2.2.3 Scale Expansion Phase (from 1998 to 2009)

In 1998, the Central Economic Work Conference designated tourism as the 'new growth driver of national economy' and established tourism's place in the economy. The whole country went into a 'tourism rush'. Also in 1998, the Ministry of Education issued the Catalog of Disciplines in Bachelor Education in Higher Education Institutes (code [1998] 8). In this catalog, disciplines in bachelor education were revised. Tourism management was established as a secondary discipline under the primary discipline of management. The fast growing tourism and favorable policies encouraged a large amount of universities to set up their tourism discipline. In 1999, schools with tourism management discipline began expanding their enrollment. In 2003, Yunnan University and Shaanxi Normal University established their tourism management PhD education center. In 2004, Sun Yat-Sen University, a university in the '985 project' program, established its School of Tourism Management. Thus, tourism as a discipline received greater recognition.

In this phase of development, tourism education generally was expanding its scale while different levels of education rose to new heights. Specifically, a pyramid system of higher tourism education came into being, featuring PhD, master, bachelor, higher vocational, and medium vocational education; the number of higher tourism education institutes and their students were increasing fast. The number of higher tourism education institutes surpassed that of medium vocational schools. Tourism education rose to new levels.

2.2.4 Quality Development Phase (from 2009 to Present)

The State Council issued Document No. 41 in October 2009. The document designated tourism as a 'strategic pillar industry' and stressed and raised the important status of tourism. The release of 12th Five-Year Plan for Tourism Human Resources (2011 – 2015) confirmed 'the priority of tourism personnels in tourism development'; pointed in the direction of 'transforming tourism development from labor-capital-intensive to quality-performance-oriented'; and set the goal of 'increasing personnel training, obtaining a competitive advantage, raising an army of highly skilled tourism managers and building the necessary tourism infrastructure capable of meeting the rising demand of tourism development'. In 2010, the Academic Degrees Committee of the State Council approved the establishment of Master of Tourism Administration (MTA). In regards to the discipline of tourism studies, the Ministry of Education issued the 2014 Catalog of Bachelor Education Disciplines in Higher Education Institutes, raising the 'tourism management' discipline to a bachelor degree level. But in the discipline catalog issued by the Academic Degrees Committee Office, 'tourism management' was still a secondary discipline under the primary discipline of 'business administration'.

Development in this phase is quality improvement in that the tourism industry is becoming so important that tourism education is regarded of greater importance and people hold it to a higher standard; the number of tourism education institutes is still growing but the number of students is decreasing, possibly reflecting that the standard of tourism education is becoming more intensive and quality-oriented.

3 Sun Yat-Sen University School of Tourism Management

3.1 Introduction

Sun Yat-Sen University established its School of Tourism Management in November, 2004. According to the Shanghai Ranking Consultancy's global first class academic disciplines ranking, Sun Yat-Sen University's hospitality and tourism management ranks No. 4 in the world, due to its complete integration into the academic syllabus, covering bachelor, master (both course-based and research-based) and PhD level education alongside a postdoctoral researcher center. Currently, the School of Tourism Management has 2 bachelor majors: tourism management (including hotel management), and exhibition economics and management; the School collaborates with international renowned universities in their 2 + 2 and 3 + 1 international bachelor education programs, and in their 3 + 2, 4 + 1, and 3 + 1 + 1 bachelor-to-master education programs; the School's tourism management faculty also has international student classes composed of only overseas students.

The School of Tourism Management therefore operates at a large-scale: currently it has 34 teachers, 29 researchers and postdoctoral researchers, 1,303 students (bachelors, masters, and PhDs); teachers are diverse, young, and international: all teachers have PhD degrees, 21.4% of them are professors, 58.8% are associate professors, 48% are below the age of 35, 21% are from overseas, one of the teachers is a Changjiang Scholar, another one of them is a Pearl River Scholar; To date, the school has cultivated 3,025 bachelors, 308 masters and PhDs. The School emphasizes both the quality and quantity of its research: in 2019, 11 projects of the School received funding from the National Natural Science Foundation; 5 projects received funding from the National Social Science Fund; 2 projects received funding from the Ministry of Education's Cultural and Social Science Fund.

The School of Tourism Management has a high standard that is 'based on academic research', 'meets the demand of tourism', offers international education, and uses research-led teaching practices. The School devotes itself to cultivating a faculty of comprehensive, application-oriented, and international high-standard tourism management personnel.

After many years of effort and dynamic adjustments, the School has built an education model featuring teaching, research, and social service, and has pioneered four paths of bachelor education discipline construction. The School's detailed course systems and discipline construction paths are as follows.

3.2 Course Systems

The School of Tourism Management's course systems fall into three categories: university level, school level, and faculty level. The university-level courses are mainly general education courses including languages, physical education, and politics. The courses' content covers Chinese civilization, basic knowledge of culture, global perspective, technology, economy, and society; the school-level courses are mainly foundation-laying courses and core courses of the discipline. Subjects are mathematics and statistics, geography, and management. These courses are interdisciplinary; the faculty-level courses are mainly optional courses of the discipline, interdisciplinary optional courses, and practice courses of the discipline. Content of the courses includes tourism planning and tourist destination management, sustainable tourism, and new technology and new methods. Such courses focus on the research and application aspects of education.

In addition, the School's Tourism Geography course is an example of education reform for the 3-level qualification. The course requires students to comprehend the core theories and concepts of tourism geography, understand the research and interpretation methods, and work in groups to develop their analysis and decision making abilities as well as teamwork.

3.3 Setting Up Paths

3.3.1 Path 1: Special Classes to Increase Attraction of Tourism Discipline

Special classes are set up in collaboration with internationally renowned schools. The School of Tourism Management has three traditional disciplines of tourism management and planning, exhibition economics and management, and hotel and club management. In addition, the School also has a special discipline of international tourism (in collaboration with School of International Studies Sun Yat-Sen University). In terms of international collaborated education, the School of Tourism Management works together with the University of Queensland in Australia in their 2 + 2 program (exhibition economics and management), and with the University of Angers in France in their 3 + 1 program (tourism management). Special classes not only attract more attention to the tourism discipline but also produce more visionary and open-minded tourism personnels with a solid foundation of knowledge.

Take the Sun Yat-Sen University & University of Queensland 2 + 2 program for example. Students in this program spend their first two years in Sun Yat-Sen University School of Tourism Management before moving on to the University of Queensland Business School. When they graduate they will receive diplomas of both universities and the graduation certificate of Sun Yat-Sen University; the program enrolls around 40 students each year and by 2017 the program has produced around 300 graduates; most of the graduates opt for further education abroad. The program is favored by the University of Queensland.

3.3.2 Path 2: Multi-Aspect Practice-Oriented Teaching System

The School's tourism education is not limited to in-class teaching but also stresses the importance of guiding students through multi-aspect practice. Students will turn their knowledge into abilities through research-based practice and course-based practice. Through such multi-aspect practice, students' basic understanding of tourism is transformed into in-depth knowledge. Eventually, their tourism management ability is improved.

The School's practice-based teaching system is centered around the in-depth analysis of tourism and destinations. The School has held and is holding 310 social consultancy projects, among which are 4 inter-provincial planning projects, 2 provincial planning projects, and over 60 planning projects in national key tourism cities and tourist destinations. The School is working with tourism enterprises and tourist destinations to establish teaching and research bases. Such bases include Chimelong Group, OCT East, Ecwalk, Yangshuo, Zhangjiajie, Kanas, and Kaiping Diaolou and Villages. The School's Azheke project is a great example and receives praise from the Ministry of Education.

In addition to the above projects, the School has also established a partnership with the United Nations World Tourism Organization Monitoring Center for Sustainable Tourism Observatories (UNWTO MCSTO). The two parties regularly conduct field trips to Yangshuo Guangxi, Huangshan Anhui, Zhangjiajie Hunan, Kanas Xinjiang, Chengdu Sichuan, Kaifeng Henan, Xishuangbanna Yunnan, Changshu Jiangsu, and Kaiping Guangdong, and return with survey reports. Advice on tourism development is given to the locals so as to boost development with knowledge and drive the sustainable development of tourism.

Thanks to partners in the tourism industry, students have the opportunity to understand the industry and put their knowledge to practice. Take the discipline of tourism management for example which involves an internship in its first year. The School arranges students' field trips to well-known hotels, the world heritage Kaiping Diaolou, and the exhibition center of Canton Fair. Through field trips, students will gain a deeper understanding of the tourism industry; in the students' first academic practice, they go to the front line of tourism and experience the work there firsthand. For example, the bachelor classes of 2017 spent 40 days of their first summer vacation in Chimelong Zhuhai, where they gained front-line work experience; students' second academic practice focuses on improving their research ability. For example, the bachelor classes of 2017 spent 6 days of their second summer vacation in Yuanyang terrace, where they utilized their knowledge to survey and analyze the current conditions of and existing problems with Yuanyang's tourism development.

3.3.3 Path 3: Localized and All-Round International Teaching Model

The School's localization focuses on understanding localized cases, localized systems, and environment interpretation. Its all-round internalization focuses on cultivating international thinking and conducting international research. The School aims to combine localization with internalization.

With regard to localization, the School delves deeper into domestic tourism and bases its education on Chinese theories and practices. Teachers follow up with domestic typical cases (such as Yangshuo, Xidi and Hongcun, and other tourism monitoring sites) and feed back teaching with such cases. In practice, teachers search for and then refine academic questions. Under their guidance, students conduct surveys and write reports on site.

With regard to the international teaching model, Sun Yat-Sen University has introduced international theories, developed international collaboration in education, exchange student programs internships, and recruitment of international faculties. In terms of international theories, the School received UNWTO TedQual in 2010 and 2015, the highest qualification given by UNWTO so far. In regards to international collaborations, the School has established cooperative relationships with 47 universities in 22 countries by December, 2017. Their programs include exchange student programs, research cooperation, and teachers' mutual visits, etc. In addition, the School constantly sends its students abroad for exchange programs and overseas internships. Its staff also frequently travels abroad for experience exchanges. The School is constantly seeking to become more international in its outlook and strives to employ international staff too.

To facilitate students' engagement in global tourism, the School has established profound and diverse cooperation and exchange with other schools around the world. The School is currently working with 35 universities in 22 countries. Programs include the double-diploma programs with the University of Queensland and with the University of Angers; the bachelor-to-master programs with the University of Surrey, the Temple University, and the University of Illinois at Urbana-Champaign; and the School has exchange student and overseas internship programs with Leeds Beckett University and with a variety of other international universities.

Generally speaking, the School maintains its stable exchange programs and overseas internships. The number of its students seeking overseas education is growing steadily. Many foreign counterparts frequently send their staff to visit the School and in return the School also frequently sends its staff abroad for exchange purposes. The School has also held many conferences and meetings that have an international importance and boast a global influence. All of these efforts demonstrate the international outlook of Sun Yat-Sen University and its School of Tourism Management.

3.3.4 Path 4: Integration of Teaching and Research, Emphasis on Quality

In terms of the integration of teaching and research, the School of Tourism Management has a 'three-prong integration' approach. First, the School mixes its rich research activities and concrete research results with its teaching, thus boosting teaching with research and integrating research with teaching. This creates a two-way transfer channel between teaching and research. Second, the School incorporates industry-leading resources and practice opportunities into its teaching system, utilizing opportunities to work with first-class tourist attractions and tourism enterprises. Third, the School facilitates teaching with prestigious teachers and industry-leading operatives. Classes are taught by famous professors, elites, and influential alumni. Under the guidance of teachers, students take part in all kinds of research, conducting in-depth surveys of various tourism enterprises across many different tourist destinations and attending all kinds of lectures and extra-curricular activities. Students gain experience from practice while improving their academic competence, thus bringing them a deeper understanding of the discipline.

Besides the integration of research and teaching, the School also stresses the importance of improving teaching quality. For instance, the School has overhauled research method courses and connected them together, taking into consideration students' progressive needs for knowledge of research methods during their school years from bachelor to master to PhD. The School provides bachelor students in their early school years with basic courses (Basic Research Method, Basic Statistic Analysis & Application) and provides bachelor students in their late school years and master students with medium-level classes in the directions of quantitative research, qualitative research, and academic competence. Also, the School has an incentive system to encourage students to apply for and take part in all kinds of research projects so students can develop a well-rounded skillset. It is a tradition that bachelor students take part in research projects. In recent years, 99 of students' projects above the university level have been approved. Students' study and practice are integrated with teachers' guidance.

3.4 Summary

In its many years of tourism education practice, Sun Yat-Sen University's School of Tourism Management continues to improve itself. At present it has a three-pronged education model integrating teaching, research, and social service, and four discipline construction paths. The School utilizes educational and social resources to make a proper arrangement of in-class learning and social practice so that its teaching guideline, teaching content, and practice meet the demand of social progress. By improving students' social practice ability, research ability, and comprehensive competence, the School produces students and staff of high quality. Many graduates from the School opt for research or further education or take social responsibility into their own hands and become a new driving force for tourism development.

4 Conclusion

China's tourism education has developed for over seven decades and has now entered its quality improvement phase, but many problems still exist. One of the problems is that although there has been progress in China's personnel training and the status of the tourism discipline, further improvements are yet to be made. Educators and funding are lacking and the infrastructure of tourism teaching still needs to be improved; another major problem is that the threshold to enter the tourism service industry has generally been too low. Due to surplus in labor, there is more supply than demand in the industry leading to low wages. Thus tourism is not attracting graduates, reducing the potential of the workforce. Since tourism has been designated as a national pillar industry, the education of tourism deserves more attention. This report introduces and analyzes the case of Sun Yat-Sen University's School of Tourism Management in the hope of providing China's continuing development of tourism education with experience and solutions.

马来西亚旅游教育：基于个人的反思

Amran Bin Hamzah　马来西亚理工大学

1　引言

马来西亚的旅游教育是一个相对较新的领域，自20世纪90年代以来，随着旅游业的增长才迅速发展起来。旅游教育和培训最初由公立大学推动，为旅游业提供"半专业化"教育，随后也在私立大学和培训机构中兴起。本文基于作者作为学者、研究者、实践者在旅游学界、业界30多年的工作经验，对马来西亚旅游教育进行介绍与反思。

本文的旅游教育定义包含旅游教育和旅游培训两部分，二者有着明确的区别。马来西亚的许多大学、学院和技术学校均在本科和研究生教学中提供旅游相关的教育课程和项目培训，导致它们在提供教育（学问）、培训（技能）或两者兼有的教育模式上出现了角色分工模糊的问题。本文中作者的反思仅基于其在讲授式课程中的经验，不包括研究型硕博培养的经验，因为后者需要更细致的思考。

2　旅游作为普通职业的历史缘由

旅游作为一个行业以及普通职业的历史给马来西亚的旅游教育以及学科发展留下了深刻的印记。结果就是，在马来西亚很难找到另一种专业仍希望其毕业生从事"卑微"的工作——如加入酒店当服务员。一纸学历证书在20世纪80年代被认为是新奇的事物，而从服务员开始一路成长为总经理一直被视为旅游接待业的榜样。

这种对旅游教育的态度使当时的玛拉工艺大学（Universiti Teknologi MARA，UiTM）花了25年多的时间才在1993年开设了马来西亚首个酒店和餐饮本科项目，而首个专科项目早在1967年就已经设立。

在1990年首个"马来西亚旅游年"取得巨大成功之前，马来西亚被认为是"新进入者"，只是包括新加坡、印度尼西亚和泰国在内的"更广泛的旅游线路"中的一个要素。1957年，马来西亚脱离英国独立之前，旅游住宿主要由政府的招待所和经济型酒店提供。20世纪70年代，假日酒店等国际连锁酒店开始在马来西亚运营，但旅游产品仅限于旅游住宿和招待。毋庸置疑，几乎所有国际连锁酒店的总经理都是外籍人士，不过酒店工作人员如服务员得到晋升的机会并不少见，最高可升至中层经理。

在20世纪80年代，对于备受鼓舞的初级和中级管理人员来说，一纸证书是他们获得令人垂涎的总经理职位的先决条件，却也是一个巨大的挑战。许多人采取了值得信赖的途径，从当时被认为是服务业佼佼者的瑞士的培训机构获得酒店管理或接待业证书。

如前所述，玛拉工艺大学是第一个认识到旅游和酒店业日益增长的需求，并开办了酒店和餐饮业资质和文凭课程的公共机构。其主要目的是为酒店业提供所需的人力资源，并赋予布米普特拉（马来西亚原住民，意为"大地之子"）青年权力，作为与1970年实行的新经济政策相关的扶持行动的一部分。尽管受训者在高中的学习成绩平平，但玛拉工艺大学提供的证书和文凭培训的实用性和实操性能够将他们培养成高素质的专业人才。尽管如此，直到马来西亚政府在第六个马来西亚五年计划（1991—1995）中将旅游业作为重要的经济门类后，旅游教育（学习而不是获得技能）才被视为优先事项。对于旅游业的重视程度日益提高，玛拉工艺大学认为有必要在1993年提供马来西亚的第一个旅游教育项目。该项目的早期毕业生都成为旅游和酒店业的领导者，并在与旅游有关的政府机构中担任高级职务。

尽管如此，旅游和酒店业的普通员工职业晋升通道仍然存在诸多阻碍，"反纸质资格证书"的态度一直持续到今天，特别是对于经历了普通员工制度的当地总经理而言。此外，与医学、法律、工程等相反，旅游和酒店教育一直被视为次等的领域。

3 马来西亚旅游和酒店教育的发展

从2000年起，马来西亚的旅游和酒店教育突飞猛进。公立大学如玛拉工艺大学和马来西亚北方大学首开先河，提供各种旅游相关本科项目。遵循这一趋势，一些公立大学也开展了类似的项目，主要是在旅游和酒店管理领域，目前有8所公立大学提供与旅游有关的本科教育。此外，马来西亚目前大约有16类与旅游相关的研究生项目，大部分由公立大学提供。

除了旅游教育项目外，全国还有12所技术学校以专科和项目结业证书的形式提供职业培训，主要是在酒店和旅游管理方面。此外，自2000年以来，有40多所社区学院提供证书级培训。虽然技术学校遵循全国通用的教学大纲，但社区学院更加灵活地提供适合特定领域需求的项目，如糕点制作、服装设计和动画等。有趣的是，有一所社区大学为有学习障碍的学生提供了一个在旅游区内经营食品摊档的教育项目。

旅游教育和培训的增长在私立院校更为普遍，大约有 36 所私立学院和大学提供各类专科、本科和研究生层次的教育项目。与国际大学联合培养的项目很常见；还有一些外国大学，如莫纳什大学（Monash University）、斯威本大学（Swinburne University）和科廷大学（Curtin University）等也会选择设立马来西亚校区（均提供旅游教育项目）。必须指出的是，私立大学的水准参差不齐，一些大学如泰勒大学（Taylor's University）和双威大学（Sunway University）是世界著名大学，但也有一些针对外国学生的普通大学。（见表1）

表 1　马来西亚提供旅游相关课程的机构

职业培训	本科教育	研究生教育
技术学校：12 所	公立大学：8 所	公立大学：16 所
社区大学：40 所	私立学院和大学：36 所	—

总体而言，自 2000 年以来，在政府的倡议和私立院校的推动下，马来西亚的旅游教育取得了巨大的发展。然而，必须强调的是，与旅游有关的项目准入资格相对低于医药、法律、建筑、会计等的准入资格。因此，旅游教育一直存在着形象刻板的问题，它无法吸引当今年轻人的眼球。泰勒大学的旅游管理项目就是一个例子，尽管其在 2019 年 QS 世界酒店和休闲管理专业排名很高，但如何吸引和维持当地和国际学生仍然存在不少挑战。

4　旅游业和接待业的负面形象

如前所述，马来西亚的旅游教育通常被视为"不得已而为之"的选择，这反映在相对较低的入学资格要求上。此外，马来西亚部分严格的穆斯林家庭总是对旅游业持负面看法，因为旅游业与酒精、恶习和少数游客的享乐行为有着密切的联系。需要注意的是，马来西亚穆斯林友好酒店越来越受欢迎，不仅反映了需求方面的增长，还可看出父母辈对这一增长趋势的认可。

马来西亚旅游、艺术和文化部最近颁发的《国家旅游政策（2020—2030）》表明，拥有稳定发展和回报的职业道路是旅游业和酒店业留住人才的主要因素。根据该政策，马来西亚旅游业人力资本发展的核心是解决旅游业和酒店业的形象问题。具有挑战性的障碍之一是水疗行业的负面形象，即使它可能是一个高价值的产品，但同时也受到所谓的脚底按摩中心不良做法的冲击。因此，尽管政府和协会在建立水疗培训中心方面采取了各种举措和提供了各种支持，但还是因当地从业人员短缺而不得不依赖外国理疗师。可以说，马来西亚的旅游教育和培训一直被持续到今天的一些不良形象问题所困扰。

5 马来西亚的旅游研究生教育是否有回报

马来西亚的旅游研究生教育是一个相对较新的领域。马来西亚理工大学（Universiti Teknologi Malaysia，UTM）提供的旅游规划硕士项目是首个旅游研究生教育项目，这是一个独立的项目，不附属于通常的 MBA 项目。从 1998 年开始，该项目的目的是提供一个不同于以往以酒店和旅游管理为重点的典型旅游管理专业课程。这个项目与马来西亚理科大学（Universiti Sains Malaysia，USM）提供的旅游发展硕士项目是仅有的专注于旅游政策规划和旅游地一级空间规划的研究生项目。

如前所述，大约有 16 所公立和私立大学提供硕博旅游教育。然而，这些专业大多是作为 MBA 项目的一部分提供的，在第一年是通用课程，在最后一年或最后一学期提供专业课程或者开展研究。

马来西亚的旅游研究生教育项目一直在逐步增长，并试图提供生态旅游、可持续旅游甚至伊斯兰旅游方面的专业项目。然而，由于担心招收不到足够的学生，这些项目未能真正落地。在马来西亚，接受旅游研究生教育并不是一项有益的投资。因为马来西亚的公共服务是基于轮换制度的，服务期间，官员可以多次被调任到不同的机构，所以很少有在旅游相关领域工作的公共部门官员愿意通过参加旅游硕士项目来提高他们的专业知识。此外，许多政府官员更愿意在周末学习，这样他们就不必申请可能影响其工作和晋升的学习时间。值得说明的是，拥有硕士学位并不能使政府官员获得晋升或加薪的资格，因此过去接受旅游研究生教育的人主要是出于自我满足和对知识的热爱。

针对这一需求，马来西亚各大学提供了所谓的离岸项目，这类项目针对特定的政府官员或学者，每两周在周末举办一次讲座。另一个尝试是引入模块化系统，在这个系统中，学生可以选择"模块"，以积累足够的学分，从而能够获得硕士学位。从本质上讲，这些采用更灵活的方式开展旅游教育项目的创新方法反映了马来西亚政府建立国际教育中心的愿景。大学也被鼓励采取更灵活的方式，包括与国际知名大学联合授予双学位，开展旅游教育。

尽管本地学生在公立和私立大学的研究生入学人数中仍占大部分，但越来越多的国际学生，特别是来自发展中国家的学生被吸引到马来西亚学习旅游专业，这证明政府已经初步将马来西亚转变成了教育中心。在马来西亚接受旅游研究生教育的外国学生中，印度尼西亚的人数最多，其中大多数是在旅游教育中寻求平稳职业道路的年轻学者。

　　非洲国家，特别是尼日利亚，自2000年以来一直向马来西亚派遣研究生。此外，马来西亚有大量来自中东地区的学生。由于地缘政治，过去有相当多的伊朗学生来马来西亚学习，因为他们在西方学习的机会有限。马来西亚对伊朗学生来说就像一个"绿洲"，但这种流动在几年前西方取消限制后就停止了，不过这种变化也可能随着国际局势的发展而发生改变。最近的一个现象是来自中国的研究生人数的增加。国际学生来马来西亚学习的主要原因是马来西亚大学的良好质量、可负担的学费和生活费用以及安全舒适的生活环境。但是，仍有个别案例表明，普通私立培训机构会被用作少数外国学生从事非法活动（如非法毒品分销和卖淫）的基地。

　　由于旅游职业的普遍性，旅游专业研究生教育没有受到重视，也难以得到足够的教育投资回报。很少有酒店或旅游经营者会考虑赞助员工深造——接受研究生教育，自费获得硕士学位的员工也很少被晋升或加薪。综上，马来西亚旅游业似乎对旅游专业研究生教育无动于衷。

6　旅游教育和培训的类型

　　基本上，目前马来西亚的大多数旅游教育和培训课程侧重于酒店管理、旅游管理和烹饪艺术等传统课程。这些课程被认为是"安全课程"，相对容易获得教育部和马来西亚资格认证局（Malaysian Qualifications Agency，MQA）的批准。这类项目也具有明显的职业性质，可以使毕业生掌握行业所需的技能，如管理酒店预订、组织出境旅游和预订航班等。具体来说，这些技能符合酒店经营者和旅行社从业人员的工作要求。为了将其项目与其他大学提供的项目区分开来，各大学通过强调特定的重点领域（如旅游创业）来增加其通用项目的价值，但是这往往只反映在最后一学期提供的少数选修课程中。

　　在过去10年中，会展管理作为传统课程中的新增课程值得关注。因为政府越来越重视会展和商业活动，这是一个潜在的高价值旅游活动。尽管马来西亚是一个享有盛誉的自然和生态旅游目的地，但是马来西亚的大学没有专门的生态旅游或可持续旅游本科或研究生项目。唯一的例外是马来西亚博特拉大学（Universiti Putra Malaysia，UPM）提供的公园和娱乐管理学位。至今该教育项目已有超过30年的历史。随着在传统酒店和旅游管理项目的舒适区内相互竞争，公立和私立大学对生态旅游和可持续旅游等专门旅游教育项目的忽视愈发明显。值得一提的是，马来西亚的资深旅游学者已经讨论了是否可能推出伊斯兰旅游及其变体——清真旅游和穆斯林友好旅游教育项目。

7 拥抱智慧旅游的需要

马来西亚国家旅游政策建议，马来西亚的旅游教育应在课程和教学大纲中充分纳入智慧旅游知识体系。然而，在该政策制定过程中，通过对选定的公立和私立大学的访谈调查发现，在智慧旅游的课程和模块方面存在空心化现象。一个共同的问题是信息技术的有限纳入，如 AR（augmented reality，指增强现实技术）、VR（virtual reality，指虚拟现实技术）、物联网、GIS（geographic information system，指地理信息系统）等。因此，现有的旅游教育课程和教学大纲往往被批评为"不是为明天而是为昨天储备旅游人力资本"。

现有课程和教学大纲中教授的旅游创业要素只侧重于培养"往日"的旅行社运营商，而不是"明天"的旅游顾问。此外，新的创业机会，如旅游技术初创企业，没有得到足够的重视。在全国初创企业总数中，与旅游业有关的初创企业不到5%，这不仅反映了旅游创业公司的稀少，还反映了他们缺乏支持。相比之下，韩国的旅游创业公司得到了韩国政府旅游创业公司加速器计划和定期比赛等支持。

国家旅游政策也推荐使用大数据分析，这是马来西亚走向智慧旅游的一部分。为实现这一目标，需要有能力的数据科学家，但旅游教育的储存性质未能引起信息技术专业学生的兴趣，也无法给他们提供机会，难以让他们选修旅游科目。大学在制订课程和教学大纲方面与旅游业产生了强大的协同作用，大多数应邀提供咨询的从业人员都是资深酒店经营者和旅游公司负责人。随着旅游业朝着智慧旅游的方向发展，大学并未意识到任命 IT 界的旅游教育顾问的必要性，也错失了一些与第四次工业革命相关的新机会。毋庸置疑，从长远来看，采用更加灵活的旅游教育方式将能扩宽旅游毕业生的职业道路，并提升旅游教育的形象。

8 展望

马来西亚的旅游教育和培训陷入了舒适区。如前所述，公立和私立大学以及学院的旅游教育的蓬勃发展预示着旅游行业人力资本的发展。然而，旅游教育和培训尚未涉足令人兴奋的新领域，如生态旅游、可持续旅游和智慧旅游等领域。马来西亚的旅游教育和实践似乎脱节，特别是在国家生态旅游规划和国家旅游政策所强调的旅游战略方向转型的大背景下。从本质上讲，马来西亚的旅游教育并没有与时俱进，这反过来又可能会影响未来旅游业的竞争力。为应对这些挑战，笔者提出以下建议。

8.1 改善旅游行业的职业形象

改善旅游行业的职业形象将有助于吸引有才华的青年学习旅游和酒店课程，而不是被其作为最后的选择。这可以通过积极和吸引眼球的方式推广旅游职业来实现。为此，真人秀节目可以作为一种媒介，突出与旅游行业相关的令人兴奋的事、有形和无形的收益和职业道路。此外，应定期举办旅游教育博览会，在此期间行业领袖可充当旅游业"大使"。

8.2 将旅游教育与智慧旅游相结合

随着旅游的专业化，旅游预订和定制（旅行社的角色）已经由旅游顾问接管。因此，旅游顾问的技能应包括熟练使用信息技术和社交媒体。大学和其他培训机构应探索将智慧旅游整合进课程和教学大纲中，这里不是指作为一门或两门课程，而是将第四次工业革命作为转变旅游业人力资本发展的基础。

8.3 聚焦旅游科技创业

与智慧旅游接轨，未来旅游教育的重点应该是释放年轻人创立和运营旅游科创企业的能量和创造力。只有大量旅游创业公司出现，并利用信息和数字化技术从根本上改变旅游业，马来西亚旅游业的创新和创造力才能有所突破。应该强调的是，内容、讲故事的能力和服务质量对于旅游初创企业的发展同样至关重要。

9 结论

马来西亚的正规旅游教育自 20 世纪 60 年代首次推出以来，已经走了很长的路。尽管马来西亚旅游和酒店业有着负面形象，社会对旅游研究生教育比较漠然，但马来西亚的旅游和酒店教育的发展仍令人振奋。当下马来西亚旅游业的前进方向是拥抱智慧旅游，改善旅游业的形象，使其成为一个令人兴奋的、充满机会和理想的行业。这将鼓舞马来西亚青年通过旅游初创企业提出新的想法，释放其创造力，推动旅游业在接下来十年间的发展。

Tourism Education in Malaysia: A Personal Reflection

Amran Bin Hamzah, University of Technology Malaysia

1 Introduction

Tourism education in Malaysia is relatively a new field which has been growing fast in tandem with the growth of the tourism industry since the 1990s. Initially driven by public universities to provide the industry with 'semi-professionals', tourism education and training are also mushrooming in private universities and training institutions. This paper will present the personal reflection of the author based on his 38 years of experience as a tourism academic, researcher and practitioner in Malaysia as well as in the region.

The definition of tourism education used in this paper covers both tourism education and training despite the clear distinction between them. Many universities, university-colleges and polytechnics in Malaysia offer a mix of tourism-related programmes and courses at the undergraduate and postgraduate levels, thus creating a blurring of their roles in either offering education (learning), training (skills) or both. The reflections of the author are purely based on his experience in running taught courses and exclude research programmes at the Master's and Ph. D. levels, which require a more nuanced contemplation.

2 The Legacy of Tourism as a Rank and File Profession

In order to understand tourism education in Malaysia, it has to be acknowledged that its history as a trade as well as a rank and file profession has left a definite mark on its development as a discipline. As a consequence, it is difficult to find another profession in Malaysia that still expects its graduates to carry out menial jobs—for instance, as waiters upon joining a hotel. A paper qualification in the 1980s was considered a novelty while the general manager who made it through the rank and file, having started as a bellboy, was always regarded as the role model in the tourism and hospitality industry.

Such was the attitude towards tourism education that it took more than 25 years for the Universiti Teknologi MARA (UiTM) to offer Malaysia's first undergraduate programme in hotel and catering in 1993, having started the country's first certificate and diploma level programmes in the same field way back in 1967.

Prior to the resounding success of the first Visit Malaysia Year in 1990, Malaysia was considered as a 'late entrant' and just an element of a 'wider tourism circuit' comprising Singapore, Indonesia and Thailand (King, 1993). Tourism accommodation, even before Malaysia became independent from Britain in 1957, was dominated by government rest houses and budget hotels. In the 1970s, international hotel chains such as the Holiday Inn started to operate in Malaysia but the tourism offerings were limited to tourism accommodation and hospitality. Needless to say, almost all the general managers of the international hotel chains were expatriates and it was not uncommon for hotel staff members to move up the rank and file from a waiter or bellboy to become, at most, a mid-level manager.

For the inspiring junior/mid-level managers, getting a paper qualification as a prerequisite for being promoted to the coveted general manager position was a huge challenge in the 1980s. Many took the trusted path of getting a hotel management or hospitality certificate from training institutions in Switzerland, a country which was then regarded as top notch for the service industry.

As highlighted earlier, the MARA Institute of Technology was the first public institution to recognize the growing needs of the tourism and hospitality industry by starting certificate and diploma level courses in hotel and catering. The main aim was to supply the manpower requirements for the hospitality industry as well as to empower the Bumiputra youth (son of the soil) as part of the affirmative actions associated with the New Economic Policy (NEP), which was introduced in 1970 (Government of Malaysia, 1970). Despite their average academic performance in high school, the practical and hands on nature of the certificate and diploma training that MARA Institute of Technology offered was able to produce a pool of quality sub professionals.

Despite this, tourism education (learning instead of acquiring skills) was not considered as a priority until Malaysia fully embraced tourism as a key economic sector as reflected in the 6th. Malaysia Plan (1991 – 1995) (Economic Planning Unit, 1991). In relation to the growing importance of the tourism sector, MARA Institute of Technology saw the need to offer Malaysia's first tourism education programme in 1993. Its early graduates were to become captains of the tourism and hospitality industry as well as having top posts in tourism-related government agencies.

Despite this, the rank and file career path in tourism and hospitality persisted, and a kind of 'anti-paper qualification' attitude remains until today, especially among the local general managers who had gone through the ranks and file system. Furthermore, tourism and hospitality education has always been looked down as an inferior field as opposed to medicine, law, engineering, etc.

3 The Growth of Tourism and Hospitality Education in Malaysia

Tourism and hospitality education in Malaysia has grown by leaps and bounds from 2000 onwards. Public universities such as Universiti Teknologi MARA (UiTM) (renamed from MARA Institute of Technology) and Universiti Utara Malaysia were the trailblazers by offering a wide range of tourism related undergraduate programmes. Following this trend, several public universities have also started similar programmes, mainly in the field of tourism and hotel management. Currently there are eight public universities offering tourism related undergraduate programmes. Interestingly there are around 16 postgraduate tourism-related programmes that are mostly being offered by public universities.

In addition to the tourism education programmes, there are 12 polytechnics nationwide that offer vocational training in the form of diploma and certificate level programmes mainly in hotel and tourism management. Furthermore, there are more than 40 community colleges offering certificate level training since 2000. While the polytechnics follow a common syllabus nationwide, the community colleges are given the flexibility to offer programmes that are appropriate to the needs of youth in the particular area such as pastry making, fashion design and animation, etc. Interestingly there is one community college that offers a programme for students with learning disability to operate food kiosks within tourism areas.

The growth in tourism education and training is more prevalent in the private sector in which there are around 36 private colleges and universities offering a wide range of programmes at the diploma, undergraduate and graduate levels. Twinning programmes with international universities are common and so are the setting up of Malaysian campuses for foreign universities such as Monash University, Swinburne

University and Curtin University (all offering tourism programmes). It has to be noted that the standard of the private universities is uneven—several universities such as Taylor's University and Sunway University are world renowned but there are also run-of-the-mill colleges that target foreign students. (See Table 1)

Table 1　Institutions offering tourism-related courses in Malaysia

Vocational Training	Undergraduate Education	Postgraduate Education
Twelve (12) Polytechnics	Eight (8) Public Universities	Sixteen (16) Mainly Public Universities
Forty (40) Community Colleges	Thirty-six (36) Private Colleges and Universities	—

Overall, tourism education in Malaysia has shown tremendous growth since 2000 onwards, driven by government initiatives as well as the savviness of the private sector. However, it has to be highlighted that the entry qualification for tourism-related programmes are relatively lower than that for medicine, law, architecture, accountancy, etc. As a consequence, tourism education has been suffering from an image problem and its inability to attract the so-called cream of today's youth. An example is the tourism management programme of Taylor's University—despite being ranked highly by QS World Ranking for Hospitality and Leisure Management in 2019, attracting and sustaining intake from both local and international students remain a challenge.

4　The Negative Image of the Tourism and Hospitality Profession

As mentioned earlier, tourism education in Malaysia is commonly viewed as a 'last resort' preference which is reflected in the relatively lower entrance qualification. In addition, a career in tourism has always been viewed negatively by strict Muslim families in Malaysia due to its real and perceived association with alcohol, vice and the hedonistic behavior of the minority of tourists. As a caveat, the growing popularity of Muslim-Friendly hotels in Malaysia (Islamic Tourism Centre, 2019) should not only be seen from the demand side but also as a reflection of the approval of this growing trend by parents.

The recently completed National Tourism Policy (NTP) (Ministry of Tourism, Arts and Culture, 2020) identifies that having a stable and rewarding career path as being the main factor to retain talent in the tourism and hospitality industry. Central to the human capital development for the Malaysian tourism industry, according to the NTP, is addressing the image of the tourism and hospitality profession. One of the most challenging impediments is the negative image of the spa industry, which is a paradox, because it is potentially a high value offering, but at the same time is tainted by the unsavoury practices of so-called reflexology centres. Consequently, Malaysia has to be dependent on foreign therapists despite the various initiatives and support by the government and associations in creating spa training centres. Suffice to say that tourism education and training in Malaysia has been burdened with an image problem that has persisted until today.

5 Is Postgraduate Tourism Education in Malaysia Rewarding?

Tourism postgraduate education in Malaysia is a relatively recent phenomenon. The Tourism Planning programme (master of science) offered by Universiti Teknologi Malaysia (UTM) was the first of its kind—a standalone programme that is not attached to the usual MBA programme. Commencing in 1998, this programme was aimed at offering a specialization that was different from the typical tourism management courses that focus on hotel and tourism management. Together with the Master in Tourism Development being offered by Universiti Sains Malaysia (USM), these two programmes are the only postgraduate programmes that focus on tourism policy planning and spatial planning at the destination level.

As highlighted earlier, there are around 16 public and private universities that are offering postgraduate tourism education up to the Ph. D. level. However, most of these specializations are offered either as part of MBA programmes, a generic programme in the first year followed by specialisation in the final year/semester or by research only.

Postgraduate tourism education in Malaysia has been growing at a gradual rate and there have been attempts in offering specialised programmes in ecotourism, sustainable tourism and even Islamic tourism. However, the fear of not having student numbers to sustain such programmes had impeded the actual realisation of previous attempts. Having a post graduate tourism education is not a rewarding investment in Malaysia. Few officers from the public sector who are working in tourism-related areas are willing to improve their knowledge by enrolling into a Master's programme in tourism because the public service in Malaysia is based on a rotation system in which officers could be transferred to different agencies several times during their service. Furthermore, many of the government officers prefer to study during weekends so that they do not have to apply for study leave which might affect their service and promotion. Most importantly, having a Master's degree does not qualify a government officer for a promotion or pay rise, hence those who pursued postgraduate education in tourism in the past, mainly did it for self-satisfaction and the love of knowledge.

In response to this demand, Malaysian universities have resorted to offering so-called offshore programmes that are conducted specifically for a group of government officers or academics involving lectures during weekends once every fortnight. Another variant that is being introduced is a modular system in which students could 'pick and choose' modules to accumulate enough credits to qualify for the conferment of a Master's degree. In essence, these innovative approaches involving more flexible modes of conducting such programmes reflect the aspiration of the Malaysian government in establishing the country as an education hub. In turn, universities are encouraged to be more flexible in their approach which includes the conferment of double/dual degrees with renowned international universities.

Although local students still form the bulk of the postgraduate enrolment in both public and private universities, international students especially from the Global South are increasingly being attracted to study tourism in Malaysia—which is a testimony to the government's success in transforming Malaysia into an education hub. Indonesia provides the highest number of foreign students seeking postgraduate tourism education in Malaysia, in which the majority are young academics seeking a secure career path in tourism education.

African countries, notably Nigeria, have been sending postgraduate students since 2000. In addition, the Middle East has a significant student population in Malaysia. There used to be a sizeable population of Iranian students coming to Malaysia to study due to their restricted opportunities to study in the West that were caused by geopolitics. Malaysia was like an 'oasis' for Iranian students but this flow ceased once restrictions by the West were lifted several years ago. However, the current escalating tensions between Iran and the USA might bring back the former restrictions and sanctions, and in turn, Iranian students might return in droves to Malaysia. A recent phenomenon is the increasing number of Chinese postgraduate students. The main reasons why international students are coming to study in Malaysia are the decent quality of its universities, the affordable fees and cost of living and a safe and comfortable living environment. Nonetheless there have been isolated cases where run-of-the-mill private training institutions have been used as a base for a minority of foreign students to undertake illegal activities such as the distribution of illegal drugs and prostitution.

Within the tourism industry, postgraduate education is not valued nor rewarded given the rank and file legacy of the profession. Very few hotels or tour operators would consider sponsoring their staff to pursue postgraduate education. Moreover, staff who had used their own expenses to obtain a master's degree will seldom be considered for a promotion or a pay rise. To surmise, it could be said that there seems to be an attitude of apathy towards postgraduate education within the tourism industry in Malaysia.

6 Types of Tourism Education and Training

Essentially the majority of tourism education and training courses in Malaysia are currently focused on the traditional courses such as hotel management, tourism management and culinary arts. These are considered as 'safe courses' that are relatively easy to obtain approval from the Ministry of Education and Malaysian Qualifications Agency (MQA). Such programmes are also distinctly vocational in nature to prepare graduates for the skills sets required by the industry such as managing hotel bookings, organizing outbound group travel and making flight reservations, etc. Specifically, these skills sets are suited to the job specifications of hoteliers and tour operators. To differentiate their programme from other offered by other universities, individual universities would add value to their generic programme by highlighting a specific focus area such as tourism entrepreneurship, which in reality, is only reflected in a few elective subjects offered in the final semester.

In the last 10 years, the only notable addition to the traditional courses has been event management due to the increasing focus by the government on MICE and business events as a potentially high value tourism segment. Despite Malaysia's outstanding reputation as a nature and ecotourism destination, it is perplexing that there is no specific undergraduate or postgraduate on ecotourism or sustainable tourism. The only exception is the Parks and Recreation degree being offered by Universiti Putra Malaysia (UPM) which is still attracting students more than 30 years since it was started. As both public and private universities are competing against each other within the comfort zone of traditional hotel and tourism management programmes, the neglect of ecotourism and sustainable tourism standalone programmes is becoming increasingly apparent. It is also interesting to highlight that among senior tourism academics in Malaysia, there have been discussions on the possibility of introducing programmes on Islamic Tourism and its variants, Halal Tourism and Muslim Friendly Tourism.

7　The Need to Embrace Smart Tourism

The National Tourism Policy (Ministry of Tourism, Arts and Culture, 2020) proposes that tourism education in Malaysia should fully embrace Smart Tourism in their curriculum and syllabus. Interviews conducted with selected public and private universities as part of the National Tourism Policy planning process revealed a vacuum in terms of the incorporation of Smart Tourism subjects and modules. A common area for concern is the limited inclusion of Information Technology such as AR, VR, Internet of Things, GIS, etc. As such the existing curriculum and syllabus of tourism education have often been critiqued as 'preparing the tourism human capital not for tomorrow but for yesterday'.

Elements of tourism entrepreneurship taught in the existing curriculum and syllabus focus only on conventional skills sets for producing tour operators (yesterday) and not tour advisors (tomorrow). In addition, new entrepreneurial opportunities such as tourism technology startups have not been given adequate emphasis. Out of the total number of startups nationwide, less than 5% are related to tourism, which reflects not only the negligible presence of tourism startups but also their lack of support. In comparison, tourism startups in South Korea are supported by tourism startups accelerators schemes and regular competitions, etc.

The use of Big Data Analytics is also recommended in the National Tourism Policy as part of Malaysia's journey towards Smart Tourism. To achieve this would require competent data scientists but the silo nature of tourism education has not been able to create interest and opportunities among students in Information Technology programmes to enroll for elective subjects in tourism. While universities have developed a strong synergy with the tourism industry in developing their curriculum and syllabus, most of the practitioners who are invited to give advice are veteran hoteliers and heads of travel companies. As the tourism industry is moving towards Smart Tourism, universities have not identified the need to appoint advisors from the IT fraternity for tourism education to leverage of fresh opportunities associated with the Industrial Revolution 4.0. Needless to say, having a more flexible approach to tourism education would be able to expand the career path of tourism graduates and elevate the image of tourism education in the long run.

8 The Way Forward

Tourism education and training in Malaysia is caught in a comfort zone. As described earlier, the mushrooming of public and private universities and colleges bodes well for the human capital development of the industry. However, tourism education and training have not ventured into new and exciting territories such as ecotourism, sustainable tourism and Smart Tourism. There appears to be a disconnect between tourism education and practice in Malaysia especially in the context of the strategic direction and transformation agenda contained in the National Ecotourism Plan and National Tourism Policy. In essence, tourism education in Malaysia is not moving with the times, which in turn, might affect the competitiveness of the industry in the future. The following suggestions are put forward to address these challenges:

8.1 Improving the Image of the Tourism Profession and Career

Improving the image of the tourism profession and career will entice talented youth to enroll into tourism and hospitality courses not as a 'last resort' option but as a preferred choice. This could be achieved by promoting the tourism profession and career in a positive and 'sexy' manner. Towards this end, reality TV shows could be used as a medium to highlight the excitement, tangible and intangible benefits and career paths associated with the tourism profession. In addition, tourism education fairs should be regularly organised during which captains of the industry could play an ambassadorial role.

8.2 Aligning Tourism Education with Smart Tourism

As travel becomes more specialised, bespoke and customized the role of tour operators have taken over by travel advisors. As a consequence, the skills sets of travel advisors should include a mastery in using IT and social media. Universities and other training institutions should explore the incorporation of Smart Tourism not as a subject or two in their curriculum and syllabus but as the foundation for transforming human capital development in the tourism industry in line with the Industrial Revolution 4.0.

8.3 Focusing on Tourism Technology Startups

In line with Smart Tourism, the focus of tourism education in the future should be the unlocking of the energy and creativity of youth to operate tourism technology startups. It is posited that creativity and innovation in the Malaysian tourism industry could only be achieved once a pool of successful tourism startups emerges to fundamentally transform the industry using IT and digitalization. Nonetheless, it should be stressed that content, storytelling and service quality are equally crucial in the development of successful tourism startups.

9 Conclusions

Formal tourism education in Malaysia has come a long way from its initial introduction in the 1960s. The growth of the tourism and hospitality education sector has been encouraging despite the negative image and the attitude of apathy toward postgraduate tourism education. The way forward for the sector in Malaysia today is to embrace Smart Tourism and improving the image of the tourism career as one that is exciting, full of opportunities and desirable. These will unlock the potential and creativity of Malaysia's youth in coming up with new ideas and innovations through tourism startups that will drive the tourism industry forward this decade.

References

[1] ECONOMIC PLANNING UNIT. The sixth Malaysia plan (1991 – 1995) [R]. Kuala Lumpur: Government Printers, 1991.
[2] ISLAMIC TOURISM CENTRE. Muslim-Friendly Hotel Recognition [R]. Putrajaya:

ITC, 2019.

[3] KING V T. Tourism and culture in Malaysia [M] //HITCHCOCK M, PARNWELL M. Tourism in Southeast Asia. London: Routledge, 1993.

[4] MINISTRY OF TOURISM, ARTS AND CULTURE. National Tourism Policy 2020-2030 [R]. Putrajaya: Ministry of Tourism, Arts and Culture, 2020.

缅甸旅游教育

Thida Aung　曼德勒大学法学系

1　定义

旅游是指为人们到某地游玩时提供服务的行业。这一表述包括旅游经营、酒店和旅馆业务、导游和其他与旅游有关的服务。[《2018年缅甸旅游法》第2（a）条]

旅游是休闲旅行或商业旅行；也是旅游的理论和实践，吸引、容纳游客和为游客提供娱乐的业务，以及经营旅游的业务。（维基百科）

2　缅甸

缅甸是东南亚的一个主权国家，拥有一条沿孟加拉湾和安达曼海分布的长1930千米的海岸线（占缅甸国土周长的近1/3），以及与5个国家毗邻的长达5876千米的陆地边界线。缅甸的邻国包括孟加拉国、印度、中国、老挝和泰国。

缅甸的国土总面积为676 578平方千米，居世界第四十，也是东盟的第二大国，仅次于印度尼西亚。行政上分为7个州和7个地区。缅甸拥有丰富的自然资源，如耕地、林业资源、矿产、天然气、石油、淡水和海洋资源，也是宝石和玉石的主要来源国。

此外，缅甸有丰富多样的文化资产，包括物质和非物质的遗产，特别是与宗教习俗和乡土生活密切相关的遗产，是传统遗产与现代生活方式共存的鲜活例证。

缅甸的人口约5500万（2013年），是世界上第二十五大人口大国，官方承认的民族有135个，具有民族多元性。

缅甸拥有长达1930千米的海岸线、大量的历史地标和多元文化传统，因而有许多潜在的旅游景点。

政府已经制订了旅游发展总体规划，旨在将缅甸建设成东南亚的主要旅游国，满足其日益增长的国际游客的需求。

3 旅游教育

旅游业是缅甸的新兴行业。尽管缅甸在许多领域具有巨大的旅游潜力和吸引力，但旅游教育的许多方面仍待发展。

2008年《缅甸联邦宪法》：阐述了联邦政府在教育方面的义务和所有缅甸公民受教育的权利。

2014年《国家教育法》和2015年修正案：根据国家战略规划（2016—2021年）中的国家教育法（NEL）的规定，在2017—2018学年，国家将采用K-12教育体系，将学校教育延长两年，并且还将提供免费教育。这不仅会增加国民受教育的机会，也让适龄儿童有条件继续上学。

文学士（旅游）：自2012年以来，仰光的国家管理学院和曼德勒的曼达拉尔学院开设了为期4年的全日制旅游课程，每年招收100名学生，条件是学生至少有60分的英语成绩和400分的总成绩。

国家管理学位学院（NMDC）：向学生提供了一系列多样化的适用课程，包括商业管理、新闻学、旅游和酒店管理以及专业英语。通过多种方式来评估模块的学习成果，包括完成书面作业、期末考试和导师指导的展示报告、短期作业和实操。

旅游管理文凭：在此之前，仰光的国家管理学院和曼德勒的曼德勒大学从2006年开始提供旅游管理专业的研究生文凭。按照曼德勒大学人力资源开发项目，文凭课程历时9个月，上课时间为每周一到周五的上午7时至9时。

4 《缅甸旅游总体规划2013—2020》

为了缅甸旅游业的可持续发展，缅甸政府组织编制了第一个全国旅游发展规划——《缅甸旅游总体规划2013—2020》。该规划由酒店与旅游部编制，得到了缅甸国内各利益相关群体、挪威政府、亚洲开发银行以及许多专家团队的大力支持。

《缅甸旅游总体规划2013—2020》（以下简称《总规划》）与2012—2015年的《经济和社会改革框架》以及即将出台的《国家综合发展计划》的政策保持一致，以负责任旅游和《缅甸负责任政策》的愿景与九大目标作为其核心指导原则。《总规划》的目标是最大限度地提高旅游业对国民就业和创收的贡献，并确保旅游业的社会和经济利益得到公平分配。

《总规划》指出，缅甸将努力打造成全天候、全地域旅游目的地，欢迎来自世界各地的游客,并将继续促进旅客入境的便利化和高效化。值得一提的是,提升旅游业的价值和收益将优先于简单地增加国际游客的数量。

此外,缅甸将在确保东道主社区福祉和自然与文化遗产保护,与发展旅游业增进外汇收入和提高国内生产总值(GDP)之间取得平衡。

5 酒店与旅游部

仰光酒店培训学校(Hospitality Training School,HTS)于2016年6月1日在酒店与旅游部的指导下及缅甸旅游联合会和卢森堡发展合作署的协助下成立。

酒店与旅游部设有一个培训中心,提供导游培训、基本旅游和接待业管理以及沉浸式语言等短期课程。

根据《总规划》,2020年缅甸国际游客的目标接待量为748万。这对酒店服务的要求很高,酒店服务需要进一步改进以实现缅甸旅游业的规划目标。虽然缅甸旅游业蓬勃发展,但政府需要改善各方面的基础设施以达到国际标准。缅甸酒店与旅游部根据政府的改革战略和经济自由化政策,强调要以可持续和负责任的方式发展和管理旅游业。

6 结论

旅游业在推动缅甸社会经济发展方面发挥了重要作用,旅游教育的重要性自然不言而喻。缅甸也正努力通过扩大财政预算、制定新的国家教育法和免除公立学校学费等政策优先推进全面教育改革,提升国民素质。需要指出的是,缅甸正试图改革其教育体系以与东盟其他国家的教育体系保持一致。当然,这些改革难免面临挑战。

Tourism Education in Myanmar

Thida Aung, Department of Law, University of Mandalay

1 Definition

Tourism means the business of providing services for people visiting places for their pleasure. This expression includes provisions of tour operation, hotel and guest-house business, tour guiding and other services related to tourism. (Section 2 (a) of the Myanmar Tourism Law 2018)

Tourism is travel for pleasure or business; also the theory and practice of touring, the business of attracting, accommodating, and entertaining tourists, and the business of operating tours.

2 Myanmar

Myanmar, a sovereign state in Southeast Asia, has about 1/3 of its total perimeter of 1,930 kilometers (1,200 miles) forming a continuous coastline along the Bay of Bengal and the Andaman Sea and also about 5,876 kilometers of land boundaries shared with 5 nations. The neighboring countries are Bangladesh, India, China, Laos and Thailand.

It is the world's 40th largest country and the 2nd largest in the Association of Southeast Asian Nations (ASEAN) after Indonesia with a total area of 676,578 square kilometers. It is administratively divided into seven states and seven regions. Myanmar is endowed with abundance of natural resources, for example, arable land, forestry, minerals, natural gas, oil, freshwater and marine resources, and is a leading source of gems and jade.

Also, their rich and diverse cultural assets, both tangible and intangible heritages, especially those closely related to religious practices and vernacular living, are still the vivid evidences of the co-existing between their heritages and the ways of life at present.

Myanmar has a population of about 55 million (in 2013), making it the world's 25th most populous country with ethnic diversity of distinct 135 ethnic groups officially recognized by the government.

Myanmar is endowed with many potential tourist attractions arising from its 1,930 km coastline, its historical landmarks and a variety of cultural traditions.

The government has drawn up a tourism development master plan, which seeks to build Myanmar into a leading tourist destination in Southeast Asia, and to cater to the increasing number of tourists arriving in Myanmar.

3 Tourism Education

Tourism in Myanmar is a developing sector. Although Myanmar possesses great tourist potential and attractions in many fields, much of the industry remains to be developed.

The Constitution of the Union of Myanmar 2008: The constitution of the Union of Myanmar 2008 describes those obligations of the Union regarding education and the rights of all Myanmar citizens to an education.

National Education Law 2014 and the Amendment 2015: In the 2017 – 2018 academic year, the country will adopt the K – 12 structure, extending schooling by two years, and education will also be made free, as stipulated in the NEL under the National Strategic Plan (2016 – 2021). That will also be taken to improve not only access to education, but also creating the conditions that will keep children in school.

BA (Tourism): Tourism courses have been available since 2012 at the National Management Degree College in Yangon and Mandalar College in Mandalay the four-year, full-time course, which also admits 100 students a year, provided they have scored at least 60 in English and 400 in total.

National Management Degree College (NMDC): National Management Degree College (NMDC) is now offering a diverse set of applicable subjects: Business Management, Journalism, Tourism and Hospitality Management and English for Professional Purposes to the students.

The learning outcomes of modules are assessed in a number of ways including through the completion of written assignments, final examinations and tutorial led presentations, short assignments and practical application of learning.

Diploma in Tourism Studies and Management (DTSM): Prior to that, a postgraduate diploma in Tourism Studies Management was offered by the National Management Degree College in Yangon and University of Mandalay in Mandalay starting in 2006. Diploma course has taken nine months, from 7 to 9 am on Monday to Friday under the Human Resources Development Programme in University of Mandalay.

4 The Myanmar Tourism Master Plan 2013-2020

In order to create a roadmap to shape the sustainable tourism future in Myanmar, the Government of Myanmar decided to formulate the first Myanmar Tourism Master Plan 2013-2020, which was prepared by the Ministry of Hotel and Tourism with closely collaborative involvement or aid-assisted by various internal stakeholders, the Government of Norway, the Asian Development Bank and many expert teams.

The Master Plan, aligning with the 2012-2015 policy priorities of the Framework for Economic and Social Reforms and the parameters of the forthcoming National Comprehensive Development Plan, mainly adopts the Responsible Tourism approach and the vision and the 9 aims of the Myanmar Responsible Policy, which was developed through an extensive consultative process and with broad support from national stakeholders, as its core guiding principle. The goal of the Master Plan is to maximize tourism's contribution to national employment and income generation, and ensure that social and economic benefits of tourism are distributed equitably.

The Master Plan states that Myanmar will work to develop Myanmar as a year-round destination with a geographically spread product base. It welcomes tourists from around the world and will continue to facilitate smooth and efficient access to the country. Importantly, the value and yield of tourism will take precedence over simply increasing the volume of international visitors.

Furthermore, Myanmar will balance the need to ensure the well-being of host communities and the protection of its natural and cultural heritage with the need to boost tourism's contribution to foreign exchange earnings and gross domestic product (GDP) growth.

5 The Ministry of Hotels and Tourism

The Hospitality Training School (HTS) Yangon was founded on 1st June,

2016 under the guidance of the Ministry of Hotels and Tourism with the assistance of the Myanmar Tourism Federation and Luxembourg Agency for Development Cooperation.

The Ministry of Hotels and Tourism runs a training center that offers short-term courses in guide training and basic tourism and hospitality management, as well as language immersion programs.

The Myanmar Tourism Master Plan 2013 – 2020 has set a target of 7.48 million international visitors in 2020. However, there is still high demand for hospitality services which need to be improved for Myanmar to achieve its target for the tourism industry. Although Myanmar has enjoyed a boom in the tourism industry, the government needs to improve infrastructure in all aspects to meet international standards.

The Ministry of Hotels and Tourism of the Republic of the Union of Myanmar has placed considerable emphasis on developing and managing tourism in sustainable and responsible ways in line with the Government's reform strategies and economic liberalization.

6 Conclusion

Myanmar is trying to make the education reform a national priority for human development with an enlarged budget, a new national education law and the removal of public school fees. However, significant challenges remain. Now, she is trying to change the education system in line with ASEAN countries. The tourism business has played a major role in driving forward Myanmar's economic development.

遗产旅游：越南近期研究和教育回顾

Dang Thi Phuong Anh　越南河内国家大学社会科学与人类学学院

遗产旅游是当今旅游业中占比最大、最受欢迎和增长最快的旅游形式之一。事实上，遗产旅游的增长速度似乎比其他形式的旅游都要快，尤其是在发展中国家，遗产旅游也因此被视为社区减贫和经济发展的重要潜在工具（UNWTO，2015）。遗产旅游通常依赖于生活方式和建筑中的文化元素，利用有形和无形的过去作为旅游资源。它涵盖了现今存在的作为遗产的文化和民俗，其他非物质遗产（音乐、舞蹈、语言、宗教、美食、艺术传统和节日），以及文化建筑遗迹（纪念碑、历史公共建筑和民居、农场、城堡、博物馆、考古遗址和文物）。尽管过去的遗产旅游主要集中在特权阶层的遗产上，但现在人们普遍认可和接受普通人（家庭、农民、工厂工人、矿工、渔民、妇女和儿童）的日常生活景观（Timothy & Boyd，2006a）作为旅游资源。自19世纪末以来，遗产一直是旅游业的关注热点。关于遗产旅游本质的学术争论仍然存在，这表明遗产是一个模糊的概念和复杂的现象。因此，不同国家对遗产旅游的研究和教育问题也将相应地具有不同的特点。在一般的旅游研究中，尤其是在遗产旅游中，人们普遍意识到旅游业及其影响、制约和管理在发达国家和发展中国家是不同的。越南是发展中国家，遗产旅游研究与教育有其自身的属性，越南政府亦可以基于这一属性确定发展方向。

1　当今越南的遗产旅游

越南是一个发展中国家，拥有丰富的遗产。越南有3 000多处遗迹被认定为国家级遗产（文化部鉴定，Nguyen Ngoc Thien，2016），包括历史遗址、宗教和信仰遗址、建筑群、博物馆、传统节日、手工艺和传统工艺村、传统音乐和艺术……这些是越南通过发展历史文化和遗产旅游来吸引游客的基础（根据1997年在新加坡举行的"越南旅游机会"会议）。在另一项针对21世纪头10年前往越南的国际游客的调查中，82%的人认为遗产旅游是当今越南具有旅游吸引力的主要因素。越南拥有独特的不同类型的文化遗产，吸引着不同类型的游客。这包括代表传统的中越文化遗址，法国殖民时期的遗址，非传统的、尚有争议的"战争旅游"遗址，以及体验世界上为数不多的共产主义社会的机会（W. Suntikul，R. Butler，D. Airey，2010）。

被联合国教科文组织列为世界遗产可能是对文化旅游地最高的认可，因为它表明这些遗址具有独特的全球文化意义。越南有8个世界遗产地，详见表1。

表1 越南世界遗产地

联合国教科文组织世界遗产地	列入年份	属性种类
顺化历史建筑群	1993	文化
下龙湾	1994，2000	自然
会安古镇	1999	文化
美山圣地	1999	文化
方芽—科邦国家公园	2003，2015	自然
河内升龙皇城	2010	文化
胡朝时期的城堡	2011	文化
长安名胜群	2014	混合

资料来源：https://whc.unesco.org/en/statesparties/vn

在过去几年中，这些世界遗产地不仅在越南家喻户晓，也成了外国游客关注的焦点。

鉴于文化遗产具有如此大的发展潜力，越南政府着眼于促进遗产地发展来带动旅游发展。政府文件、指导方针、政策和社会经济发展战略中均提到了遗产旅游，如《旅游法》《文化遗产法》《近期至2020年、远期至2030年的越南旅游发展战略》《近期至2020年、远期至2030年的越南文化产业发展战略》《近期至2025年、远期至2030年的旅游产品发展战略》。值得一提的是，2017年的08-NQ/TW号决议提出，"将旅游业发展成为国家重点产业"。这些文件提到了以下重要问题：具有民族文化特征的旅游产品是吸引游客、提高越南旅游业区域和国际竞争力的重要因素；旅游业的发展必须以保护和提升越南的文化价值为目标；大力发展遗产旅游，保质保量显著发展，为经济增长做出积极贡献。

这些政策促进了近年来越南旅游业的发展。联合国世界旅游组织指出，东南亚是所有亚洲次区域中旅游人数增长最快的地区，2017年新增了900万国际游客。亚洲东北部客源市场的强劲需求推动了东南亚各旅游目的地的发展。

越南的入境人数增长最快,而这个次区域最大的旅游目的地——泰国则增加了300万人次。免签和更加便利的航空联通也有效带动了该次区域旅游的发展(UNWTO,2018)。过去三年来,越南国际游客人数增长迅猛,根据《贸易经济学》的统计数据,在2019年10月达到了161.83万人,创历年之最。(如图1所示)

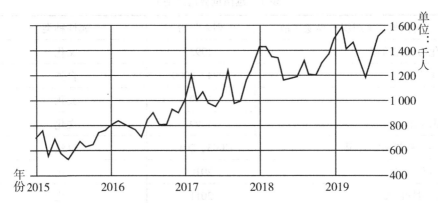

图1 越南国际游客人数增长

资料来源:https://tradingeconomics.com/vietnam/tourist-arrivals

因此,越南旅游总收入显著增长。越南的旅游收入在2018年12月达到270亿美元,创下历史新高(前一年同期为230亿美元)。[①] 这表明旅游业已经成为越南国民经济的重要支柱,为经济增长做出了积极贡献。值得一提的是,遗产旅游被定位为越南旅游产品的四大基石之一。遗产旅游是仅次于休闲旅游的第二大旅游产品。遗产旅游业的收入占2019年越南旅游总收入的10%~25%。

遗产旅游的快速发展带来了一些积极和消极的影响。其中,积极影响包括以下几点。

(1) 保护和保留重要的遗产。
(2) 带动地方经济发展。
(3) 旅游业的收入可用于改善地方基础设施。
(4) 可以振兴传统文化。

此外,不可避免地会产生一些负面影响。

(1) 游客对设施和资源的过度使用,如景区过度拥挤,停车、垃圾和噪

---

① 数据来源为司尔亚司数据信息有限公司(CEIC)全球数据库。

音问题等，使公共资源难堪重负。

（2）对旅游业的过度依赖导致一些自负盈亏的传统劳动方式消失。

（3）部分游客缺乏礼貌和文化敏感性。

（4）无序的旅游基础设施建设会影响社区的生活设施、地区的旅游吸引力以及游客体验。

（5）收入流向少数行业。

（6）失去对文化财产的控制。

这些现象表明，旅游与文化遗产的关系并不总是和谐的。在越南这样的旅游业正蓬勃发展的国家，这些因素相互作用所产生的问题变得越来越复杂。在这样的背景下，遗产旅游研究和教育正在兴起。那么，越南的遗产旅游研究和教育进展如何呢？本文通过对越南遗产旅游研究和教育的回顾来回应这一问题。

2 近期研究回顾

遗产旅游研究可以从旅游研究和文化遗产研究两个方面来展开。但从旅游的角度看，越南的研究尚未对"遗产旅游"进行具体的阐释。而在越南学者的研究中，文化遗产仅被描述为文化旅游产品的一个组成部分。遗产旅游被理解为一个以文化资源为开发对象的过程，服务于理解、享受、体验和感受目的地文化、社会和人类价值观的需求。（Tran Thuy Anh，2011；Nguyen Pham Hung，2016）因此，人们常常从文化遗产的角度来研究遗产旅游。这些研究大致可以分为以下三类。

第一，一些研究阐释了当代社会中遗产的概念、角色和重要性。学者们根据联合国教科文组织的定义、越南《文化遗产法》（2001）以及《文化遗产法》若干修正和补充条款（2009）重新阐释遗产的内涵，强调遗产在当前背景下的作用和价值。Nguyen Thi Kim Loan（2014）和她的同事认为，文化遗产是一项国家资产和发展资源，是团结人民的灵魂，是文化认同的载体，是人类文化多样性和丰富性的表达，是形成新价值体系的重要因素。Nguyen Thi Thu Ha（2013）认为，随着科学技术的发展，将遗产纳入文化产业是帮助遗产提升其价值的一种重要方式。Nguyen Quoc Hung（2006）表示，文化遗产对越南的发展越来越重要。许多遗产地已成为旅游线路中的重要目的地，对国家和地方财政收入（通过门票收入、创造就业机会、吸引外国投资、促进地方基础设施升级）做出了重大贡献。Le Hong Ly 及其同事 Duong Van Sau、Dang Hoai Thu（2010）也强调了文化遗产在越南旅游发展中的重要性，他们提到了许多遗产，并说明了它们的特点以证明它们是文化旅游产品。此外，Nguyen Pham-Hung（2016）也阐述了文化遗产在旅游发展中的作用，但他认为所有的旅游活动都包含文化元素，因而遗产存在于所有形式的旅游之中。

第二，还有研究对遗产管理进行了探讨。遗产既然具有如此重要的作用和价值，因此，文化遗产的管理一直是越南国内研究的重要议题。大多数研究聚焦越南工业化和现代化发展背景之下的遗产管理理论与实践、文化遗产保护与利用等议题，并针对具体案例提出解决方案和建议。首先，有学者介绍了遗产管理的理论，希望以这些理论来指导文化遗产管理和保护。（Bui Hoai Son，2005）还有一种观点认为，越南当前文化遗产管理需要采取跨学科视角来进行。（Dang VanBai，2010）基于国际经验的本土化创新，不少研究旨在提出切实可行的管理模式、方法和措施。遗产管理通常涉及两个方面：①国家管理，包括颁布法律文件等，显示党和国家在保护文化遗产方面的指导方针和政策；②非商业发展，重点分析古迹保护的好处，如国家为革命遗产保护和修复投入大量资金，不少革命遗址已成为激动人心的景点等。（Phan Hong Giang，Bui Hoai Son，2014）需要指出的是，这些研究最为关注的是国家在遗产管理中的角色。这是一个重要议题，因为国家的法律文件（包括关于保护和提升文化遗产价值的法律文件，关于规划机制、组织和发展计划的决定，管理权力下放的决定……）、历史遗迹管理权下放、遗产保护产业组织体系和遗产管理机构财政预算等是影响遗产管理效率的决定性因素。（Dang Van Bai，2001）总之，无论具体议题如何，学者们一致认为，文化遗产管理要在遗产保护和利用中找到平衡点（Ngo Duc Thinh，2001；Dang Van Bai，2007；Bui Hoai Son，2009）。

第三，一些研究探讨了遗产与旅游的关系，以及遗产旅游这种形式。在越南，目前虽然已有一些研究论文或在旅游和遗产相关会议上发表的文章探讨了旅游业在保护和提升遗产价值方面的作用，但对遗产管理与旅游发展之间关系的系统性和长期性的研究还不多。现有研究主要厘清了以下问题：旅游与文化遗产之间的有机或二元关系（Bui Hoai Son，2010）；旅游业带来的影响，如旅游业对社区、遗产和环境的积极和消极影响（Dang Van Bai，2001，2013）；文化遗产在旅游业中的发展潜力（Nguyen Quoc Hung，2004，2006）；管控旅游业影响的发展思路（Nguyen Thi Thu Ha，2013）。自越南共产党中央政治局2017年第08-NQ/TW号决议提出"发展旅游业成为重要经济行业"以来，为了充分利用各种文化遗产的潜在价值以满足游客需求，利用文化遗产发展旅游业这一议题日益受到学界关注（Lethi Thu Phuong，2017；Trinh Le Anh，2018）。值得一提的是，Nguyen Thi Thu Ha基于McKercher B和du Cros H（2002）的冲突—合作模型探讨了文化遗产管理与旅游发展之间的关系。该文章描述了二者间积极或消极的关系,以及对遗产的影响(Nguyen Thi Thu Ha, 2016)。

上述研究涵盖了当前遗产旅游地的理论和实践议题。然而,现有研究在将国际上的理论方法应用于越南遗产旅游地时往往缺乏足够的解释力,将一般旅游研究范式用于遗产旅游研究时会发现二者仍然存在差距,无法彻底解决旅游开发与遗产保护之间的矛盾。这些不足就是今后越南遗产旅游研究的基本方向。

3 旅游教育综述

遗产旅游地的可持续发展涉及教育、员工培训、从业者、地方居民和游客等方方面面,需要将旅游的负面影响最小化。

越南遗产旅游地的发展现状表明,导游和讲解员短缺,能满足游客期望的合格导游更是稀缺。遗产地的导游是对遗产、历史、文化、自然保护区、博物馆等进行讲解、引导、介绍、传播和教育的人。他们是对遗产地最为了解的群体之一,其使命不仅是履行遗产地旅游大使的职责,而且要有助于弘扬当地文化价值。他们还需要拥有实践技能,不仅要尽可能满足游客的需求,而且还要能够指引游客,确保游客在遗产地获得知识并且行为举止得体。此外,在国际知名遗产地,导游人员必须满足游客的外语导览需求。事实上,尽管导游群体在越南的遗产旅游地发展中担任如此重要的角色,但他们还没有满足市场的需求。在游客人数快速增长的知名景点,专业导游的人数不足以为每位游客提供周到而专业的服务。例如,2016年下龙湾接待了290多万游客,其中国际游客190万,与2015年相比增长了12.6%。然而,下龙湾管理委员会配备的解说团队只有22人,其中1/4会说流利的外语,主要是英语和汉语,而其他外语几乎没有。在著名的遗产旅游景点,导游的水平也有差异。一个优秀的导游,需要兼具知识与技能。在小型旅游景点或当地遗迹中,一些未经培训的导游被雇佣上岗,这损害了旅游地旅游产品的服务质量。

这一问题与越南过去数年的遗产旅游教育和培训不无关系。越南有一套包括大学、旅游专业学校和职业学校的旅游教育体系。在大学里,有一些与旅游业密切相关的培训课程,如文化研究、越南研究和历史科学等。然而,在这些培训方案中,没有专门针对遗产旅游的方案,甚至没有任何关于遗产旅游的课程。遗产旅游只在旅游文化、可持续旅游发展、目的地管理或文化遗产管理等课程中被提及。此外,这些课程只存在于大学或更高级别的教育体系中,这导致专科院校和职高毕业生对遗产旅游缺乏深入了解。相比之下,深度的学科理论学习又会导致学生缺乏旅游实操技能。对此,《近期至2020年、远期至2030年的越南文化产业发展战略》中提出了解决办法和培养目标,即"培训和开发文化旅游人力资源,特别是人力资源管理人员、导游、讲解员和其他一线服务人员。按照东盟职业标准提升文化旅游业职业培训质量"。最近,越南国家旅游局制定了相当多的解决方案,以逐步实现导游和讲解员的标准化,充分利用欧盟和联合国教科文组织在技术和经费方面的支持,为导游和讲解员制定培养方案,规划专业知识、专业技能及外语等培训内容。越南国家旅游局还致力于研究和开发一套针对13个职业(包括导游和讲解员)的越南旅游技能标准(Vietnam's tourism skills standards,VTOS)。在不久的将来,越南国家旅游局将与劳动、荣军和社会事务部合作,制定和引入国家职业技能标准,包括旅游解说员职业技能标准。许多国际组织也一直在支持越南的遗产地开发和讲解员培训。例如,联合国教科文组织和国际劳工组织设置专家培训班,举办世界遗产地导游讲解越南知名遗产地(即河内、广南、顺化、岘港)的活动(Dinh Thi Hong Nhung,2018)。

遗产旅游教育不仅面向在遗产地工作和管理的相关人员,还面向其他利益相关者。遗产地旅游形象的恶化也与当地居民在遗产旅游发展中寻求短期利益、缺乏对遗产价值的认知不无关系。因此,在现今越南的遗产旅游目的地,典型的世界遗产地如会安古镇、下龙湾、顺化等,遗产管理委员会定期举办培训课程,以提高当地居民对遗产保护的认识、社区参与遗产保护的积极性和居民与旅游企业合作的意愿,通过这些培训让旅游更好地惠及当地社区。每个当地人都可以成为遗产地导游。在一些遗产资源丰富但尚未进行旅游开发的地区,居民生活仍然很困难,越南国家旅游局、地方旅游部门等政府组织将与旅游教育培训机构或非政府组织进行协调,以惠及地方社区。他们组织了培训、再培训和指导人们从事旅游业,在老街、安沛、河江等少数民族省份,这些努力已初见成效。

游客对遗产地保护意识不足会给遗产地带来压力,包括环境污染、环境超载、不尊重当地文化、不遵守法律法规等问题。越南正在开展针对这些问题的教育活动,在遗产地实行更严格的规定,并通过标志牌、传单、讲座等来提供更详细的说明和警示。值得一提的是,提高游客意识的教育还通过具体的旅游产品反映出来,如"扮演"当地居民的一日游、旨在使用环保工具的绿色旅游、有明确主题的教育旅游和志愿旅游。对游客的教育不仅要在遗产地进行,还需要产品营销员、旅行社代表、全陪导游和当地居民等方方面面加以配合,以确保游客在进入遗产地之前获得"绿色通行证"。

近年来,越南的遗产旅游教育虽然尚未完善,也没能完全跟上旅游业快速发展的步伐，但相关群体已经在为管控和减少遗产旅游的负面影响而努力。

4 结论

旅游是一种多层次、多构面的现象，涵盖了许多不同类型的活动。游客带着不同的动机前往不同的目的地。在文化景点中，如历史场所、纪念碑、建筑和艺术是旅行的首要选择。许多类型的景点都属于遗产旅游，占旅游业的很大一部分。遗产旅游快速发展，可以使公众和官方更广泛地承认文化遗产地的重要地位。在旅游情境中，"遗产"一词包括目的地文化和自然两方面因素。但是，文化被认为是遗产景点的必要组成部分。因此，遗产旅游不仅是一种将游客带到遗产地的活动，也包括当地居民、游客、旅游企业在遗产地的社会互动。因此，遗产旅游是一种特殊的旅游类型，它体现了遗产地与旅游发展之间的复杂关系。当旅游活动蓬勃发展时，遗产地会受到很多影响，这让遗产旅游研究和教育有用武之地。如果研究和教育不能跟上现实的发展，就会导致遗产保护与发展之间的组织结构断裂，不利于可持续发展。每个国家在这方面都有不同的研究和教育背景。对于一个像越南这样的旅游业蓬勃发展的国家来说，遗产地和拥有遗产的社区所承受的压力更大。本文通过对越南近期遗产旅游研究和教育的回顾，力图呈现越南遗产旅游发展的现状，为未来越南遗产旅游研究和教育提供了借鉴，以期促进越南遗产旅游的可持续发展。

Heritage Tourism: A Review of Recent Research and Education in Vietnam

Dang Thi Phuong Anh, University of Social Sciences and Humanities, Vietnam National University, Hanoi

People visiting cultural and historical resources is one of the largest, most popular, and fastest growing sectors of the tourism industry today. In fact, heritage tourism appears to be growing much faster than all other forms of tourism, particularly in the developing world, and is thus viewed as an important potential tool for poverty alleviation and community economic development (UNWTO, 2015). Heritage tourism typically relies on living and built elements of culture and refers to the use of tangible and intangible past as tourism resources. It encompasses existing cultures and folkways of today, as they are inheritances from the past; other immaterial heritage elements (music, dance, language, religion, cuisine, artistic traditions and festivals); and material vestiges of the built cultural environment (monuments, historic public buildings and homes, farms, castles, museums, archeological ruins and relics). Although the heritage industry has in the past focused overwhelmingly on the patrimony of the privileged, there is now widespread acknowledgment and acceptance of everyday landscapes that depict the lives of ordinary people (families, farmers, factory workers, miners, fishers, women and children) (Timothy and Boyd 2006a). Heritage has been a buzzword in tourism since the late nineteenth century. Much scholarly debate with regard to the nature of heritage tourism still persists, suggesting that heritage is an amorphous concept and a complex phenomenon. Therefore, the matter of research and education on heritage tourism in different countries will have accordingly different characteristics. There is recognition in tourism studies in general, and heritage tourism in particular, that tourism and its impacts, constraints, and management implications are different in the developing world from conditions in the developed world. Vietnam is being a developing country, thus, in recent years, shaping issues for research and education on heritage tourism has played a vital role in comparison with other neighboring countries in the global context, from which the government can make a development orientation.

1 Heritage Tourism in Vietnam Today

Vietnam is a developing country and Vietnam is proud of having the diversity of heritages. There are over 3,000 relics recognized as national heritage in Vietnam (as identified by Ministry of Culture, Nguyen Ngoc Thien, 2016), including historical sites, religious and belief sites, complex of architectural monuments, museums, traditional festivals, handicraft and traditional craft villages, traditional music and art, etc. This is considered the basis whose historical culture and heritage Vietnam should make better use of to attract tourists (according to 'Opportunities of tourism in Vietnam' conducted in Singapore, 1997). In another survey targeted at international visitors to Vietnam in the 2000s, 82 percent cited heritage as a major factor in contemporary Vietnam's attractiveness. Vietnam possesses a unique mixture of different types of heritage sites, appealing to different groups of visitors. These include sites representing traditonal Sino-Vietnamese culture and the romantic relics of French colonialism as well as less conventional types of capitalizing on the controversial trend of 'war tourism' and the chance to experience one of the world's last surviving communist societies (Wantanee Suntikul, R. Butler, D. Airey, 2010).

Listing as a UNESCO World Heritage site is possibly the most outstanding designation for a cultural attraction, as it indicates that such a site is of unique and global cultural significance. Vietnam has eight such sites (Table 1).

Table 1 Vietnam UNESCO World Heritage Sites

UNESCO World Heritage Sites	Year of Listing	Kind of Properties
Complex of Hué Monuments	1993	cultural
Ha Long Bay	1994, 2000	natural
Hoi An Ancient Town	1999	cultural
My Son Sanctuary	1999	cultural
Phong Nha-Ke Bang National Park	2003, 2015	natural
Central Sector of the Imperial Citadel of Thang Long-Hanoi	2010	cultural
Citadel of the Ho Dynasty	2011	cultural
Trang An Landscape Complex	2014	mixed

Source: https://whc.unesco.org/en/statesparties/vn

Besides being the focus of attention that interests foreign tourists over the last few years, these world heritage sites also highlighted their name on Vietnam's destination map.

With such great tourism potential emerging from cultural heritage, Vietnam government orients to promote heritage for tourism development. Heritage tourism is mentioned in government documents, guidelines, policies and strategies for socio-economic development, for example, Law on tourism; Law on cultural heritage; Strategy on Vietnam Tourism Development until 2020, vision to 2030; Strategy for development of Vietnam's cultural industries until 2020, vision to 2030; Strategy for development tourism product until 2025, vision to 2030; especially, 08 – NQ/TW Resolution in 2017 named 'Grow tourism into a national key industry'. These documents have mentioned such highlight issues as: 1) Tourism products imbued with national cultural identity are factors that attract and enhance the competitiveness of Vietnam's tourism with other countries in the region and around the world; 2) Tourism development must aim to preserve and promote the cultural values of Vietnam; 3) Promoting heritage tourism to be one of the important service economic sectors, developing markedly in quality and quantity, making a positive contribution to economic growth.

This has urged the growth of tourism in Vietnam recently. UNWTO noted that Southeast Asia enjoyed the highest growth of all Asian subregions, with an additional nine million international tourist in 2017. Growth across destinations was fuelled by robust demand from Northeast Asian source markets. Vietnam recorded the fastest growth in arrivals, while Thailand, the subregions' largest destinations, added three million more arrivals. Visa exemptions and improved air connectivity also contributed to the positive results (UNWTO, 2018)[①]. Therein, the growth in international tourist arrivals have rocketed over the last three years, notably, it reached a record of 1 618.30 thousand in October, 2019 (according to statistics of Trading Economics) (Figure 1).

---

① https://www.e-unwto.org/doi/pdf/10.18111/9789284419876.

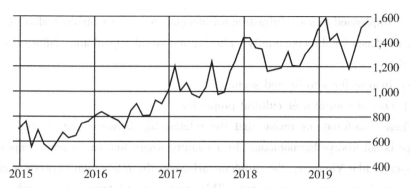

Figure 1 Chart of the growth in international tourist arrivals (thousands)
Source: https://tradingeconomics.com/vietnam/tourist-arrivals

Hence, total revenue from tourists has been remarkably growing. Vietnam's tourism revenue reached 27 billion USD in December, 2018, compared with 23 billion USD in the previous year. The data reached an all-time high of 27,431 million USD in December, 2018 (CEIC①). This proves that tourism has become an important economic sector, developing both quality and quantity, contributing positively to economic growth. Particularly, heritage tourism is positioned as one of the four pillars in Vietnam tourism products. Heritage sightseeing activities are the second most popular tourist attraction after leisure travel. Revenue from heritage tourism accounts for 10% – 25% of the gross return from tourists to Vietnam today.

The strong and rapid growth of heritage tourism has brought about some positive and negative impacts. Examples of positive impacts are listed as below:

a) The need for conservation and retention of important heritage assets in general.

b) Opportunities can arise to develop local economies.

c) Revenue from tourism can be directed to local infrastructure improvement.

d) Reinvigoration of traditional culture can occur.

Besides, there are unavoidably some negative impacts:

a) Overuse by tourists: overcrowding; parking, litter and noise problem; overburdens shared resources.

b) Tourism dependency: lead to loss of self-reliance and traditional-style activities.

c) Tourist behavior: lack of courtesy and sensitivity to local custom.

---

① https://www.ceicdata.com/en/indicator/vietnam/tourism-revenue.

d) Unplanned tourism infrastructure development: this involves altering the amenity of places for the community; altering the visual appeal and visitor experience for tourists.

e) Income flows to limited sectors.

f) Loss of control over cultural properties

These manifestations reveal that the relationship between tourism and cultural heritage is not always harmonious. In a country where tourism is amid leapfrogging development like Vietnam, the problems arisen in the interaction between such factors become increasingly complicated. This creates great interest for research and education activities at the heritage tourist site. How has this activity recently been taken place in Vietnam? A review of research and education on heritage tourism will bring out the answer.

2　A Review of Recent Research

Heritage tourism can be approached through two perspectives: tourism studies and cultural heritage studies.

From the perspective of tourism, studies in Vietnam have yet to show that there is a specific interpretation for the 'heritage tourism'. In those studies, cultural heritage is only described as a component of cultural tourism products. It is understood as the process of taking cultural resources as an object of exploitation to serve the needs of understanding, enjoying, experiencing and feeling the cultural, social and human values at the destination (Tran Thuy Anh, 2011; Nguyen Pham Hung, 2016).

Therefore, heritage tourism is often studied from the perspective of cultural heritage. These studies can be categorized into three most common trends.

Firstly, these are studies which interpret the concept, role and importance of heritage in the contemporary context. Apart from re-interpreting the concept of heritage on the basis of the UNESCO's definition, the *Vietnam Cultural Heritage Law 2001* and the *Law amending and supplementing a number of articles of the 2009 Cultural Heritage Law*, these studies have emphasized the role and value of heritage in the current context. Nguyen Thi Kim Loan and her colleagues believe that cultural heritage is a national asset and a development resource; is the soul that unites the people; embodies the cultural identity; is an expression of the diversity and richness of human culture; is a factor for the formation of new value systems (Nguyen Thi Kim Loan, 2014). Nguyen Thi Thu Ha sees that with the current development of science and technology, the inclusion of heritage forms into cultural industries is a way to help heritage promote their values (Nguyen Thi Thu Ha, 2013). Nguyen Quoc Hung affirmed that cultural heritage is increasingly making important contributions to the development of Vietnam. Many heritage sites have become important destinations in tourism routes, contributing significantly to the national and local budget revenues (through the revenue from entrance tickets, jobs creation, foreign investment, local infrastructure upgradation) (Nguyen Quoc Hung, 2006). Also in the direction of identifying cultural heritage as of great importance in the process of tourism development in Vietnam, Le Hong Ly and his partners also affirmed the essential position of cultural heritage in the formation of tourism. The authors have listed a number of heritage and stated their appropriate characteristics which prove them to be cultural tourism products (Le Hong Ly, Duong Van Sau, Dang Hoai Thu, 2010). As a continuation of point of view, Nguyen Pham Hung also mentioned the role of cultural heritage in tourism development, but according to him, all activities in tourism include cultural value and heritage's role exist in all types of tourism (Nguyen Pham Hung, 2016).

Secondly, studies discuss about the management of heritage. With such an important role and value, the management of cultural heritage is always a question for domestic studies. Most of them are focused on theoretical issues, practical experience of managing, preserving and promoting the value of cultural heritage in the period of industrialization and modernization, integration and development, from which propose solutions and recommendations for each specific case. The first is the research in the direction of introducing theoretical perspectives on heritage management, taking that as a needle for measures to manage and conserve specific cultural heritage (Bui Hoai Son, 2005). One of such viewpoints is referring the interdisciplinary approach as a necessary and appropriate solution to the current practice of the cultural heritage management system in Vietnam (Dang Van Bai, 2010). From a theoretical point of view, applied in the context of extensive innovation and international integration in Vietnam, the research aims to propose practical management models, methods and measures. The management content is mentioned in two aspects: 1) State management: including the promulgation of legal documents, which show guidelines and policies of the Party and State on cultural heritage conservation; 2) Non-business development: focusing on analyzing the advantages of monuments conservation activities. For example, the state has invested all funding for the revolutionary relics and relics which received investment for restoration and anti-degradation and have become thrilling attractions (Phan Hong Giang, Bui Hoai Son, 2014). In particular, the more concerned issue is the role of state management with heritage. Considering this as a key issue, state management, through legal documents (including legal documents on the protection and promotion of cultural heritage values; decisions on planning mechanisms, organizations and development plan; management decentralization decision…); the decentralization of monuments management; the organizational system of conservation industry and budget investments for the monuments management agencies—are decisive factors to enhance management efficiency (Dang Van Bai, 2001). In conclusion, regardless of the trend, the studies come to a consensus in the view of managing cultural heritage as a balance between 'preserving' and 'promoting' their values (Ngo Duc Thinh, 2001; Dang Van Bai, 2007; Bui Hoai Son, 2009).

Thirdly, some studies discuss about the relationship between heritage and tourism, also about one type of tourism—heritage tourism. In Vietnam so far, there have not been many systematic and long-term studies on the relationship between heritage management and tourism development besides some articles discussing the role of tourism in conservation and promoting heritage values in some research journals or in conferences about tourism and heritage. The works mentioned and considered this relationship but mainly clarified issues such as: the organic/dual relationship between tourism and cultural heritage (Bui Hoai Son, 2010); reciprocal impacts between the two sectors such as the positive and negative impacts of tourism on the community, heritage and environment (Dang Van Bai, 2001, 2013); cultural heritage potential in tourism development (Nguyen Quoc Hung, 2004, 2006); development orientation to limit the impact of tourism (Nguyen Thi Thu Ha, 2013). Since the Politburo's Resolution No. 08-NQ/TW of 2017 on 'Developing tourism to become a key economic sector', the issue of promoting the value of cultural heritage for tourism development has been increasingly receiving attention from essay writers and researchers in the direction of exploiting the potential values of each type of heritage to meet the needs of tourists (Le Thi Thu Phuong, 2017; Trinh Le Anh, 2018). In particular, Nguyen Thi Thu Ha's thesis initially mentions the relationship between cultural heritage management and tourism development based on the conflict/cooperation model of McKercher B and du Cros H (2002). This work approaches from a perspective describing the relationship at the destination on the positive to negative dimensions and recognizes what the above effects have brought to the heritage (Nguyen Thi Thu Ha, 2016).

The above studies have covered both theory and practice of ongoing issues at heritage tourism sites. However, still, there are gaps when applying international theoretical approaches to practical explanations at heritage tourism sites in Vietnam, when adapting tourism research approach for heritage tourism or not thoroughly solving issues that arise in the relationship between tourism development and heritage sites. This is the basis, the suggestion, and the way forward for other studies on heritage tourism in Vietnam in the future.

3 Review of Education

Dominant tourism activities at heritage tourism sites also raise the questions of education, staff training, workers, local residents and visitors to minimize the negative impacts, aiming at sustainable development.

The current situation at the heritage tourist sites in Vietnam suggests that there is a shortage of tour guides / presenters and even the qualified among them to meet visitors' expectation. Tour guides at the heritage sites are those who explain, guide, introduce, propagate and educate about relics, history, culture, nature conservation zones, museums, etc. This is the team with the most in-depth knowledge of the destination whose mission is not only fulfill the role of ambassador at the heritage site but also contribute to the promotion of local cultural values. Additionally, they also need to own practical skills, not only to serve the needs of tourists as much as possible but also be able to guide and instruct visitors in order for them to have the knowledge and correct behavior at the heritage site. Moreover, at the outstanding and attractive heritage sites, the guide team must meet the foreign language requirements. Playing such an important role, at heritage tourism destinations in Vietnam, yet the guide team has not reached the standard. At the famous spots with a rapidly increasing number of visitors, the number of specialist guides is not enough to serve each one of them thoughtfully and professionally. For example, in 2016, Ha Long Bay welcomed more than 2.9 million visitors, of which 1.9 million are international visitors, enjoying an increase of 12.6% compared with 2015. Even so the interpreters team equipped by the Management Board of Ha Long Bay had only 22 people, of which a quarter could speak fluent foreign languages, mainly English and Chinese, while other foreign languages are almost none (Source: Vietnam National Administration of Tourism). In famous heritage tourist sites, there are differences in the level of tour guides. One may have the knowledge but lack skills, and vice versa. In small tourist sites or in local relics, there are record of untrained guides hired, which leads to a decline in the quality of tourism products at the destination.

This is a consequence of heritage tourism education and training over the last few years. In Vietnam, there is a system of universities, colleges majoring at tourism and vocational colleges. Besides, at the universities, there are training programs relating to the tourism industry such as culture study, Vietnamese study, and historical sciences. However, among these training programs, there are no programs specializing in heritage tourism. What's more, there is not even any subject about 'heritage tourism'. Heritage tourism is only mentioned in subjects such as 'Tourism culture' 'Sustainable tourism development' 'Destination management' or 'Cultural heritage management'. Moreover, these subjects are only trained at university or higher level. This will lead to the fact that students trained in colleges and high schools will lack intensive knowledge about heritage when the local heritage tourist administrator hires them. In contrast, the in-depth training disciplines lack tourism skills. Therefore, one of the tasks and solutions given in the Strategy for development of Vietnam's cultural industries by 2020, with a vision to 2030, is 'training and developing human resources for cultural tourism, especially for manpower management, tour guides, interpreters and human resources directly interact with tourists and improving the quality of cultural tourism vocational training according to ASEAN occupational standards'. Recently, the Vietnam National Administration of Tourism has implemented quite a lot of solutions to standardize the tour guides and interpreters step by step, taking advantage of the support from the European Union (EU) and UNESCO in terms of techniques and expense to develop programs, content of training, and retrain professional knowledge, professional skills and foreign languages for tour guides and speakers. The Vietnam National Administration of Tourism has also focused on researching and developing a set of Vietnam's tourism skills standards (VTOS) for 13 occupations, including tour guides and interpreters. In the near future, the Vietnam National Administration of Tourism will cooperate with the Ministry of Labor, War Invalids and Social Affairs in formulating and introducing national occupational skills standards, including the profession of tourist narrator. A number of international organizations have also been supporting Vietnam in developing programs and training interpreters at heritage sites. The United Nations Educational, Scientific and Cultural Organization (UNESCO) and the International Labor Organization (ILO), for example, set up a training course for experts, or a program for tour guides at world heritage sites was held in famous cultural heritages destinations of Vietnam, namely Hanoi, Quang Nam, Hue, Da Nang, etc. (Dinh Thi Hong Nhung, 2018).

Heritage tourism education is not only oriented towards the workforce working and managing at heritage tourism sites but also towards other stakeholders. The deterioration of the heritage tourism image is also caused by local residents seeking profit from heritage in their homeland, due to the lacking awareness of tourists about the value of the heritage. Therefore, nowadays at heritage tourism destinations in Vietnam, typically the world heritage sites such as Hoi An the ancient town, Ha Long Bay, Hue, etc. the Heritage Management Board regularly organizes training courses to raise awareness for local people about heritage conservation, participation and cooperation with tourism business units to bring benefits from tourism for themselves and their local. Each indigenous person can become a heritage guide at the same time as a living heritage. Therefore, in some localities which are rich in heritage resources yet have not been exploited for tourism development, people's life is still difficult, government organizations such as the Vietnam National Administration of Tourism, local Department of Tourism will coordinate with tourism training institutions or non-governmental organizations for community benefits. They have organized training, retraining and guiding people to do tourism. This has reached its initial success in provinces with ethnic minorities such as Lao Cai, Yen Bai and Ha Giang.

For tourists, their lack of awareness at the site can cause problems, such as environmental pollution, overload, disrespect for indigenous culture, and by non-compliance with regulations. Educational activities for tourists are being carried out in Vietnam with more stringent regulations at the destination, with more detailed warnings and instructions through signs, leaflets, and lecture presentations and friendly reminders from other officials and local people. In particular, the awareness-raising education of visitors is also reflected through specific tourism products such as one-day-trip disguised as local residents, green tourism geared towards using environmental protection tools, educational and volunteer tourism. Such activities contribute to improving economic and intellectual life for indigenous people. The education of visitors must not only be done at the heritage site, but also systematically carried out from marketing products, to travel agent representatives, to guides throughout the route and to each local residents to ensure that they provide visitors with a 'green passport' before entering the heritage site.

In recent times, although heritage tourism education activities in Vietnam are not yet complete and are not able to keep up with the rapid development of tourism activities, they have shown the efforts of stakeholders in curbing the restrictions and negative impacts that are happening every day in heritage tourist sites.

4　Conclusion

Tourism is a multi-dimensional, multi-faced phenomenon covering many different types of activities. Tourists travel to different destinations with different motivations. Cultural attractions such as historical places, monuments, architecture, people and art are important motivators to travel. Many types of attractions fall into the heritage tourism which accounts for a considerable portion of tourism. It has been noted that tourism to heritage attractions can play a role in their gaining wider public and official acknowledgement of their status as cultural heritage sites. In the context of tourism, the term 'heritage' has been used in connection with both cultural and natural aspects of a destination. However, culture is known as a necessary component of a heritage attraction. Therefore, heritage tourism is not just an activity that brings tourists to the heritage site but also the social interaction at the destination among indigenous people and tourists and business travelers. Accordingly, heritage tourism is a specific type of tourism that demonstrates the complex relationship between heritage sites and tourism development. When tourism activities thrive, there will be many consequences at the heritage site. This places an important role for heritage tourism research and education. In case that research and education cannot keep up with the fluctuations of reality, and go beyond practice, it will lead to the structure disruption of the balance between conservation and development at the heritage site and go against sustainable development. Each country will have different research and educational backgrounds in this regard. For a country where tourism is in a thriving period like Vietnam, the pressure on the heritage and the community that owns them is even greater. This review of research and education in Vietnam recently aims to provide an overview of heritage tourism in Vietnam, with its pros and cons. This is the basis for future heritage tourism research and education orientations for sustainable development goals.

References

[1] DUC THANH T. Nhập môn khoa học du lịch [R]. Hà Nội: Nxb Đại học Quốc gia Hà Nội, 2009.

[2] DUC MINH V. Tổng quan du lịch [R]. Hà Nội: Nxb Thống kê, 1996.

[3] GIANG P H, SON B H. Quản lý văn hóa Việt Nam trong tiến trình đổi mới và hội nhập quốc tế [R]. Hà Nội: Nxb Chính trị quốc gia, 2014.

[4] HA N T T. Bảo tồn di sản văn hóa ở Việt Nam: phát triển ngành công nghiệp văn hóa [R]. Ha Noi: Nxb Văn hóa Thông tin, 2013.

[5] HA N T T. Managing cultural heritage and developing tourism in Hoi An ancient town, Quang Nam province [D]. Ha Noi: Luận án Tiến sĩ Văn hóa học, 2016.

[6] HUNG N P. Văn hóa du lịch [R]. Hà Nội: Nxb Đại học Quốc gia Hà Nội, 2016.

[7] HUNG N Q. Tầm nhìn tương lai đối với Di sản văn hóa và hệ thống bảo vệ di tích ở nước ta [J]. Tạp chí di sản văn hóa, 2004 (4): 8 – 18.

[8] HUNG N Q. Bảo tồn, phát huy giá trị các di sản văn hóa-thiên nhiên thế giới phục vụ phát triển ở nước ta [J]. Tạp chí di sản văn hóa, 2006 (4): 14 – 21.

[9] KIEN D T. Bài giảng Văn hoá quản lý và kinh doanh du lịch [R]. Hà Nội: ĐHQG Hà Nội, 2005.

[10] LE ANH T. Quản lý lễ hội truyền thống gắn với phát triển sản phẩm du lịch qua khảo sát lễ hội Kiếp Bạc (Hải Dương) và lễ hội Tịch Điền (Hà Nam) [D]. Hà Nội: Viện Văn hóa Nghệ thuật Quốc gia Việt Nam, 2018.

[11] LE HONG LY, VAN SAU D, THU D H. Quản lý di sản văn hóa và phát triển du lịch [R]. Hà Nội: Nxb Đại học Quốc gia, 2010.

[12] LE THI THU PHUONG. Bảo tồn và phát huy các giá trị văn hóa tộc người trong mối quan hệ với phát triển du lịch [D]. Hà Nội: Viện Văn hóa Nghệ thuật Quốc gia Việt Nam, 2017.

[13] LOAN N T K. Quản lý di sản văn hóa [R]. Hà Nội: Nxb Văn hóa thông tin, 2014.

[14] MCKERCHER B, Du CROS H. Cultural tourism: The partnership between tourism and cultural heritage management [M]. New York: Routledge, 2002.

[15] THIEN N N. Linking conservation and promotion of cultural heritage values for sustainable tourism development [J]. The communist review, 2016 (886): 1 – 10.

[16] SON B H. Quản lý lễ hội truyền thống của người Việt [R]. Hà Nội: Nxb Văn hóa dân

tộc, 2009.

[17] SON B H. Di sản để làm gì và một số câu chuyện quản lý di sản ở Việt Nam [J]. Tạp chí Di sản văn hóa, 2010 (3): 10 – 14.

[18] TIMOTHY D J, BOYD S W. Heritage tourism in the 21st century: Valued traditions and new perspectives [J]. Journal of heritage tourism, 2006, 1 (1): 1 – 16.

[19] VAN BAI D. Bảo tồn di sản văn hóa phi vật thể-từ góc nhìn toàn cầu hóa [J]. Tạp chí Di sản văn hóa số, 2007 (21): 12 – 18.

菲律宾旅游和酒店教育：挑战与机遇

Evangeline E. Timbang 菲律宾圣托马斯大学旅游与酒店管理学院

1 引言

菲律宾是东南亚的一个群岛国家，拥有 7 000 多个岛屿。截至 2019 年，菲律宾人口约为 1.08 亿。菲律宾受到了西班牙近 400 年的影响和美国 50 年的影响，文化上呈现出鲜明的东西交融特征。尽管就种族出身而言，当地人基本上是南岛民族，但菲律宾人中有中国人、日本人、印度人、西班牙人和美国人的混合血统。中国人、印度人和日本人组成外国少数民族，纯西班牙人和其他欧洲人的比例很小。英语被认为是菲律宾的第二语言，但岛屿上有171种语言和方言。

2 菲律宾国家旅游局

菲律宾国家旅游局的主要职责是通过推动旅游发展，促进外汇增收和就业发展，惠及公私行业。《2016—2022 年国家旅游发展规划》的愿景是推动菲律宾成为"亚洲必游之地"，发展具有全球竞争力和环境可持续性的旅游业。

根据菲律宾国家旅游局数据，2018 年菲律宾接待了 720 万国际游客，超过了 2017 年 660 万的记录（增长 7.5%）。据 2019 年 1—4 月的统计数据，菲律宾共接待 2 867 551 名游客，中国、韩国、美国和澳大利亚是菲律宾主要的客源国市场。菲律宾 2017 年的旅游出口总额为 3797 亿比索，旅游业投资额为 951 亿比索。根据菲律宾统计局 2019 年 6 月的数据，旅游业直接增加值（TDGVA）占国内生产总值（GDP）的 12.7%，提供了 540 万个就业机会。旅游业是菲律宾经济和房地产行业的亮点，因为国内外游客的涌入推动了酒店和度假村的建设。

作为发展中国家，菲律宾认为旅游业有潜力成为促进菲律宾经济发展的引擎行业之一，因此，旅游业被列为优先发展产业。旅游业的发展将促进投资并创造商机,产生新的就业机会,因而需要知识丰富和技术熟练的劳动力。因此,提高国家旅游教育质量,保证旅游专业毕业生稳定就业,提高旅游从业人员的专业能力,使之具有国际竞争力已成为当务之急。

3 菲律宾教育

菲律宾国会教育委员会(The Philippines Congressional Commission)对国家的教育体系进行了广泛的改革,重点是针对3个层次的教育设置3个管理机构:负责大专和研究生教育的高等教育委员会(Commission on Higher Education,CHED)、基础教育教育部(Department of Education,DepEd)和负责该国的技术职业和中级教育的技术教育与技能发展局(Technical Education and Skills Development Authority,TESDA)。

3.1 高等教育委员会

高等教育委员会是总统办公室的附属机构,由1名主席和4名委员领导。1997年,为了建立完整、适当和综合的高等教育体系,通过了被称为"1997年高等教育现代化法案"的菲律宾共和国第8298号法案。菲律宾宪法第十四条第一款规定高等教育委员会的任务是"保护和促进所有公民接受各级优质教育的权利,并使所有人都能获得这种教育"。

截至2019年8月,菲律宾共有2 393所高等教育机构(见表1)。表2列出了提供旅游和酒店管理教育的私立和公立学校数量。按人口计算,工商管理(包括酒店和餐厅管理项目)的注册人数最多(2018—2019学年为896494人)。

表1 菲律宾高等教育机构分布概况(2018—2019学年)

类型	数量/所	占比/%
私立	1721	72
公立	672	28
总数	2 393	100

表2 菲律宾提供旅游和酒店管理教育的高等教育机构

单位：所

项目	私立高等教育机构	公立高等教育机构	总数
旅游	350	95	445
酒店管理	671	272	943
总数	1 021	367	1 388

截至目前，只有5所有酒店管理专业的大学和3所有旅游管理专业的大学被高等教育委员会评为卓越中心，另有2所大学被评为发展中心。

3.2 技术教育与技能发展局

技术教育与技能发展局是政府机构，其任务是制订全面的发展计划，以促进和发展中级人力技能，批准技能标准、资助技术教育和技能开发项目，测试和制定机构认证制度。它分别与培训伙伴和地方政府部门合作，共同管理职业技术学校、企业和社区培训中心。

旅游和酒店业登记的行业培训机构最多，最受欢迎的课程是与酒店和餐厅有关的技能课程（食品、饮料和家政），以女性学生为主。旅游和酒店业也是就业人数最多的行业，达393 353人，就业率为57%。国家技术教育与技能发展局将旅游业确定为主要的创造就业机会的行业，预计2018—2022年将创造150万个就业机会。

3.3 旅游和酒店管理学士项目

菲律宾的旅游和酒店教育在20世纪70年代初作为短期技能课程应运而生，目的是为新兴旅游业培养酒店经营者。随后国家实施了认证计划，以确保行业中高层管理人员的资质。20世纪80年代，菲律宾政府在马尼拉举办国际货币基金组织会议时发现，合格的旅游专业人力资源短缺，一些教育机构随后被赋予提供旅游、酒店和饭店管理学位教育的职责。

根据菲律宾共和国第7722号法案（又称"1994年高等教育行动"），高等教育委员会的任务之一是促进素质教育。方案和标准厅的职责之一是制定标准并落实，以监测政策、规范和准则的执行情况。2001年9月24日，经修订的旅游和酒店管理学士（以前称为旅游学士/酒店和餐厅管理学士）最低课程要求生效，并载于高等教育委员会2001年第31号备忘录中，对酒店管理核心课程、工商管理核心课程和主要课程进行了修订。

为了遵循2012年高等教育委员会第46号备忘录中提倡的基于结果的质量保证体系，高等教育委员会通过并颁布了旅游和酒店管理学士的新准则、政策和标准，以跟上全球竞争激烈的旅游和酒店行业。

4 挑战和改革

4.1 2017年高等教育委员会第62号备忘录

为了满足旅游行业对知识丰富和技能熟练的劳动力的需求，修订和更新这些方案势在必行。高等教育机构的重要任务是，根据行业的使命、愿景和目标，在课程中引入创新理念，以达到最佳的学习成果。2017年高等教育委员会第62号备忘录提供的旅游学士（BST）和酒店管理学士（BSHM）学位纳入各个利益相关方的需求，其中包括：①菲律宾教育资历认证框架，②国家旅游规划，③劳动和就业部（DOLE）的"工作匹配"项目，④教育部K-12基础教育体制，⑤菲律宾商业教育（PBEd）提供的美国国际开发署编制课程（DACUM）报告，⑥由旅游局、亚洲开发银行（ADB）和加拿大政府牵头的菲律宾提升旅游竞争力项目。

图1是菲律宾的全国教育资历认证架构（PQF），明确了教育资历的等级和标准。这一国家架构是基于工人或学习者以不同的方式获得的知识、技能和价值观标准来发展、评估和授予教育资历的。菲律宾教育资历认证框架鼓励终身学习，允许学员从适合个人的水平开始学习，直到获得相应的教育资历。

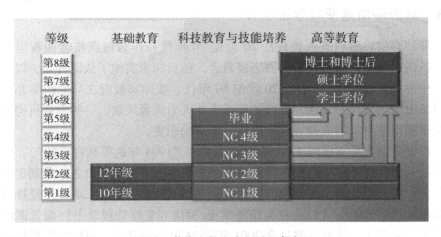

图1 菲律宾教育资历认证框架

K-12基础教育体制让学生通过学习相应的技能来获得相应的菲律宾教育资历（纳入东盟教育资历互认框架）。随着就业专业化，K-12教育体制旨在帮助大学生找到工作。

4.2 高等教育委员会和技术教育与技能发展局

2010年，高等教育委员会前主席Patricia Licuanan博士发布了高等教育委员会第32号备忘录，要求暂停自2011—2012学年生效的包括酒店和餐厅管理的新项目。提供本科和研究生酒店和餐饮管理项目（HRM）的学校激增可能导致毕业生质量下降，因此，政府机构采取了行动。

该禁令于2016年解除，但要求相关机构在开设酒店和餐厅管理相关教育项目之前，需要具备下列资质。

（1）具备自主权的私立高等教育机构和达到（SUC）Ⅲ级水平的公立大学和学院。

（2）具备酒店和餐饮管理卓越中心/发展中心资质。

（3）已从高等教育委员会认定的认证机构获得教育项目二级认证。酒店和餐饮管理相关的教育项目有工商管理、行政管理、旅游、差旅管理、会计、办公管理、创业、房地产管理。

此外，高等教育委员会根据国家发展计划、人力需求状况以及劳动和就业部的相关研究更新了重点课程清单。劳动和就业部的研究明确了2020年重点行业所需的紧缺和重要课程、技能和工种。

菲律宾高等教育机构面临的挑战包括：①教育质量问题，②学生缺乏所需的能力，③缺乏健全的师资队伍，④缺乏先进的研究，⑤需要改善获得优质教育的机会，⑥国际化程度不高。为了解决这些问题，高等教育委员会已经进行了制度化改革。

为了提高学生获得优质教育的机会和公平性，2017—2018学年全国111所州立大学和学院为至少100万学生免除了学费。菲律宾公私部门也为大学的研究生教育、研究和行业实践提供了更多的资助。为了持续提高国家的教育质量，对符合卓越中心和发展中心标准的院校进行了表彰和奖励。

表3　菲律宾高等教育机构的QS世界大学排名

排名	学校名称
384	菲律宾大学
651—700	马尼拉大学
801—1 000	德拉萨大学
801—1 000	圣托马斯大学

菲律宾国家发展计划指出，"菲律宾高等教育机构的数量是其邻国的十倍"。然而，在目前的知识经济时代，高等教育机构仍需培养更多的研究人员、创新者、学者和解决方案提供者。随着菲律宾高等教育研究网络和高等教育区域研究能力建设中心的建立，这一问题将得到解决。

另一方面，菲律宾社会普遍认为国家技术教育与技能发展局在培养低技能人才，因为职业教育毕业生普遍从事低价值工作，就业能力较差。因此，第四次工业革命的来临无疑是一大挑战（需要高技能人才）。设施设备、培训师资、评估人员等的缺乏则进一步加剧了菲律职业技术教育面临的挑战。

因此，国家技术教育与技能发展局应当启动新方案，确保职业教育对技术变革有积极的响应，扩大和强化技术教育与培训，以满足社会对熟练和有责任心的劳动力的需求，并充分考虑和照顾社会边缘、弱势群体的（教育）需求。

国家高等教育委员会和技术教育与技能发展局应致力于协调职业技术教育以及高等教育的实践，可以实行下列举措：

（1）基于文凭课程的菲律宾教育资历认证框架（PQF）；
（2）菲律宾学分转换系统；
（3）菲律宾教育资质信息系统（PhQuaR）。

4.3　东盟一体化、东盟相互承认协议和东盟教育资历参考框架

随着2015年东盟一体化进程的启动，菲律宾在实施旨在允许区域内熟练劳动力自由流动的东盟相互承认协议的过程中做出了重要努力。东盟相互承认协议确立了东盟各国共同的技能和资历认可标准。旅游是2012年东盟各国签署的教育资历互认协议的7个领域之一，为区域旅游人才流动铺平了道路。截至目前，协议涉及旅游人才的242项技能、23个酒店服务职位和7个旅游服务职位。

此外，通过协调和标准化、课程审查和教师资格认证，东盟教育资历参考框架（AQRF）将使东盟成员国之间能够进行比较，以建立一个强大的区域共同体。

上述教育变革涉及菲律宾教育领域中不同的机构和利益相关方，建立起符合当地需要和全球协调的课程目标必将有利于菲律宾的经济发展。希望这些变革能扩大菲律宾国民的就业机会，提高国民的终身学习能力。

The Philippine Tourism and Hospitality Management Education: Challenges and Opportunities

Assoc. Prof. Evangeline E. Timbang, CHE, CGSP Asst. Dean
College of Tourism and Hospitality Management
University of Santo Tomas Manila, Philippines

1 Introduction

The Philippines is an archipelago country in Southeast Asia with more than seven thousand islands. As of 2019, the Philippines has a population of around 108 million. From its almost 400 years of western influence by the Spaniards and 50 years by the Americans, the Filipino race is proud of its unique blend of East and West culture. Although the natives are largely Austronesian in terms of its ethnic origin, the Filipinos have Chinese, Japanese, Indian, Spanish and American culture mixtures in their blood. The Chinese, Indian, and the Japanese consist the foreign minority with a small percentage from pure Spaniards and other Europeans. Although English is considered as a second language in the country, there are 171 languages and dialects in the islands.

2 The Philippine Department of Tourism

The Department of Tourism has the major responsibility to encourage and promote tourism as a major socio-economic activity in order to generate foreign currency and employment benefiting both private and public sectors in the country. The 2016 – 2022 National Tourism Development Plan vision is to develop globally competitive and environmentally sustainable tourism industry as the country becomes a 'must destination to visit in Asia'.

As of 2018, there were 7.2 million foreign travelers in the country which is over the 6.6 million record in 2017 (7.5 % increase). The January-April, 2019 statistics show 2,867,551 tourists in the country with the top travel markets coming from China, South Korea, the United States of America and Australia. The Philippine tourism exports in 2017 totaled to 379.7 billion pesos while Philippine tourism investments was at 95.1 billion pesos. According to the June, 2019 data of the Philippine Statistics Authority, the share of tourism direct gross value added (TDGVA) to gross domestic product (GDP) was 12.7% and tourism has provided 5.4 million jobs. Back to back with the domestic travel statistics, tourism continue to register a bright spot in the Philippine economy and real estate industry as the influx of local and foreign travelers push up demand for construction of hotels and resorts.

As a developing country, the Philippines recognizes tourism as among the industries that has a potential to boost the Philippine economy and serve as a powerful economic growth engine, hence placed it as a priority industry. These tourism developments prompt investments and create businesses leading to new job opportunities requiring highly knowledgeable and skilled workforce. To achieve this goal, it becomes imperative that quality tourism education in the country assures a steady supply of job ready and competent graduates towards global competitiveness.

3 The Philippine Education

The Philippine Congressional Commission on education introduced broad reforms in the country's education system focused on the education into three governing bodies: the Commission on Higher Education (CHED) for tertiary and graduate education, the Department of Education (DepEd) for basic education and the Technical Education and Skills Development Authority (TESDA) for technical-vocational and middle-level education in the country.

3.1 Commission on Higher Education

CHED is an attached agency to the Office of the President headed by a Chairperson and four Commissioners. In 1997, Republic Act (RA) No. 8292, otherwise known as the 'Higher Education Modernization Act of 1997' was passed to establish a complete, adequate and integrated system of higher education. The mandate of CHED as provided in Article XIV, section 1 of the Philippine Constitution is 'to protect and promote the right of all citizens to quality education at all levels and make such education accessible to all'.

As of August, 2019, there are 2,393 (see Table 1) higher educational institutions. Table 2 shows the number of tourism and hospitality schools in both private and public schools. By population, the Business Administration cluster (including the hotel and restaurant management program) has the most number of enrollees (896,494 in the school year 2018 – 2019).

Table 1　Summary of Higher Education Institutions Distribution in the Philippines

Distribution of Higher Education Institutions (Academic year 2018 – 2019)		
Private	1,721	72%
Public	672	28%
Grand total	2,393	100%

To date, there are only five universities in Hospitality Management and three universities in Tourism Management recognized as Center of Excellence and two universities as Center of Development by CHED.

Table 2　HEIs offering Tourism and Hospitality Education in the Philippines

HEIs Offering Tourism and Hospitality Management Programs			
Program	Private HEIs	Public HEIs	Total
Tourism	350	95	445
Hospitality management	671	272	943
Grand total	1,021	367	1,388

3.2　Technical Education and Skills Development Authority

The Technical Education and Skills Development Authority (TESDA) is the government agency mandated to formulate a comprehensive development plan for the promotion and development of middle level manpower skills, approval of skill standards, fund programs and projects for the technical education and skills development and tests and formulation of accreditation system for institutions. It administers technical-vocational schools and enterprise and community based training centers in cooperation with dual training partners and local government units respectively.

The tourism and hospitality sector registers the highest number of industry training partners. The most popular courses are hotel and restaurant related skills (food beverage and housekeeping) with female students dominating the enrolment. It is also the sector with the highest employment record of 393,353 or 57% employment rate. The National Technical Education and Skills Development Authority Plan of 2018 – 2022 has identified key employment generators with tourism sector projected to produce 1.5 million jobs.

3.3 The Bachelor of Science in Tourism and Hospitality Management Program (the Philippines)

The tourism and hospitality education in the Philippines came into being as a short term skill courses to prepare hoteliers in the emerging tourism industry in the early 70's. The certification programs followed to ensure qualifications of middle to top managers in the industry. A number of educational institutions were challenged to offer degree programs on tourism, hotel and restaurant management after the country felt the shortage of qualified manpower in the 80's during the International Monetary Fund meeting in Manila.

The Commission on Higher Education (CHED), pursuant to Republic Act (RA) No. 7722, otherwise known as 'the Higher Education ACT OF 1994' is mandated to promote quality education as one of its basic tasks. The Office of Programs and Standards (OPS) had the development of criteria and instruments for monitoring the enforcement of Policies, Standards and Guidelines (PSGs) as one of its responsibilities. In September 24, 2001, the Revised Minimum Curricular Requirements for the Bachelor of Science in Hospitality Management/Tourism (formerly known as B.S. Tourism / B.S. Hotel and Restaurant Management) took effect as contained in CHED Memorandum No. 31, s. 2001. Revisions were made in the Hospitality Management Core, Business Management Core and the major courses.

In pursuance of an outcomes-based quality assurance system advocated under CHED Memorandum No. 46 series of 2012, the Commission on Higher education adopted and promulgated new guidelines, policies and standards for the programs of Bachelor of Science in Tourism and Hospitality Management in keeping abreast with the globally competitive world of travel and lodging.

4　Challenges and Reforms

4.1　CHED Memo No. 62 series of 2017

The need to revise and update the said programs became imperative to meet the demand for more knowledgeable and skillful workforce. As such, higher education institutions are challenged to introduce innovations in the curriculum thru best learning outcomes based on their respective mission, vision and objectives. The latest CHED Memo No. 62 series of 2017 offers Bachelor of Science in Tourism (BST) and Bachelor of Science in Hospitality Management (BSHM) which incorporate inputs from various stakeholders which include the following:

a) Philippine Qualification Framework;

b) National Tourism Plan;

c) Project Job Fit of the Department of Labor and Employment (DOLE);

d) K to 12 program of the Department of Education;

e) Developing a Curriculum (DACUM) report from USAID provided by Philippine Business for Education (PBEd);

f) The Philippine Improving Competitiveness Tourism Project led by the Department of Tourism, Asian Development Bank (ADB) and Government of Canada.

Figure 1 illustrates the Philippine national policy which describes the levels of educational qualifications and sets the standards for qualification outcomes. It is a national system for the development, recognition and award of qualification based on standard of knowledge, skills and values acquired in different ways by workers or learners of a certain country. The Philippine Qualifications Framework (PQF) encourages lifelong learning allowing the person to start at a level suitable to him until he builds his qualification over time.

The offering of the K to 12 program allows the students to develop the necessary qualifications by acquiring competencies at each level of the PQF vis-à-vis the ASEAN Qualifications Reference Framework (AQRF). With specialization for employment, the K – 12 program aims to help college students find jobs.

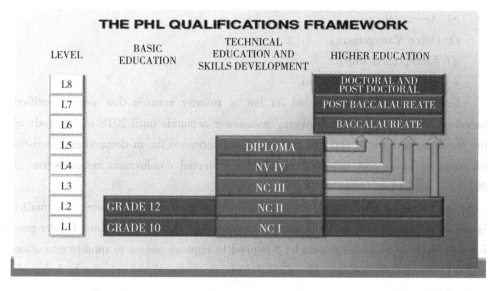

Figure 1 The Philippine Qualification Framework

4.2 CHED and TESDA

In the year 2010, Dr. Patricia Licuanan, the former CHED Chairman, issued a CHED Memo No. 32 imposing a moratorium on offering new programs including Hotel and Restaurant Management program effective since academic year 2011 – 2012. The government agency took action on the proliferation of schools offering undergraduate and graduate HRM programs which may lead to poor quality graduates.

However, the suspension was lifted in 2016. The following qualifications were required prior to the opening of Hotel and Restaurant Management related programs:

a) Autonomous /Deregulated status for private HEIs and SUC Level Ⅲ for state universities and colleges;

b) Center of Excellence /Center of Development in HRM;

c) Level II accredited status of programs from CHED recognized accrediting agencies.

For HRM, allied programs are:

a) Business Administration;

b) Public Administration;

c) Tourism;

d) Travel Management;

e) Accountancy;
f) Office Management;
g) Entrepreneurship;
h) Real Estate Management.

Furthermore, CHED updated its list of priority courses that were identified based on national development plans, manpower demands until 2018 and a study of the Department of Labor and Employment that determined the in-demand and hard-to-fill courses, skills and jobs that match the projected employment requirements of 2020 key industries.

The identified challenges faced by higher education institutions are: 1) quality issues in education; 2) lack of desired competencies; 3) lack of robust faculty profile; 4) lack in advanced research; 5) need to improve access to quality education and 6) internationalization. The CHED have institutionalized reforms to help address these issues.

To improve access and equity to quality education, tuition fee was offered to at least a target of 1,000,000 students in school year 2017 – 2018 at 111 state colleges and universities nationwide. There were more faculty grants provided in both private and public sectors for graduate degrees, research and industry immersion. To continue upgrading the quality of education in the country, schools which met the criteria for center of excellence and center of development were recognized and awarded (Table 3).

Table 3 Philippine Higher Educational Institutions with QS Rankings
(2019 QS World University Rankings of Philippine HEIs)

Rank	Name of Higher Education Institution
384	University of the Philippines
651 – 700	Ateneo de Manila University
801 – 1 000	De La Salle University (St Benilde)
801 – 1 000	University of Santo Tomas

The Philippine National Development Plan cites that 'the number of Philippine higher education institutions is ten times more than its neighboring countries'. However, it remains a fact that there is a need to produce more researchers, innovators, scholars and solution providers in the present knowledge economy.

This concern will be addressed with the creation of the Philippine Higher Education Research Network and Higher Education Regional Research Center for Research Capacity Building.

On the other hand, it is perceived that TESDA produces low level skills characterized with the prevalence of low value work and low employability of TVET graduates. In addition, the onset of the 4th industrial revolution poses challenges demanding advanced work skills. The lack of facilities, equipment, qualified trainers and assessors add to job and skills mismatch and underemployment.

However, TESDA shall embark on a program that shall ensure prompt and innovative response to the advent of technology, scale up and intensify TVET programs to address demand for skilled and conscientious workforce and engage in culturally sensitive approaches to cater the needs of the marginalized members of the society.

CHED and TESDA shall work on harmonizing the Technical-Vocational Education and Training and Higher Education practices in the implementation of the following:

a) Philippine Qualifications Framework (PQF) through the Diploma Programs;

b) Philippine Credit Transfer System;

c) Philippine Qualifications Register (PhQuaR).

4.3 ASEAN Integration, MRAs and AQRF

With the introduction of ASEAN Integration in 2015, the Philippines continue to assume important roles in various capacities in the implementation of the ASEAN Mutual Agreements (MRAs) which aims to allow free flow of skilled labor within the region. The MRAs establish common skills and recognition of qualifications. The MRA on tourism is among the seven qualifications which have been signed in 2012 paving the way to regional mobility. To date, there are 23 hotel services job titles and 7 travel services job titles in the MRA for Tourism Professional (TP) with 242 unit competencies.

Furthermore, through harmonization and standardization, curricular review and faculty qualification accreditation, the ASEAN Qualifications Reference Framework (AQRF) shall enable comparison across ASEAN member states towards building a strong regional community.

With all these reforms in place involving the dynamic leaders and stakeholders in Philippine education, the goal towards achieving a locally responsive and globally attuned curricula will surely benefit the country towards its economic development.

Hopefully, the good news will expand career opportunities and enhance competencies for life long learning.

菲律宾旅游和酒店教育：
基于能力的培养模式

Guerrero, RGIG, Guggenheim, LJG, and Ramos-Tumanan, MA

1 引言

菲律宾旅游和酒店管理高等教育始于20世纪70年代，当时菲律宾大学率先开设了酒店和餐饮管理科学学士（bachelor of science in hotel and restaurant administration, BS HRA）项目。菲律宾大学的BS HRA项目创设于1969年，于1970—1971学年正式启动。该教育项目的开设源于菲律宾酒店和餐饮业协会要求学术界为蓬勃发展的酒店和餐饮业提供中层管理人员（Paz-Guzman, 1982）。此外，在菲律宾国家旅游局的倡议下，菲律宾大学于1976年又开设了旅游科学学士学位项目（UP Gazette, 1976）。此后，越来越多的菲律宾高等教育机构开设这两类教育项目。截至2012年，有978所大学提供酒店管理学位，346所大学提供旅游学士学位（Aquino和Aragon, 2015）。

菲律宾旅游和酒店教育以能力（competency-based education, CBE）和结果（outcomes-based education, OBE）为导向。Nodine和Johnstone（2015）将CBE定义为"基于学生学习或能力的证据，而不是基于一门课程所花费的时间来提供学分的在线和混合课程及项目"。菲律宾旅游和酒店教育中的能力导向理念，是在与菲律宾-澳大利亚优质技术职业教育和培训委员会（受澳大利亚国际发展署和菲律宾技术教育技能发展司指导）进行了一系列磋商之后实施的（Guggenheim和Ramos-Tumanan, 2007）。该项目旨在为旅游业和酒店业的未来员工提供所需的能力。

Spady（1994）认为，OBE"始于清楚地了解学生能够学会做什么是重要的，然后组织课程、教学和评估，以确保这种学习效果最终会发生"。2012年，高等教育委员会（CHED）发布了《CHED备忘录令》（CHED Mermorandum Order, CMO）2012年系列第42号，题为《通过基于结果和基于类型的质量保证，提高菲律宾高等教育质量的政策标准》，为OBE铺平了道路。

2 东南亚国家联盟相互承认协议

东盟成立于1967年，由菲律宾、马来西亚、泰国、印度尼西亚和新加坡5个成员国组成。文莱、越南、老挝、缅甸和柬埔寨后来也加入了该组织。

该组织的目标可以概括为"同一个愿景、同一个身份、同一个共同体"。为了实现这些目标，东盟各成员国已经达成了几项协议。其中之一是东盟相互承认协议，目标是"促进商务人员和熟练劳动力及人才的流动"（Aquino 和 Aragon，2015）。东盟为不同的工作领域创建了若干互认协议，《东盟旅游专业人员互认协议》（ASEAN MRA TP）于2009年签署，并于2012年完成（Aquino 和 Aragon，2015）。

《东盟旅游专业人员互认协议》的目标如下：促进旅游专业人员/工人的流动；就旅游专业人员能力教育和培训的最佳实践进行分享；为东盟成员国之间的合作和能力建设提供机会（TESDA，2016）。《东盟旅游专业人员互认协议》已经确定了6个类别和32个职位（如图1所示），并且基于这些职位制定了242项东盟旅游专业人员共同能力标准（Aquino 和 Aragon，2015；Jotikasthira 等，2016），从而建立了东盟共同旅游课程（CATC）。

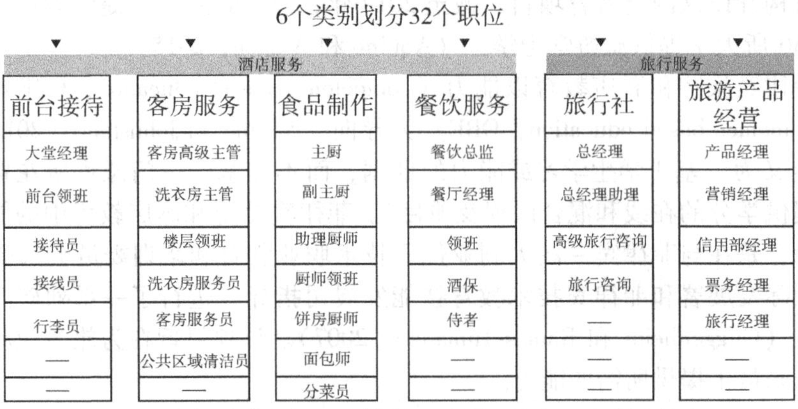

6个类别划分32个职位

酒店服务				旅行服务	
前台接待	客房服务	食品制作	餐饮服务	旅行社	旅游产品经营
大堂经理	客房高级主管	主厨	餐饮总监	总经理	产品经理
前台领班	洗衣房主管	副主厨	餐厅经理	总经理助理	营销经理
接待员	楼层领班	助理厨师	领班	高级旅行咨询	信用部经理
接线员	洗衣房服务员	厨师领班	酒保	旅行咨询	票务经理
行李员	客房服务员	饼房厨师	侍者	—	旅行经理
—	公共区域清洁员	面包师	—	—	—
—	—	分菜员	—	—	—

图1 面向旅游专业人士的东盟互认协议框架[①]

菲律宾政府指定了3个部门来实施《东盟旅游专业人员互认协议》，分别是国家旅游局、旅游产业委员基金会和技术教育与技能发展局（Aquino 和

---

① 资料来源：《东盟相互承认协议手册》（2013年）。

Aragon，2015；技术教育与技能发展局，2016）。国家旅游局的作用是制订、协调和实施工作计划，加强东盟成员国在旅游领域的合作，同时是菲律宾在东盟旅游专业监督委员会的官方代表（Aquino，Arogon，2015）。旅游产业委员基金会的作用是提高民众对东盟相互承认协议的认识并传播这方面的信息，并确保该协议和东盟共同旅游课程得到维护和实行（Aquino 和 Aragon，2015）。

技术教育与技能发展局的角色是根据东盟旅游专业人员共同能力标准对旅游专业人员进行评估和认证（Aquino 和 Aragon，2015）。对于基础教育和中等教育，菲律宾于 2016 年实施了从幼儿园到 12 年级（K-12）的培养方案。它有 4 个路径：学术路径，技术—职业—生计（technical – vocational – livelihood，TVL）路径，运动路径，艺术和设计路径。旅游和酒店课程属于 TVL 路径下的家政学领域。旅游和酒店课程有烹饪、商业烹饪、会展管理、餐饮服务、前台服务、管家服务、地方导览服务、旅游推广服务等。高等教育委员会的旅游和酒店教育技术小组发布了 2018 年系列第 62 号 CMO，为旅游和酒店课程体系设计提供指南。该政策指南考虑了 K-12 教育体系和《东盟旅游专业人员互认协议》。

3　明确学习成效

1994 年，在转向行业导向和需求驱动的技术和职业教育与培训（technical and vocational education and training，TVET）的同时，菲律宾对基于能力的评估进行了探索。这一举措得到了菲律宾－澳大利亚优质技术职业教育和培训（the Philippines – Australia quality technical vocational education and training，PAQTVET）双边项目的支持。通过澳大利亚国际开发署的援助，该项目向菲律宾国家、地区和省一级的技术教育与技能发展局官员提供了技术援助，以改造菲律宾的技术和职业教育与培训系统。PAQTVET 的目标是促进减贫，因为高质量的技术和职业教育与培训有助于减少失业问题，PAQTVET 通过有效地促进项目或方案提供了一个安全网。值得一提的是，该项目是行业制订技能提升计划、制定能力标准和确定职业资格的载体，最初涉及由菲律宾国家技术教育与技能发展局指定的 3 个行业，即卫生、信息技术和旅游行业。

菲律宾旅游业委员基金会监督并着手制定菲律宾旅游业的能力标准和资格。在不断深入的小组讨论和内容分析过程中，基金会对采用和调整能力教育方案、设置能力单元优先顺序的关键步骤有了全面的理解，并且对能力标准有了彻底的审视。澳大利亚的顾问和菲律宾国家技术教育与技能发展局的代表，利用基于亚洲和太平洋技能发展计划的区域模型促进了能力标准的发展。旅游业工作组根据菲律宾酒店和餐馆职业的现行培训条例（1998年系列），审查了食品和饮料服务提供商的标准。该培训条例规定了酒店和餐馆职业能力的最低标准，用来指导课程开发、培训材料开发、认证、行业培训认可、培训机构的注册和监督、学习者的评估和认证。

根据 PAQTVET 第二阶段的计划，下一步工作是根据行业能力标准和资质制定国家课程和评估指南及范例。这些指南为能力导向的课程体系的操作计划和方法提供质量保障，内容涉及实际教学材料和评估工具。制定指南的相关人员包括负责规划和实施与指定行业相关的所有技术教育和技能发展课程/计划指南的人员。

4 理论框架

能力代表了个人为实现工作所需的产出而具备的累积技能、知识、行为和态度（Wynne 和 Stringer，1997）。胜任意味着个人具备足够的工作所需的知识、技能和态度（Saunders 和 Race，1992；Wolf，1995；Chu 等，2001）。Dubois（1998）在其编撰的《能力案例》一书中解释道，业务运营的类型、技术和组织角色以及主动性决定了工作场所需要的具体能力。有趣的是，Wynne 和 Stringer（1997）指出，在英国，研究人员会将能力与工作产出联系起来；而在美国，大多数研究人员评价能力时会参考工作投入程度。产出相关意味着能力是根据员工是否达到或超过工作标准和期望来衡量的。而投入相关则反映了影响员工工作能力的知识、技能和态度。但是，由于大多数员工的考核和奖励是根据员工对组织的实际贡献来衡量的，因此，本文将在产出相关的背景下讨论能力。

教育、培训和经验都有助于能力的形成（Saunders 和 Race，1992）。教育提供一般知识，发展智力，能够为形成能力提供所需的深层知识、技能和态度打下基础。从文化角度来说，文凭是一种优势，低于大学本科学历的文凭通常不受重视。Rohini 等人（2005）的政策研究工作表明，许多国家对受过中等教育的工人的需求与偏重技能的技术变革相关联。世界银行和亚洲开发银行在过去几年中进行的产业研究结果表明，职业教育和短期课程的毕业生与接受正规或高等教育的同龄人相比，失业率很高。因此，许多职业教育机构的毕业生会接受额外的培训，以获得更高薪酬的海外工作，或者为了在当地劳动市场中得到公正的对待和良好的报酬。

Williams 和 Hua（2000）的一项关于能力的研究强调了能力的3个指标：一个人有效地从事各种行业相关工作的能力，一个人在不断变化的角色和情况下发挥专业作用的能力，以及一个人不断学习、发展和变革的意愿。Li 和 Kivela（1998）在 117 名学生和 71 名酒店经理中进行了一项调查，重点调查酒店经理和学生对酒店毕业生的能力水平的看法。这项研究旨在检验哪些接待技能与职业高度相关。结果显示，学生认为任务/工作分析、采购管理、饮料生产、客房管理、营销管理、职位描述和人际交往技能是酒店工作场所的重要技能。然而，酒店经理认为营销管理能力、制定工作规范及描述的能力是酒店员工应该具备的关键技能。

在设计基于能力的课程时，需要对能力标准进行全面分析和阐释。基于能力的课程框架包含整体课程设计和学习模块，是教师在规划课程和授课时的指南（Ablett，2006）。图 2 为技术教育和技能发展局颁布的基于能力的课程框架，该框架采用了亚太技能发展计划区域模型中的能力标准的核心组成部分。

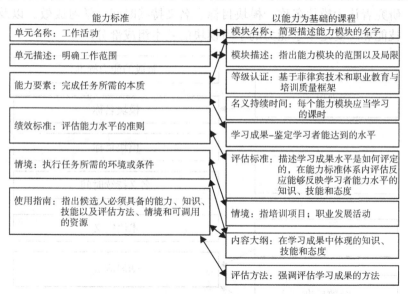

图 2　能力标准的组成部分和基于能力的课程的联系

从该框架中可以看出，能力标准的关键组成部分是单元名称、单元描述、能力要素、绩效标准、情境和使用指南。

能力标准的名称是用来界定能力单元所对应的工作范围。单元描述用来明确工作场所中的工作内容，并阐明能力单元的范围和目标。要素描述行动或结果，或者在特定工作领域中的一个人能起到的作用。因此，要素是可论证的，并且是能够被评估的。绩效标准是指评估能力水平的准则。绩效标准涉及能够显示能力的每个要素的技能、知识和行为。情境则指执行工作任务的环境或条件。工具和设备列表、学习资源和设备手册的获取、设施类型也属于情境因素。最后,使用指南会明确学习者能够胜任的事情,旨在指导工作场所和/或培训计划中能力单元的评估(Casey,2003)。通过对比可以发现,以能力为基础的课程框架的核心内容与行业制定的能力标准中规定的工作场所要求是一致的,如此确保行业所需的所有能力都能在培训和评估后实现(Ablett,2006)。

5 操作框架

本文的作者修改了基于能力的课程框架,使之成为更完善、更具有响应性的学习模块,以契合菲律宾大学酒店、餐厅和机构管理专业学生的需求。如图3所示,学习模块的开发是在彻底分析能力标准的深度和复杂性之后开展的。此外,研究者认为模块名称、模块目标、名义持续时间、学习成效,以及基础知识、技能和态度是基于能力的学习模块的基本组成部分。

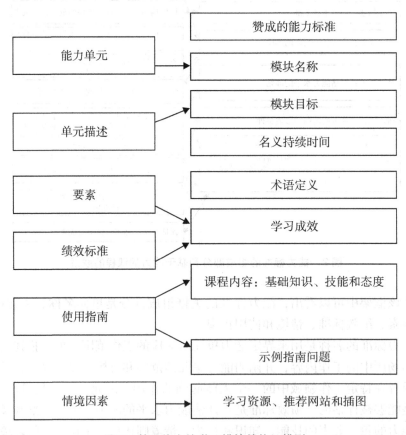

图3 基于能力的学习模块的修正模型

总的来说，学生希望以能力为基础的培养模式能用本地语言来阐释，这样他们就能完全理解课程主题。因此，支持者将术语定义策略性地纳入学习模块，以打造对学生友好的学习模块。另外，通过示例指南问题、学习资源、推荐网站和插图等提升学生的学习能力。可以注意到，尽管对理论框架进行了修改，学习模块仍然符合菲律宾技术教育与技能发展局根据工作场所的需求和标准制定的基于能力的课程形式。

在一个单一的基于能力的学习模块的基础上，这个操作框架催生了一个完整的基于能力的餐饮管理学习指南（Guggenheim 和 Ramos-Tumanan，2007）。这份指南是菲律宾大学酒店、餐厅和机构管理（HRIM）下的105个餐饮管理学生使用的实验室手册。有了这份学习材料，学生们将学习几个与葡萄酒和烈酒以及本地和国际上的非酒精饮料产品相关的模块，习得满足酒店行业所需的相关知识、技能和态度。

有意地接触东盟邻国的本地酒精和非酒精饮料，研究他们独特的饮酒文化，强调未来专业人员的能力建设，可以成为课程设计和教育传递的有效策略，以推进和影响东盟相互承认协定的目标——"促进专业人员的流动，分享基于能力的教育和培训的最佳实践，并为东盟成员国之间的能力建设提供机会"。

6 一项实证研究

为完成提供高质量的酒店和旅游专业毕业生的任务，研究者采取行业需求导向战略，鼓励行业、学术界和地方政府机构积极参与，以确保大学和其他学习机构能够使学生具备适当的知识、技能和态度。这项描述性研究于2007年进行，旨在比较菲律宾技术教育与技能发展局颁布的基于能力的课程框架，与亚太技能发展计划区域模型制定的能力标准的核心内容之间的相关性，目标是制定一个经过修改的学习模块，该模块有助于确保酒店和旅游教育的质量和响应性。该研究的对象是菲律宾大学机构和酒店、餐厅的管理专业的本科生；研究重点是基于能力的课程的关键要素，以及每个要素如何响应行业的技能需求。调查结果显示，学生们支持在餐饮课程中采用基于能力的学习和教育方法。作为学习模块实施中的主要行动者，学生们对新的学习和教育方法做出了极具启发性的回应。他们赞赏新的教学模式，并详细阐述了学习模块完成后的预期成效。该研究建议加强并倡导在菲律宾建立面向行业需求的餐饮课程学习模块。

6.1 样本情况

菲律宾大学酒店、餐饮和机构管理（HRIM）专业的学生组成了105人的样本群体。被调查者是所有符合饮料管理、采购管理和定量食品生产系列课程的学术要求的HRIM大三、大四学生。（见表1、表2、表3）

表1 受访者的性别

性别	数量/人	百分比	有效百分比	累计百分比
男性	26	24.8	24.8	24.8
女性	79	75.2	75.2	100.0
总数	105	100.0	100.0	—

表2 受访者的学年

学年	数量/人	百分比	有效百分比	累计百分比
第二年	1	1.0	1.0	1.0
第三年	53	50.4	50.4	51.4
第四年	42	40.0	40.0	91.4
第五年	8	7.6	7.6	99.0
第六年	1	1.0	1.0	100.0
总数	105	100.0	100.0	—

表3 受访者年龄

年龄	数量/人	百分比	有效百分比	累计百分比
18	3	2.8	2.8	2.8
19	27	25.7	25.7	28.5
20	42	40.0	40.0	68.5
21	21	20.0	20.0	88.5
22	9	8.5	8.5	97.0
23	1	1.0	1.0	98.0
24	1	1.0	1.0	99.0
29	1	1.0	1.0	100.0
总数	105	100.0	100.0	—

6.2 数据收集

在菲律宾-澳大利亚优质技术职业教育和培训项目二（Casey，2003）期间，课程和评估专家 Sonya Casey 编写了一份关于在旅游部门试行基于能力的课程评估报告，在此基础上形成了用于衡量基于能力的课程相关性的调查问卷。调查问卷包括三部分：第一部分涉及受访者的人口统计学特征；第二部分对评估的学习模块进行详细和深入的分析，如此可以获得重要信息，来评估学习模块的有效性；第三部分是收集对该模块一般化的评价。"李克特量表"对量表中的项进行评分，1分为不充分、最不重要和最不可接受，4分为非常充分、最重要和高度可接受。

6.3 数据分析

对统计数据进行描述性分析，如频数分布、百分比、平均值和标准差，用于描述收集的数据。利用 SPSS 数据分析软件（11.5.0版）（美国 LEAD 技术公司开发）进行独立样本 t 检验，来识别调查对象在不同主题方面的显著差异（$P<0.05$）。

6.4 调查结果的讨论

数据显示，在抽样调查的学生中，女性占主导，其中大多数是19～20岁的大三学生。

首先，研究者向受访者解释了本研究的目的及其与优质教育的关联性。随后，研究者向学生们发放了概念框架和"对餐酒进行感官评估"这一案例学习模块的资料，以确保学生们理解调查的每个主题。然而，在调查问卷的发放过程中出现了一些问题，因为一些学生显然误解了能力标准的一些关键组成部分。学生需要得到基于能力的培养模式的更全面的介绍，以及了解它如何满足学生和行业的需求。这是有益的，由于研究者非常熟悉能力标准的关键要素，所以他们能够相应地回答受访者的询问。

如图4所示，从回答中可以明显看出，学生非常支持学习模块。作为实施基于能力的学习模块的主要行动者，他们对这种新的学习和教育方法做出了非常有启发性的回应。

受访者赞赏新的教学模式，并详细阐述了预期的学习成效。一些学生在调查问卷中表示，该方法将有助于有效学习，课堂互动会更加积极，因为必要的知识、技能和态度都包含在基于能力的学习模块中。

图4、图5和图6说明了基于能力的方法的战略实施的基石是学生对课程

主题的清晰理解和认同，反映了工作场所所需的基础知识、技能和态度。研究结果还强调，机构或学校成员（即教师、学生和实验室工作人员）参与的程度和积极性被视为这一方法成功的关键因素。

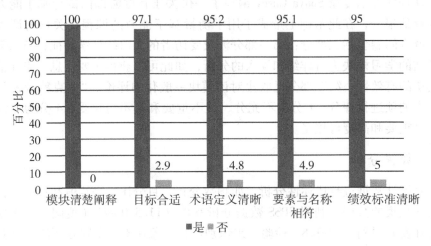

图 4　对调查主题的回应总结

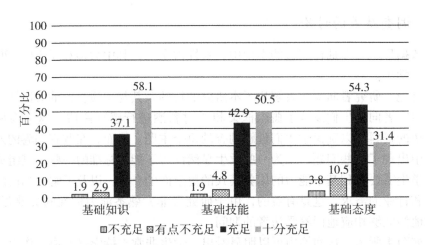

图 5　基础知识、技能和态度充分性方面的回应总结

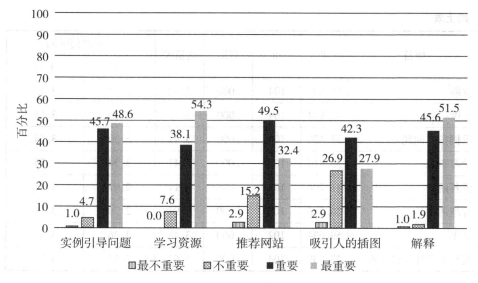

图 6 对调查主题的回应总结

表 4 显示，修订后的基于能力的学习模块的每个关键组成部分都非常重要。下限值和上限值的小差值说明所有题项的均值和响应模式基本相同。学生对修订后的学习模块的关键组成部分的相关性和可接受性的积极响应意味着他们认可基于能力的教育方法。这将有助于学生们通过实践活动来学习，帮他们建立符合行业水准的执行能力的信心。

表 4 独立样本 t 检验

项目	T	df	双尾	均值差	95% 置信区间	
					下限	上限
受访者学年	52.931	104	.000	3.57	3.44	3.71
受访者年龄	150.316	104	.000	20.21	19.94	20.48
性别	41.403	104	.000	1.75	1.67	1.84
适当的目标	59.464	104	.000	.97	.94	1.00
术语定义清晰	45.607	104	.000	.95	.91	.99
要素与名称相符	44.265	101	.000	.95	.91	.99
绩效标准清晰	43.818	100	.000	.95	.91	.99
基础知识	55.220	104	.000	3.51	3.39	3.64

续上表

项目	T	df	双尾	均值差	95%置信区间	
					下限	上限
技能	51.807	104	.000	3.42	3.29	3.55
态度	42.944	104	.000	3.13	2.99	3.28
示例指南问题	55.420	104	.000	3.42	3.30	3.54
学习资源	55.810	104	.000	3.47	3.34	3.59
推荐网站	41.796	104	.000	3.11	2.97	3.26
有趣的琐事	36.845	103	.000	2.95	2.79	3.11
插图	59.634	102	.000	3.48	3.36	3.59
模块的总体可接受性	73.639	104	.000	3.63	3.53	3.73

6.5 挑战

尽管大多数受访者认为引入基于能力的学习模块将为学生带来积极影响，但其实施方面仍存在一些挑战。首先，学习模块的准备需要花费大量的时间和精力。其次，教师推进基于能力的教学模式的能力和有效性是需要解决的问题。就研究者提供的样本学习模块而言，受访者的准备程度和成熟度是理解能力标准核心组成部分的关键所在。因此，学习机构应当通过提供最新的教学材料和设备供学生和教师使用，以此推进实施基于能力的培养模式。

6.6 建议

各利益相关群体，尤其是全国各地的培训提供者，包括行业工作组，有必要审视、理解和实施相关政策指南（Ablett，2006）。这些政策指南应当明确《培训条例》的内涵，特别是其颁布的能力标准。此外，学校和行业应签署协议备忘录，建立强有力的合作伙伴关系，以此推进基于能力的学习模式。协议备忘录可以涉及在职培训和评估等项目，以及任何一方可提供的其他支持服务，如招聘合格的酒店和旅游专业毕业生。

相关方可以实行一系列项目来厘清参与设计和对提供基于能力的课程的人员及其角色的期望。学校管理人员、教职人员、行业代表和课程开发人员参与的项目可能包括基于能力的教授系统的指南或简介、能力标准开发的导向、基于能力的课程开发、基于能力的学习材料开发、基于能力的评估以及教员－培训师开发和沉浸式项目（Ablett，2006）。

提供基于能力的课程的学校非常有必要根据《培训条例》（2005 系列）中认可的能力标准来开发课程。此外，校方应该有足够的基于能力的学习材料和资源。因此，教师应该在专业领域有相关的工作场所或行业经验，在提供加强与行业联系的计划之前，应制定一份协议备忘录（Ablett，2006）。

为了实施基于能力的教授系统，学校可以考虑与当地政府部门协调以促进项目推广和获取赞助。学术界和业界合作举办各种论坛、对话和信息分享会，通过基于能力的培养模式促进优质教育。在统计数据充分和准确的情况下，必须开展有效的研究，以确定旅游和酒店行业目前对相关技能的需求。

7 结论和启示

2007 年收集的实证数据为采用基于能力的餐饮管理课程铺平了道路，惠及菲律宾众多大学和培训机构，推动了基于能力的课程和培训模块在全国范围内的普及。

研究表明，地方政府部门、学术界和行业合作伙伴之间的合作对于从传统教育模式转向基于能力的教育模式至关重要，有助于完善菲律宾的教育体系。研究结果也表明，学生们渴望成为具有全球竞争力的酒店管理专业毕业生。类似的研究可以进一步开展，以确保今后在教育和培训中更有组织、更有效地实施基于能力的教育模式。

可能因为评估人员群体比较单一和有限，因此在评估过程中他们可能"超负荷运行"。而且，由于评估的指导原则植根于经验，当评估人员本身缺乏必要的技能和资格时，这可能会影响评估结果。在确定技能和要求的过程中，设施等资源对于确保基于能力的教育在菲律宾的普及至关重要。最后，能力发展计划是必要的，以便厘清参与设计和对提供基于能力的课程的人员及其角色的期望。

致　谢

感谢菲律宾 - 澳大利亚优质技术职业教育和培训的顾问，特别是 Sonia Casey 女士和 Patrick Cummings，感谢他们在能力标准和基于能力的课程开发方面的专业知识。此外，菲律宾技术教育与技能发展局是基于能力的课程的主要推动者，促使作者写了这个案例研究。

Tourism and Hospitality Education in the Philippines: A Competency-Based Approach

Guerrero, RGIG, Guggenheim, LJG, and Ramos-Tumanan, MA

1 Introduction

Tertiary Education in tourism and hospitality in the Philippines started the 1970s with the Bachelor of Science in Hotel and Restaurant Administration (BS HRA) at the University of the Philippines (UP). The BS HRA program at the UP was created in 1969 and first offered during the school year of 70 – 71. It was a request by the Hotel and Restaurant Association of the Philippines for academe to provide them with middle-management for the booming hotel and restaurant industry (Paz-Guzman, 1982). The Bachelor of Science in Tourism, on the other hand, also started in UP in 1976 (UP Gazette, 1976). It was initiated by the Department of Tourism. Since then, both degree programs have been offered by the different higher education institutions (HEI). As of year 2012, there are 978 HEIs offering the hospitality degree and 346 HEIs offering the tourism degree (Aquino and Aragon, 2015).

In the Philippines, tourism and hospitality education are guided by the principle of competency-based education (CBE) and outcomes-based education (OBE). CBE is defined by Nodine and Johnstone (2015) as 'online and hybrid courses and programs that offer credit based on evidence of student learning, or competencies, rather than on the amount of time spent in a course'. The CBE concept in the Philippine tourism and hospitality education was implemented after a series of consultation with the Philippines-Australia Quality Technical Vocational Education and Training (PAQTVET) operating under the Aus-Aid and TESDA (Guggenheim and Ramos-Tumanan, 2007). This project provided the competencies needed for the future workers in the tourism and hospitality industry.

Spady (1994) defines OBE as 'starting with a clear picture of what is important for students to be able to do, then organizing the curriculum, instruction and assessment to make sure this learning ultimately happens'. In 2012, the Commission on Higher Education (CHED) issued CHED Memorandum Order (CMO) No. 42, Series of 2012 titled Policy Standard to Enhance Quality Assurance (QA) in Philippine Higher Education Through an Outcomes-Based and Typology-Based QA that paved the way for OBE.

2 The Association of Southeast Asian Nations Mutual Recognition Arrangement (ASEAN MRA)

The ASEAN is an organization establishing in 1967 with five member states: the Philippines, Malaysia, Thailand, Indonesia and Singapore. Brunei, Vietnam, Laos, Myanmar and Cambodia also joined the organization later (https://www.asean.org/storage/images/2013/economic/handbook% 20mra% 20tourism _ opt.pdf).

The organization's aims could be summarized as its motto 'One Vision, One Identity, One Community', and in order to achieve the aims several agreements were put in place. One of this is the ASEAN MRA with the objective to 'facilitate movement of business persons and skilled labor and talents' (Aquino and Aragon, 2015). Several MRAs were created for the different work field, the MRA for the Tourism Professionals was signed on 2009 and completed on 2012 (Aquino and Aragon, 2015).

The objectives of the ASEAN MRA for Tourism Professionals (https://www.asean.org/storage/images/2013/economic/handbook% 20mra% 20tourism _ opt.pdf) are as follows: ①to facilitate mobility of Tourism Professionals / Workers; ②to exchange information on best practices in competency-based education and training for Tourism Professionals; ③to provide opportunities of corporation and capacity building across ASEAN member states (TESDA, 2016). The ASEAN MRA TP has identified 6 labor divisions and 32 job titles (Figure 1). It has established the Common ASEAN Tourism Curriculum (CATC) by establishing 242 common competencies in these job titles called ASEAN Common Competency Standard for Tourism Professionals (ACCSTP) (Aquino and Aragon, 2015; Jotikasthira, et al, 2016).

32 Job Titles–Six Labour Divisions

HOTEL SERVICES				TRAVEL SERVICES	
Front Office	House Keeping	Food Production	Food and Bevarage Service	Travel Agencies	Tour Operation
Front Office Manager	Executive Housekeeper	Executive Chef	F & B Director	General Manager	Product Manager
Front Office Supervisor	Laundry Manager	Demi Chef	F & B Outlet Manager	Assistant General Manager	Sales & Marketing Manager
Receptionist	Floor Supervisor	Commis Chef	Head Waiter	Senior Travel Consultant	Credit Manager
Telephone Operator	Laundry Attendant	Chef de Partie	Bartender	Travel Consultant	Ticketing Manager
Bell Boy	Room Attendant	Commis Pastry	Waiter	—	Tour Manager
—	Public Area Cleaner	Baker	—	—	—
—	—	Butcher	—	—	—

Figure 1 The ASEAN MRA Framework for tourism professionals
Source: ASEAN MRA TP Handbook (2013)

Three lead agencies were tapped to implement this ASEAN MRA-TP in the Philippines; they are the Department of Tourism (DOT), Tourism Industry Board Foundation (TIBFI) and the Technical Education and Skills Development Authority (TESDA) (Aquino and Aragon, 2015, TESDA, 2016). The DOT's role is to develop, coordinate and implement work programs/plans to enhance cooperation in tourism. It shall be the official representative of the Philippines to the ASEAN Tourism Professional Monitoring Committee (Aquino and Aragon, 2015). TIBFI's role is to create awareness and disseminate information about the ASEAN MRA and to make sure that the ACCSTP and CATC are maintained and monitored (Aquino and Aragon, 2015).

TESDA's role is to perform the assessment and certification of the tourism professionals based on the ACCSTP (Aquino and Aragon, 2015). For the basic and secondary education, the K to 12 Program (Kindergarten to Grade 12 Program) was implemented in the Philippines in 2016. It has four tracks: ①Academic Track; ②Technical-Vocational-Livelihood (TVL) Track; ③Sports Track; ④Arts and Design Track. The tourism and hospitality courses are under the home economics specialization of the TVL strand. Tourism and hospitality courses are: ①Cookery; ②Commercial Cookery; ③Events Management; ④Food & Beverage Services; ⑤Front Office Services; ⑥Housekeeping; ⑦Local Guiding Services; ⑧Tourism

Promotion Services; ⑨Travel Services for the tertiary level. The Commission on Higher Education's (CHED) technical panel for the Tourism and Hospitality education had issued CMO No. 62 Series of 2018 that provides the guides for the Tourism and Hospitality Curriculum. This issuance has considered as inputs the K to 12 Curriculum and the ASEAN MRA-TP's CATC.

3 An Evidence of Clear Learning Outcomes

The Philippines made its own foray into competency based assessment in 1994, alongside the shift towards a more industry responsive and demand-driven approach to Technical and Vocational Education and Training (TVET) delivery. This move was supported by a bilateral project called the Philippines-Australia Quality Technical Vocational Education and Training (PAQTVET). Through the aid of the Australian Agency for International Development, technical assistance was given to Technical Education and Skills Development Authority (TESDA) officials at the national, regional and provincial levels to the transformation of the TVET system in the Philippines. It was the objective of PAQTVET to contribute to poverty alleviation since quality technical and vocational education and training reduce problems of unemployment and provide a safety net through effective facilitated projects or programs. Principally, the project was a vehicle to the establishment of sectoral industry working groups to develop skill plans, competency standards and qualifications initially for each three economic sectors identified by TESDA, namely, health, information technology and the tourism sectors.

The Tourism Industry Board Foundation Incorporated has overseen and undertaken the development of competency standards and qualifications for the Philippine tourism industry. During the focused group discussions and progressive content analyses, a comprehensive understanding of the key steps in adopt and adapt approach, prioritization of units of competencies and a thorough examination of components of a competency standard transpired. The Australian consultants and representatives from TESDA facilitated the development of competency standards utilizing the regional model based on the Asian and Pacific Skills Development Program. The tourism industry working groups likewise reviewed the existing Training Regulations (series 1998) for the hotel and restaurant occupations in the Philippines in order to examine standards for food and beverage providers. It provides minimum standards to competencies in the hotel and restaurant occupations, which serve as guides to curriculum development, training materials development, accreditation, industry training recognition, registration and monitoring of training providers, assessment of learning and certification.

As proposed in Phase II of the PAQTVET project, the next step was to develop National Curriculum and Assessment Guides and Exemplars based on competency standards and qualifications. These guides aimed to provide a quality assurance approach to the development of operational plans and methodologies in developing competency-based curriculum that would include actual instructional materials and assessment instruments. The people involved were the key players who were responsible for the planning and implementation of the guides prepared for all TVET courses/programs relevant to the selected industry sector.

4　Theoretical Frame

Competencies represent the accumulated skills, knowledge, behavior and attitude which individuals apply in achieving the outputs required on the job (Wynne and Stringer, 1997). Being competent means that the individual is equipped with adequate knowledge, skills and attitudes required in the workplace (Saunders and Race, 1992; Wolf, 1995; Chu et al., 2001). In the *Competency Case* edited by Dubois (1998), he explained that the type of business operation, technology and organizational role and initiative dictate the specific competencies needed in the workplace. Interestingly, Wynne and Stringer (1997) explicated that in the United Kingdom, researchers would relate competency to job outputs, whereas in the United States of America most refer to job inputs. Output-related means that competencies are measured in relation to whether or not an employee meets or exceeds work standards and expectations. On the other hand, input-related reflects the knowledge, skills and attitudes that affect the employee's ability to perform. But since most employees are measured and rewarded in respect of their actual contribution to the organization, competency will be discussed in this paper in the context of output-related.

Education, training and experience all contribute to the elements of competence (Saunders and Race, 1992). Education provides general knowledge and develops intellectual attributes. It provides the basis for further knowledge, skills and attitudes necessitated to establish the required competence. Culturally speaking, credentials are viewed as a cutting edge and any qualification less than a college degree is not so much held in any particular regard. The policy research working paper by Rohini et al. (2005) suggests that in many countries, the demand for workers with secondary schooling has been associated with skill biased technological change. The results of sectoral studies carried out by the World Bank and the Asian Development Bank in the last five years suggest that vocational education and graduates of short-course programs suffer from high levels of unemployment compared to individuals of the same age in formal or higher education. Not surprisingly, a number of graduates of vocational courses would result in taking additional training either in preparation for an overseas assignment for a higher remuneration, or to be fairly regarded and well compensated within the local workforce.

A study carried out by Williams and Hua (2000) on competency highlighted the three indicators of competency: the ability of a person to efficiently perform a wide-range of industry related jobs, the ability of a person to function professionally in the changing roles and situations and the desire of a person for continuous learning development and change. A survey among 117 students and 71 hotel mangers carried out by Li and Kivela (1998) focused on the perception of hotel managers and students in view of levels of competencies demonstrated by hospitality graduates. The study aimed to examine which hospitality skills were found to be highly correlated with occupation. Results showed that task/job analysis, purchasing management, beverage production, room management, marketing management, development of job description and interpersonal skills were perceived by the students to be the salient competencies in the hospitality workplace. However, hotel managers considered the competencies of marketing management and development of job specifications or descriptions as the key areas that hospitality workforce should be equipped with.

The key considerations in designing a competency based curriculum takes into account a thorough analysis and interpretation of details of competency standards. The competency based curriculum framework encapsulates the overall course design and modules of learning. It serves as a guide for teachers when planning for the design and delivery of a course (Ablett, 2006). Figure 2 illustrates key components of a competency standard adopted from the Asia Pacific Skills Development Program regional model against the competency based curriculum framework promulgated by Technical Education and Skills Development Authority.

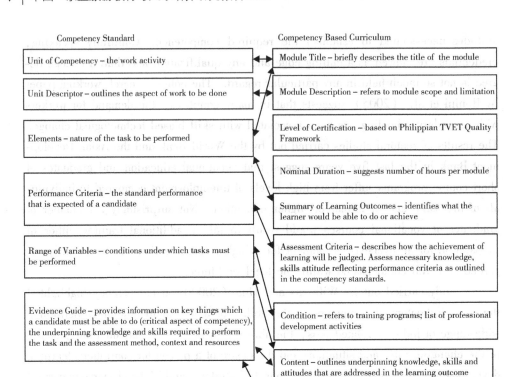

Figure 2 Relationship between components of a competency standard and competency based curriculum

Drawn from the framework, key components of a Competency Standard (CS) are Unit Title, Unit Descriptor, Elements of Competency, Performance Criteria, Range Statement and Evidence Guide.

A Title of a CS defines the scope of the work described in the unit of competency. A Unit Descriptor outlines what is done in the workplace and clarifies scope and intent of the unit of the CS. An Element describes actions or outcomes, or the function that a person in a particular area of work is able to perform. It is therefore demonstrable and capable of being assessed. Performance Criteria are evaluative statements that specify how to assess the level of competency. Performance criteria refer to skills, knowledge and behavior that provide evidence of competent performance for each element of competency. Range of Variables depicts the circumstances or conditions under which the task must be performed. List of tools and equipment, access to learning resources and equipment manuals, types of facility also fall under range of variables. Lastly, Evidence Guide provides information on key things which a learner must be able to do. Its purpose is to guide the assessment of the unit of competency in the workplace and/or training program (Casey, 2003). Comparatively, the competency based curriculum framework details key components which are consistent with the requirements of the workplace as laid down in the competency standards prepared by the industry. It is designed to ensure that all required competencies by the industry are achieved after the training and assessment (Ablett, 2006).

5 Operational Frame

The proponents of the study modified the competency based curriculum framework into a more refined and responsive learning module tailored fit to the needs of the Hotel, Restaurant and Institution Management students of the University of the Philippines. Figure 3 shows that development of a learning module begins after conducting a thorough analysis of the depth and complexity of a competency standard. Henceforth, the proponents considered module title, module objective, nominal duration, learning outcomes and underpinning knowledge, skills and attitudes as basic components of a competency based learning module.

Generally speaking, students would like to have the competency based approach written in vernacular language for them to fully understand the course topic. Thus the proponents included definition of terms as a strategy to a more user-friendly learning module. Notwithstanding that, sample guide questions, learning resources, recommended websites and illustrations facilitate students' learning capacity. It can be noted that despite modifications, the learning module is still consistent with the competency based curriculum format by the Technical Education and Skills Development Authority based on the identified needs and standards required in the workplace.

From a single competency based learning module, this operational frame has given birth to an entire Competency Based Learning Guide in Beverage Management (Guggenheim and Ramos-Tumanan, 2007), a laboratory manual for the use of 105 Beverage Management students of Hotel, Restaurant and Institution Management (HRIM) of the University of the Philippines. With this learning resource material,

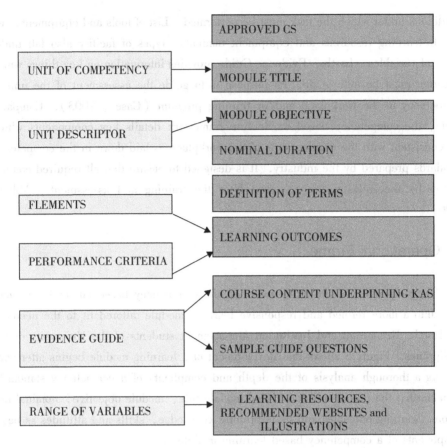

Figure 3　A revised model of a competency-based learning module

students go through several modules pertaining to wines and spirits as well as non-alcoholic beverage products of local and international origins, acquiring knowledge, attitudes and skills that build over all competency for satisfying careers in the hospitality industry.

Deliberate exposure to indigenous alcoholic and non-alcoholic beverages of our ASEAN neighbors and the study of their unique drinking cultures with emphasis on capacity building of future professionals could be an effective strategy for curriculum design and education delivery to contribute and impact the ASEAN Mutual Recognition Agreement objectives 'to facilitate mobility of professionals, exchange information on best practices in competency-based education and training and to provide opportunities of capacity building across ASEAN member nations'.

6 An Empirical Evidence

Pursuing its mandate of providing relevant and high quality hospitality and tourism graduates, the proponents adopted an industry-led strategy that encouraged the dynamic participation of industry, academe and local government institutions to ensure that appropriate knowledge, skills and attitudes are provided by the universities and other learning institutions. This descriptive study conducted in 2007 aimed to examine the relevance of the key components of competency standards developed by the Asia Pacific Skills Development Program regional model vis-à-vis the competency based curriculum framework promulgated by the Technical Education and Skills Development Authority. A final output was a modified learning module that assured quality and responsive approach to hospitality and tourism education. The units of analysis were students enrolled in the Bachelor of Science in Hotel, Restaurant and Institution Management program of the University of the Philippines. A strong mechanism involved a thorough analysis of key elements of a competency based curriculum and how each element responds to the skill needs of the industry. Findings revealed students were supportive of the competency based approach in food and beverage courses. Being the lead actors in the implementation of the module, they provided very enlightening responses to the new approach to learning and education. They appreciated the fact that the new mode of delivery spelled out in detail the expected learning outcomes upon completion of the module. Recommendations from the study enhanced and advocated the institution of an industry-driven learning module for food and beverage courses within the Philippines.

6.1 Sample Population

Students enrolled in the B.S. Hotel, Restaurant and Institution Management (HRIM) program of the University of the Philippines composed the sample population of 105. All third and fourth year undergraduate students of HRIM who had complied with academic requirements of the series courses—Beverage Management, Purchasing Management and Quantity Food Production encompassed the total number of respondents. (See Table 1 to Table 3)

Table 1 Gender of respondent

Gender	Frequency	Percent	Valid Percent	Cumulative Percent
Male	26	24.8	24.8	24.8
Female	79	75.2	75.2	100.0
Total	105	100.0	100.0	—

Table 2 Year of respondent

Year	Frequency	Percent	Valid Percent	Cumulative Percent
Second Year	1	1.0	1.0	1.0
Third Year	53	50.4	50.4	51.4
Fourth Year	42	40.0	40.0	91.4
Fifth Year	8	7.6	7.6	99.0
Sixth Year	1	1.0	1.0	100.0
Total	105	100.0	100.0	—

Table 3 Age of respondent

Age	Frequency	Percent	Valid Percent	Cumulative Percent
18	3	2.8	2.8	2.8
19	27	25.7	25.7	28.5
20	42	40.0	40.0	68.5
21	21	20.0	20.0	88.5
22	9	8.5	8.5	97.0
23	1	1.0	1.0	98.0
24	1	1.0	1.0	99.0
29	1	1.0	1.0	100.0
Total	105	100.0	100.0	—

6.2 Data Collection

The survey instrument used to measure the relevance of a competency based curriculum was patterned after the evaluation report on piloting competence based curricula in the tourism sector developed by Sonya Casey, curriculum and assessment specialist during the Philippines-Australia Quality Technical Vocational Education and Training project II (Casey, 2003). The instrument was divided into three parts. Part I dealt with demographic profile of the respondents. Part II presented a more detailed and in-depth analysis of the module being reviewed. This was done in order to obtain important notes, which would greatly affect the validity of the learning module. Part III was a more generalized approach of gathering comments on the module. Items in the scale were rated using a four-point Likert scale ranging from 1 as inadequate, least important and least acceptable to four, meaning extremely adequate, most important and highly acceptable.

6.3 Data Analysis

Descriptive statistics such as frequency distribution, percentage, mean and standard deviation were employed in the characterization of the data collected. Independent-Sample t-test using SPSS for Windows ver. 11.5.0 (LEAD Technologies, Inc., USA) was also utilized to distinguish significant differences ($P < 0.05$) among the subjects' responses on the different topics of inquiry.

6.4 Discussion of Findings

Among the students sampled, data indicated a female dominant population where most of them were junior students with 19 and 20 years of age.

Initially, objective of the study and its relevance to quality education was explained to the respondents. They were given copies of the conceptual framework and sample module on 'Conducting a Sensory Evaluation for Table Wines' to sufficiently understand each topic of inquiry. There were some problems however that surfaced during the administration of the survey instrument as the result of some students evidently misunderstanding some key components of a competency standard. Students needed a more comprehensive introduction about the competency based approach and how it addresses the needs of the students and the industries. It was advantageous, though that the proponents were well versed with the key elements of a competency standard and have been able to respond to respondents' query accordingly.

As shown in Figure 4, it is apparent in the responses that students were very supportive of the learning module. Being the lead actors in the implementation of the competency based module, they provided very enlightening responses to the new approach to learning and education.

The respondents appreciated the fact that the new mode of delivery spelled out in detail the expected learning outcomes. Some students commented in the questionnaire that this approach will facilitate effective learning, and class discussion becomes more interactive since necessary knowledge, skills and attitudes are covered in the competency based learning module.

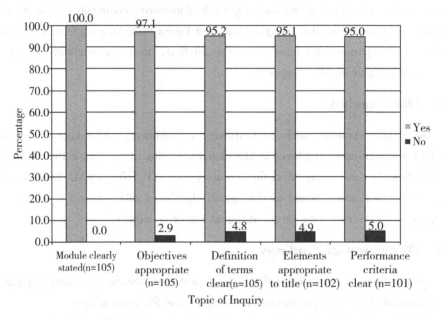

Figure 4　Summary of responses for each topic of inquiry

Figures 4, 5, and 6 explicated that the cornerstone towards a strategic implementation of a competency based approach is a clear understanding and appreciation of the course subject by the students, reflective of the underpinning knowledge, skills and attitudes needed in the workplace. Results from the study also emphasized that commitment and enthusiasm of members of the institutions/ schools (i. e. teachers, students and laboratory staff) to get involved is seen as a crucial factor to the success of this approach. Noticeably, the graphical data presented how the respondents appreciated the alternative approach to education as the next best thing to experiencing and learning.

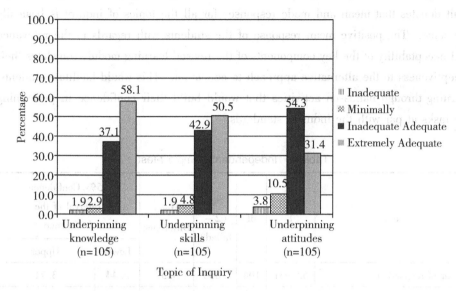

Figure 5   Summary of responses in terms of adequacy of underpinning knowledge, skills and attitudes

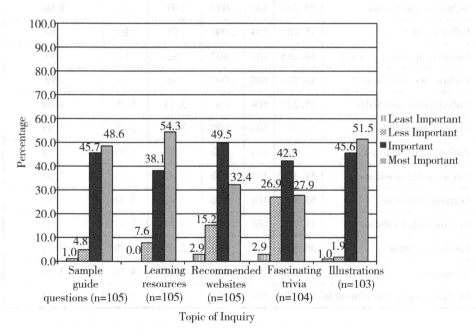

Figure 6   Summary of responses for each topic of inquiry

Table 4 revealed that each key component of the modified competency based learning module is highly significant. The small range between the lower and upper limit denotes that mean and mode responses for all the topics of inquiry is basically the same. The positive mean response of the students with regards to the relevance and acceptability of the key components of the revised learning module translates their receptiveness to the alternative approach to education. This would facilitate students' learning through hands-on activities that would build their confidence in performing the tasks at par with the industry standards.

Table 4　Independent-Sample *t*-test

Item	T	df	Sig. (2-tailed)	Mean Difference	95% Confidence Interval of the Difference	
					Lower	Upper
Year of respondent	52.931	104	.000	3.57	3.44	3.71
Age of respondent	150.316	104	.000	20.21	19.94	20.48
Gender	41.403	104	.000	1.75	1.67	1.84
Objectives appropriate	59.464	104	.000	.97	.94	1.00
Definition of terms clear	45.607	104	.000	.95	.91	.99
Elements appropriate to title	44.265	101	.000	.95	.91	.99
Performance criteria clear	43.818	100	.000	.95	.91	.99
Underpinning knowledge	55.220	104	.000	3.51	3.39	3.64
Underpinning skills	51.807	104	.000	3.42	3.29	3.55
Underpinning attitudes	42.944	104	.000	3.13	2.99	3.28
Sample guide questions	55.420	104	.000	3.42	3.30	3.54
Learning resources	55.810	104	.000	3.47	3.34	3.59
Recommended websites	41.796	104	.000	3.11	2.97	3.26
Fascinating trivia	36.845	103	.000	2.95	2.79	3.11
Illustrations	59.634	102	.000	3.48	3.36	3.59
Overall acceptability of module	73.639	104	.000	3.63	3.53	3.73

6.5 Challenges

Though most of the respondents claimed that the introduction of a competency based learning module will bring positive outcomes to students, there are some challenges to support its implementation. First, the preparation of a learning module takes enormous time and effort consuming. Second, availability and competency of the teacher to facilitate the competency based approach are issues that need to be addressed. The level of preparedness and maturity of the respondents was deemed critical in comprehending key components of a competency standard against the sample learning module provided by the proponents. Needless to say, the learning institution should also exert more effort in implementing the method by providing updated instructional materials and equipment for utilization of the students as well as the teachers.

6.6 Recommendation

It is recommended that relevant policy guidelines are reviewed, understood and implemented by all stakeholders especially for training providers across the country including the industry working groups (Ablett, 2006). These policy guidelines should provide clear understanding of the Training Regulations where the promulgated competency standards are encapsulated. It is likewise suggested that there should be a strong partnership arrangements of schools and industry partners for the implementation of competency based learning experiences through the preparation and signing of a Memorandum of Agreement that could include items such as, on-the-job training and assessment, and other support services that can be provided by either party, including the recruitment of competent hospitality and tourism graduates.

Several programs can be implemented to outline details of expectations and roles of those involved in designing and delivering competency based curriculum. Programs to be attended by school administrators, teachers/instructors, industry representatives and curriculum developers may include orientation/briefing on competency based delivery system, orientation on competency standards development, developing competency-based curriculum, developing competency-based learning materials, competency-based assessment and faculty-trainer development and immersion programs (Ablett, 2006).

It is strongly recommended that schools offering the program should have competency-based curricula developed based on approved competency standards found in the Training Regulations (series 2005). In addition, schools offering the program should have sufficient competency-based learning materials and resources. Consequently, teachers should have relevant workplace or industry experience in the area of expertise. A Memorandum of Agreement should be in place before a program is offered to strengthen linkages with industry (Ablett, 2006).

For implementation of competency based delivery systems, schools may consider to coordinate with the Local Government Units for program promotion support and sponsorship. A collaborative effort between academe and industry to conduct various forum, dialogues and information sessions to promote quality education through a competency-based approach. Effective research that determines the nature and extent of the industry's current and emerging needs for skills development in the hospitality and tourism industry must be carried out, where statistical data are sufficient and accurate.

7 Conclusions and Implications

The empirical data albeit, conducted in 2007 paved the way to the adoption of a competency-based curriculum for beverage management within which benefits accrue to different universities and training institutions in the Philippines thereby ensuring the proliferation of a competency-based curriculum and training modules throughout the country.

What the study has proven is that a collaborative work effort amongst local government units, academia and industry partners is critical in a process of change, from a traditional to a competency-based approach in strengthening the education system in the country. Inevitably, results were also reflection of the learners' desire to become globally competitive hospitality graduates. A similar study can still be replicated in order to ensure a more organized and effective implementation of a competency-based approach in education and training in the future.

While the assessors may be credible to be one, they could experience 'brain drain' in the process. Equally, the guiding principle of the assessment is rooted in experience and this could pose a challenge when the assessors themselves lack the necessary skills and qualifications. In the process of identifying the skills and requirements, resources such as facilities are premium thereby ensuring the proliferation of competency-based education in the country. Finally, Capacity development programs are necessitated in order to outline details of expectations and roles of those involved in designing and delivering competency-based curriculum.

References

[1] ABLETT D. Developing competency based curriculum: Capacity development learning program [M]. Taguig, Metro Manila: PAQTVET 2, 2006.
[2] AQUINO M C G, ARAGON L C. Finding... ASEAN MRA for tourism professionals [J]. Journal of business and economics, 2015, 6 (2): 286 – 295.
[3] ASEAN. 2018 handbook of ASEAN mutual recognition arrangement on tourism professionals (2nd edition) [M]. Jakarta: ASEAN Secretariat, 2018.
[4] ASIAN DEVELOPMENT BANK. Strengthening the management capacity of the technical education and skills development authority (AOTA ADB 3482 Phil) [EB/OL]. (2002 – 06) [2019 – 12 – 01]. http://www.adb.org/Education/tesda.pdf.
[5] GUGGENHEIM L J, RAMOS – TUMANAN M. Competency-based learning guide in beverage management [M]. Quezon City, the Philippines: C&E Publication, 2007.
[6] JOTIKASTHIRA N, PHAKDEEPHIROT N, TEERANOOT S. Thai tourism and hospitality education: Current conditions and strategic directions [J]. Rangsit journal of educational studies, 2016, 2 (3): 86 – 103.
[7] NERI R. The medium term Philippine development plan 2004 – 2010 [M/OL]. Manila, the Philippines: the National Economic and Development Authority (2004 – 10 – 11) [2019 – 12 – 01] https://openjicareport.jica.go.jp/pdf/11948882_29.pdf.
[8] NODINE T, JOHNSTONE S M. Competency-based education: Leadership challenges [M]. Philadelphia: Routledge, 2015.
[9] RACE P, SAUNDERS D. Developing and measuring competence [M]. London, UK: Kogan Page Limited, SEDA Publishing, 1992.
[10] SPADY W G. Outcome-based education: Critical issues and answers. [M]. Arlington, VA: American Association of School Administrators, 1994.
[11] The ASEAN Secretariat. ASEAN qualifications reference framework: A practical guide [M/OL]. Jarkata: The ASEAN Secretariat, 2018. https://asean.org/wp – content/uploads/2018/12/aqrf – publication – 2018 – final.pdf.
[12] TOURISM EDUCATION AND SKILLS DEVELOPMENT AUTHORITY. Labor market intelligence report tourism and economic development [EB/OL]. (2016 – 08) [2019 – 12 – 01]. http://www.tesda.gov.ph/About/Tesda/51.
[13] TOURISM INDUSTRY BOARD FOUNDATION INC. ASEAN MRA on tourism professionals [EB/OL]. (2017) [2019 – 12 – 01] https://www.tourismindustryboard.org/asean – mra.
[14] WYNNE B, STRINGER D. A competency-based approach to training and development

[M]. London, UK: PITMAN Publishing, 1997.

Acknowledgment

Acknowledgements are extended to the consultants of the Philippine Australia Quality Technical Vocational Education and Training specifically to Ms. Sonia Casey and Patrick Cummings for their expertise in the development of a competency standard and competency-based curriculum. Additionally, the Philippine Technical Education and Skills Development Authority for being the prime-mover of a competency-based curriculum, which prodded the author to write this case study.

泰国私立大学旅游和酒店教育

宗希蔓　泰国易三仓大学经济管理学院

我叫宗希蔓，这是个中文名字，但我已经在泰国住了13年，所以，可以说我现在是半个泰国人了。今天早上 Therdchai 教授分享了泰国的旅游研究近况，Korawan 博士刚刚分享了一些关于中国游客的研究。因此，我将把重点放在一所我所在的私立大学——易三仓大学的旅游教育上。

1 大学介绍

易三仓大学在泰国所有私立大学中排名第一。它是一所国际天主教大学，已经有50年的历史，是泰国第一所国际大学，学生来自世界各地。易三仓大学有4个校园，分别是 Huamak 校区、city 校区、Suvarnabhumi（素万那普）校区和 ACC 商学院 Sathorn 校区。city 校区和 ACC 商学院 Sathorn 校区位于曼谷中心，为在职的学生提供便利，方便他们下班后前来学习。HuamaK 校区是研究生院，设有硕士学位课程和博士学位课程。Suvarnabhumi 校区靠近曼谷 Suvarnabhumi（素万那普）国际机场，是为本科教育准备的，所有的学士学位教育都将在 Suvarnabhumi 校区进行。

2 酒店和旅游管理专业

酒店和旅游管理专业（HTM）隶属商学院。商学院的全名叫马丁·德图尔经济管理学院（Martin de Tours School of Management and Economics）。商学院下设12个学士学位项目、2个硕士学位项目和2个博士学位项目。商学院本科学生在获得50学分后可以确定专业，通常在他们学习的第二年进行。所有商学院学生都需要在前两年学习基础课程，如统计学、会计学、财务管理、商业研究。酒店和旅游管理是商学院最受欢迎的专业之一。酒店和旅游管理专业有3个计划，分别是计划A、B和C。计划A聚焦于酒店管理，计划B聚焦于旅游管理，计划C聚焦于商业。其中，主修酒店专业的学生会从营销、商业信息系统或国际商业管理中选择一个作为辅修专业。

对于计划A，学生重点学习酒店管理的必修课程，如餐饮服务、厨房运营、客房事业部管理、活动管理和服务管理。对于计划 B，学生将需要学习旅游管理相关课程，如旅游政策与发展、旅游目的地管理、导游和实操、文化遗产旅游和国际旅游研究。对于计划 C，学生需要从 4 个专业中选择一个作为辅修专业，这 4 个专业分别是管理信息系统（MIS）、国际商业管理（IBM）、管理领导力和企业家精神（MGT）、市场营销（MKT）。不同的辅修专业有不同的课程。例如，如果学生选择管理信息系统作为辅修专业，他们需要学习 5 门课程，包括编程和算法、数据库系统、数据通信和网络、信息系统分析和设计以及信息系统项目管理。针对酒店和旅游管理专业，学校采用了综合性的教学方法，学生在课堂上学习理论和概念，然后参加酒店业的实习和实地考察项目。

3 实习

实习是酒店和旅游管理专业的主要要求之一。学生需完成 400 小时的实习任务。对于实习，学校为学生提供建议，并帮助他们找到合适的旅游企业，如四或五星级酒店、航空公司、旅行社等。然后学生需要联系相关的公司机构并获得"录取通知书"。在他们被酒店或航空公司接受并开始工作后，学校将联系实习的学生，回答他们的问题并提供建议。学校也会与他们的主管保持联系，解决实习期间的问题。在他们完成实习之前，学校将前往他们的工作场所和他们的主管进行交流。

实习结束后，学校会让主管评估学生的工作表现。在完成实习后，学生需要给导师做一个汇报展示，包括他们做了什么、他们从实习中学到了什么。评分不仅基于学生的展示和学校相关人员的考察，主管的评价也是评分非常重要的组成部分。

4 酒店和旅游管理职业日

每学期学校都会组织职业日来帮助学生找到实习公司。职业日的目的是为学生提供与酒店行业专家和经理互动的机会。2019 年的职业日在 9 月，学校邀请了一些著名的公司参加，如曼谷暹罗安纳塔拉酒店（Anantara Siam Bangkok Hotel）、曼谷安凡妮中庭酒店（Avani Atrium Bangkok Hotel）、曼谷素坤逸万豪酒店（Bangkok Marriott Hotel Sukhumvit）等。公司代表们来到学校与学生交谈，回答有关职位空缺或工作要求的问题。在职业日，学生需要准备简历，如果他们有兴趣申请某职位，可以提交给公司代表。

5 餐饮培训实验室：水晶餐厅

除了实习外，学校还不断为学生提供培训，以期学生在旅游接待工作中具备良好的仪容仪表、专业素养和沟通能力。大学里有一个实用的餐厅培训实验室，根据两门不同课程（厨房操作和餐饮服务）的要求，学生需要在里面工作。在厨房操作课上，学生需要在厨房工作，学习如何准备食物和烹饪食物。而在餐饮服务课上，学生需要学习如何为客户服务、如何下订单、如何展示菜单、如何处理账单支付和为客人准备餐桌。在水晶餐厅工作时，学生们学会了如何做鸡尾酒、如何做蛋糕，总之，他们感到非常开心。

对于水晶餐厅的菜单，学校鼓励学生自行决定。学生需要考虑每月要推出什么样的菜单，还需要设计海报以向校内所有师生宣传新菜单。例如，学校 50 周年校庆时，同学们为校庆推出了特别菜单。特别菜单里有 3 种不同的菜品，分别是周年纪念沙拉、含虾仁和易三仓大学酱汁的意大利面以及 50 周年纪念香橙蛋糕。而常规菜单中有开胃菜、主菜、咖啡、甜点、冰沙、果汁、苏打水、无酒精鸡尾酒等。因此，学生不仅需要介绍和准备新的菜单和食物，还需要推广菜单和服务客户。

6 工作坊

为了帮助学生做好工作准备，学校每学期都会为他们提供各种类型的工作坊。例如，举办乘务员培训，研讨会的讲师是来自阿联酋航空公司和曼谷航空公司经验丰富的乘务员。这次研讨会的主题包括应聘航空公司的正确态度、如何打理自己的外形、如何建立自信、如何成为一个优秀的应聘者、面试成功的技巧等，还有模拟个人和团体面试。完成工作坊的学习后，学生将获得易三仓大学颁发的结业证书。

7 各种实地考察和研学旅行

此外，我们还有各种实地考察和研学旅行，让学生参观酒店和航空公司等，使学生在课外观察真正的服务业运作。

8 留学

我们与瑞士的大学开设了联合学位课程。此外，我们还有另一个名为"夏季交换项目"的海外交流项目。夏季，学生在瑞士学习两门课程，所得学分可转换为我们大学的学分。

9 毕业生的就业情况

根据2018年研究生就业调查，96.1%的学生在毕业后可以找到工作。泰国旅游业的大多数客户都是国际旅行者，所以，雇主偏好能够说好英语的毕业生；易三仓大学采用全英文授课，毕业生具备良好的英语水平，颇受雇主的欢迎。毕业生的就业分布占比较多的是酒店和航空业，许多学生在实习期间就从雇主那里拿到了聘书。部分学生拒绝了聘书，因为他们的家人有自营旅馆或度假区，他们毕业后需要回去经营这些家族企业。这类毕业生约占10%。旅行社也是就业选择之一，但目前在旅行社工作的毕业生占少数。

Hospitality and Tourism Education from a Private University in Thailand

Ximan Zong, Martin de Tours School of Management and Economics
Assumption University, Thailand

As you can see, my name is Ximan Zong. It seems like a Chinese name, but I come from Thailand. I've been living there for thirteen years, so I can say that I'm a half Thai now. As professor Therd talked about research in Thailand in general this morning, and Dr. Korawan just shared about some research regarding to the Chinese tourists. Therefore, I will focus on the tourism education from a private university, which is my university.

1 The Introduction of the University

The name of my university is Assumption University. It is an international catholic university. We have 50 years' history and we are the first international university in Thailand. We got students from all over the world. We have four campuses in different locations, they are Huamak Campus, City Campus, Suvarnabhumi Campus, and ACC School of Commerce Sathorn Campus. City campus and ACC Sathorn campus are in the center of Bangkok for students who have a job. Those campuses will be convenient for them to come to study after work. Huamak campus, which is the graduate school, have master degree programs and the PhD programs. The next one is the Suvarnabhumi Campus, which is near Suvarnabhumi airport. It is for the undergraduate program. So, all the bachelor degree program will be in Suvarnabhumi campus.

In terms of ranking, our university ranks number one among all the private universities in Thailand.

2 The Introduction of HTM Major

The Hospitality and Tourism major (HTM) is under the business school. The full name of our business school is Martin de Tours School of Management and Economics (MSME). Under the business school, we have twelve bachelor degree programs, two master's degree programs and two doctoral degree programs. Bachelor's degree student can declare the major after they have obtained 50 credits, which is mostly in their second year of study. All the business school students need to study the fundamental courses together in the first two years, such as Statistics, Accounting, Financial Management, Business Research. HTM major is one of the most popular majors in MSME business school. There are three plans under HTM major, which are the plan A, B and C. Plan A is hospitality management. Plan B is tourism management, and plan C is business. The students who study hospitality as a major would choose a minor from marketing, business information system, or international business management.

For plan A, hospitality management concentration students will need to study the major required subjects which is focus on the Hospitality Management. For example, Food and Beverage Service, Kitchen Operation, Room Division Management, Event Management and Service Management. For plan B, Tourism Management students will need to study the subjects regarding to the tourism management such as Tourism Policy and Development, Tourism Destination Management, Tour Guiding and Operation in Practice, Cultural Heritage Tourism and International Tourism Studies. And for plan C, students will need to choose a minor from four options, which are Management Information System (MIS), International Business Management (IBM), Management Leadership and Entrepreneurship (MGT) and Marketing (MKT). There are different courses based on different minors. For example, if the students choose MIS as the minor, they will need to study five courses including Programming and Algorithms, Database Systems, Data Communications and Networking, Information Systems Analysis and Design, and Information Systems Project Management.

For Hospitality and Tourism Management, we use an integrative blended teaching and learning method, students learn theories and concepts from the classes, and join the internship, educational field trip programs from the hospitality industry.

3 Internship

Internship is one of the major requirement of HTM major. Therefore, the students are requested to fulfill internship for 400 hours. So for the internship, we will provide the students with suggestions and help them to find the appropriate hospitality industries to work with, such as the 4-star or 5-star hotels, airlines, travel agencies, and other businesses related to hospitality and tourism.

Then the students need to contact the organization and get the 'Acceptance Letter'. After they have accepted by the hotels or air lines and started to work, we will contact internship students and respond to their question and provide advice. We will also keep in touch with their supervisors and solve any problem during the internship period. And before they finish their internship, we will visit the students, go to the workplace and talk with their supervisors.

At the end of the internship, we will let the supervisor evaluate student's work performances. After completing their internship, students need to give advisor a presentation, which including what they did and what they have learned from the internship. The grading is not only based on their presentation, advisor's observation and the evaluation of the supervisor are also very important criteria for grading.

4 HTM Career Day

Every semester we will organize career day to help our students to get a company for their internship. The purpose of the career day is to provide opportunities for students to interact with experts and managers from hospitality industries.

The career day of this semester is held in September. We have invited some famous companies to participate. For example, Anantara Siam Bangkok Hotel, Avani Atrium Bangkok Hotel, Bangkok Marriott Hotel Sukhumvit and so on. The representatives come to our university to talk with our students, answering the questions regarding to the job opening or job requirements. On career day, students are required to prepare their resumes, so they can send them to the representatives if they were interested to apply for that job position.

5 Practical Lab for Restaurant Training: Crystal Restaurant

Apart from the internship, we continuously provide training to students for well grooming, good personality, and good communication for hospitality and tourism industry. There is a practical lab for restaurant training, which means students need to work inside of the university.

Under the HTM major, we have a restaurant called Crystal Restaurant. Students will need to work in Crystal Restaurant as a requirement of two different subjects—Kitchen Operation and Food and Beverage Service. For Kitchen Operation, students need to work in the kitchen, they will learn how to prepare the food and how to cook the food from teacher. And for the Food and Beverage Service, students need to learn how to serve the customers, how to take the orders, how to present the menu, deal with the bill payment, or prepare the table for the guests. During the time working in the Crystal Restaurant, they learned how to make a cocktail and how to bake a cake. Students are very happy while they are working in the Crystal Restaurant.

Regarding Crystal Restaurant food menus, we encourage students to decide the menu by themselves. They need to consider what kind of menu they are going to introduce for every month and they need to design posters to advertise the new menu to all the teachers and students from our university. For example, this year is the 50th years anniversary of our university. So, the students introduce a special menu for the anniversary, there are three different things in the special menu—the AU Jubilee salad, spaghetti with shrimps and AU sauce, and golden Jubilee orange cake. While in the regular menu, we have appetizer, main course, coffee, dessert, frappe, juice, soda, mocktail and so on. Therefore, students not only need to introduce and prepare the new menu and foods, but also need to learn how to promote the menu and serve customers.

6　Workshop

In order to help our students to be ready for work, we also provide them with different kinds of workshops every semester. In this semester, we have a Cabin Crew Training, the lecturers for this workshop are experienced flight attendance from Emirates Airline and Bangkok Airway. The topics of this workshop include what are right attitudes and personality for your dream airlines, how to dress for success, how to build your self-confidence, how to be an outstanding candidate, tips and techniques for successful interview, mock up individual and group interview. After completing the workshop, students will be given a certificate of completion from AU.

7 Various Field Trips and Education Trips

In addition, we have various field trip and educational trip for students to visit hotels and airlines. Students will spend time together outside class to observe the real service business operation.

8 Study Abroad

We also have joint degree program with the universities in Switzerland. Besides, we have another overseas exchange program called summer exchange program. Students can study two courses in Switzerland during the summer period. After that, those credits can be transferred back to our university.

9 Our Graduates

Based on the Graduate Job Placement 2018 survey, 96.1 % of the students can secure their job after they graduate. Our graduates are quite popular when they are securing jobs, because most of the customers in the tourism sector in Thailand are international traveler, so the employer prefer the graduates who can speak English well. Our graduates are quite popular among the employers for their good English proficiency. The trends of our graduates' employment are still in hotel and airline industry, as the top two occupations. Around 10% of our students are self-employed, during the internship period many students got the offer from their employer, but some refused the offer because their family have a hotel or a resort and they need to go back and continue the family business right after graduate. Therefore, the self-employment of our graduates comes mostly from family businesses. Travel agencies are also one of the employment opportunities, but the number of the graduates who work in this business industry is still small.

泰国清迈大学旅游研究

Korawan Sangkakorn　泰国清迈大学社会研究所
旅游研究与发展中心

清迈是泰国北部最大的城市，位于具有重要战略意义的湄平河畔，靠近主要贸易路线。因此，清迈自古以来就是一个十分重要的城市。清迈是一个有许多事物可以欣赏、有许多事情可以做的地方。美丽的自然环境、古老的（兰纳）文化和原生态的山地部落每年吸引超过1 000万的国内外游客来清迈游览。

"清迈"的字面意思是"新城市"，尽管早在1996年清迈就已经庆祝了建城700周年纪念日。明莱王（King Meng Rai）和他的朋友们在建立苏霍泰王国（Sukhothai Kingdom）的同时，也建立了这座城市作为兰纳王国（Lanna Kingdom）的首都。清迈不仅是兰纳王国的首都和文化中心，也是泰国北部的佛教中心。明莱王本人是一位非常虔诚的宗教领袖，他建立了许多至今仍非常重要的寺庙。奇怪的是，在过去很长一段时间里，游客一直误以为清迈仅仅是他们徒步旅行计划、漂流到山区部落村庄和探索其他省份的中转基地。后来，游客们惊讶地发现，清迈除了有美丽的寺庙之外还有许多东西可以发掘。多样的民族部落、多元的大象营地、各种烹饪和按摩学校、大量户外活动、各种手工艺品作坊和文化表演、绝佳的自然风景等使清迈成为亚洲最有吸引力的旅游目的地之一。"在清迈的一天足以看到城镇的一切"这一观点一度甚为流行。

1 清迈大学概况

清迈大学（CMU）是清迈7所大学之一，有21个院系、3个学院、1个研究生院和5个研究所。清迈大学的愿景是成为一所致力于社会责任和创造可持续卓越发展的世界级大学。为帮助泰国应对全球化中的挑战，清迈大学肩负着5重使命：

（1）在"充足经济"哲学（Sufficiency Economy Philosophy）思想的指导下将学术卓越与高尚道德标准结合起来，提供高质量的教育和专业培训；

（2）在各个领域开展研究，以维持教学、学习和技术输出标准，促进地区和国家的社会经济发展；

(3) 根据"充足经济"哲学向全国社区提供学术服务，特别是泰国北部地区的社区；

(4) 保护和培育我们的宗教和文化遗产，可持续地开发泰国北部地区独特的自然环境资源；

(5) 在"充足经济"哲学下发展大学的行政系统和管理，实现大学的可持续发展。

清迈大学是一个集学习、研究和知识输出于一体的胜地，大学的学术自由建立在崇高道德、卓越学术、知识应用和输出以及文化艺术发展的基础上。

清迈大学是一所美丽的大学，有静心湖（Angkaew Reservoir）——一个以素帖山（Suthept mountain）为背景的大型人工湖。清迈大学已经成为一个事实上的旅游景点，许多游客会前往清迈大学参观游览，中国游客尤甚。这所大学的主要入口在怀乔路（Huey Kaew Road），是游客唯一可以进入的入口，也是一个颇受欢迎的拍照点。清迈大学提供绿色校园游览项目，即乘坐电动游览车参观清迈大学，每半小时一班车（在繁忙时段车次更多）。游览之旅的收费标准为成人60泰铢、儿童30泰铢，游览时长约40分钟。旅途中会提供建筑物、院系和大学历史的详细讲解，顾客可以拍照并欣赏大学的美丽。电动游览车中途会停一次，让游客下车拍照，欣赏校园美景。

清迈大学的人文学院旅游系开设有旅游专业，该系是泰国北部地区重要的旅游和接待业教育培训中心。该系开设了旅游导论、泰国遗产、文化旅游、旅游行为、生态旅游、导游职业规范、旅游和酒店营销、旅游管理、旅游影响管理、航空票务、酒店管理导论（前台、客房管理、餐厅管理、餐饮、酒店健身管理、人力资源管理、酒吧、饮料和葡萄酒、会展、住宿管理、活动策划和餐饮服务以及服务质量）等课程。该系还提供旅游培训课程，如年度导游培训课程、当前旅游热点培训课程（取决于每年批准的预算）和其他"按需"开展的培训课程。此外，清迈大学的艺术、媒体和科技学院的现代管理和信息技术系在其双语教育项目中开设了电子旅游、会展管理等本科课程。该学院开设了2个软件工程和知识创新管理硕士学位项目、1个创新管理博士学位项目。

清迈大学有许多学院和研究所从事旅游领域的研究。特别是社会研究所下的旅游研究与发展中心（CTRD）。旅游研究与发展中心的研究集中在旅游管理、旅游战略、社区旅游等领域，中心的研究人员发表论文并向社会开展学术服务和传播知识。在研究区域方面，中心研究人员主要关注清迈大学周边社区、清迈和泰国北部地区以及周边邻国，研究议题涉及文化旅游、康养旅游、社区旅游、旅游行为、长住旅行、智慧城市、电子旅游等。中心已完成的研究有《泰囧》后的中国游客满意度、绿色旅游服务、泰国北部旅游开发与面向中国游客的推广、兰纳文明路线清迈—琅勃拉邦旅游发展网络、琅勃拉邦对清迈地区未来申请世界遗产的启示——土地利用分区和旅游住宿改造的案例研究、泰国北部地区文化旅游市场竞争力开发、绿色旅游服务、寄宿家庭标准、老年游客慢游和泰国北部高级旅游管理。此外,中心也针对当地居民、旅游企业家、政府官员等群体开展了旅游专题研讨会和工作坊以回馈社会。中心也通过组织旅游学术活动促进泰国北部各地区旅游研究的交流。下文是中心完成的一个与中国游客相关的研究。

2 中国成为泰国的最大客源国

近年来赴泰的中国游客数量激增,中国已经成为泰国的最大客源国。在泰国到处都能见到中国游客,2012年年底在泰国多地(主要是曼谷、大城府和清迈)取景拍摄的电影《泰囧》上映后尤其如此。曾经不受中国游客欢迎的清迈,也很快迎来了大量的中国游客。这些最新的现象,无论是游客数量还是目的地选择,均表明中国游客的行为可能有了新的变化趋势。因此,本研究旨在以清迈为个案进行区域研究,调查、比较并重新思考来泰国的中国游客的变化。我们采用问卷调查的方式,对2017年6月至11月到访清迈的300名中国游客进行了调查,并将问卷调查所得数据与过去的数据进行比较。调查结果显示,大部分受访者为女性,单身和已婚者各占一半,大部分是公司员工,月收入主要在5 001~10 000元,大部分来自中国东部地区(如北京和上海)。大多数受访者第一次去泰国是为了放松。陪同的人主要是他们的家人和朋友。他们大多依靠网站、口碑和旅游指南搜集信息,自主制订旅行计划。他们最感兴趣的是历史和文化旅游,其次是自然旅游和软探险活动。他们最喜欢去的3个城市分别是清迈、曼谷和芭堤雅。大多数人每次旅行的花费在5 001~10 000元。旅行中,几乎所有人都使用智能手机或平板电脑拍照,在社交平台上发布图片和信息,搜索旅行信息和地图,翻译语言。在住宿方面,他们主要住在市内或购物中心附近的民宿、酒店和精品酒店。对于纪念品,大多数人喜欢用棉花、木头和银制作的产品。他们喜欢泰国菜(尤其是芒果糯米饭和冬阴功汤)和中国菜。他们中的大多数人乘坐飞机抵达清迈。中国的许多大城市,如北京、上海、武汉、广州、昆明、重庆、杭州、成都等,和清迈之间都有直飞航班。他们乘坐突突车或摩托车游览清迈市。他们最感兴趣的旅游活动包括传统的泰国按摩、SPA、冒险等。对这些中国游客而言,最具吸引力的五大旅游景点分别是塔佩门(Tapae Gate)、素贴寺(Wat Prathat Doi Suthep)、夜市

(Night Bazaar)、清迈大学和帕辛寺(Wat Pra Singh)。这项调查表明,目前中国游客的行为与之前集中在泰国中部地区的大规模团队游的游客的行为有所不同。

1988年,泰国成为中国公民可以到访的首批海外目的地国家之一。自此,中国赴泰国游览的人数每年不断增加。刚开始,一年只有1万人左右,接着很快攀升到了10万人,到2006年则突破了100万人大关。2012年,中国游客创下了278万人的新纪录,中国随之成为泰国第一大客源国(根据泰国旅游部2013年数据)。2018年,赴泰的中国游客数量更是突破了1 000万的大关(根据泰国旅游和体育部2019年数据)。可见,中国人赴泰国旅游在短短的20多年就实现了跨越式增长。从现在开始,泰国旅游业的图景将会迅速改变,不仅体现在游客数量上,也表现在游客结构和旅游方式上。这些变化极有可能是由中国游客驱动的,因此,我们有必要深入研究和跟踪中国游客的增长情况,以便为将来可能发生的变化做好准备。毕竟,如果我们在没有任何计划和准备的情况下等待他们的到访,大量的中国游客涌入可能会带来更多的威胁而非机遇,可能对泰国的旅游形象造成负面影响。

开泰银行研究中心(Kasikorn Bank Research Center)指出,中国许多城市到泰国主要旅游目的地直航航班的扩增是促进赴泰中国游客数量增长的一个根本性因素,因为直航极大地便利了中国游客的旅行。此外,泰国的旅游形象也通过泰国拍摄的电影作品得以广泛传播。该研究中心还预测,自由行游客(FIT)数量的增长将令人瞩目。这一群体的特点是具有高购买力,年龄超过30岁,能熟练利用信息技术获取与旅行有关的信息(包价旅游、住宿地等)。

3 清迈的中国游客的行为研究

近年来到访清迈的中国游客数量不断增长。他们中的大多数人都受电影《泰囧》和在中国播出的泰国电视剧的影响。这一趋势引发了对清迈新一代中国游客行为的研究。本研究得出的数据将用于支持文化社区的能力发展,促进"清迈创意城市"建设。

中国游客行为研究在过去几年中获得了越来越多的关注,如上文提到的开泰银行研究中心(Kasikorn Bank Research Center)的研究,Korawan(2008)所做的关于泰国和大湄公河次区域国家旅游竞争战略的研究。此外,Jakkere(2013)关于泰国旅游形象的研究专门探究了中国游客眼中的泰国,发现中国游客强调安全、物有所值和清洁度。然而,在中国游客的眼里,泰国最突出的形象是沙滩和大海,其次是夜生活、SPA和传统的泰国按摩。

本研究旨在探研中国游客在泰国的旅游模式，分析中国游客在清迈旅游的行为现状，比较中国游客过去和现在的行为模式差异。

本研究的范围包括基于对以往研究、统计数据、网站和各种相关文献资料的梳理对中国游客在泰国的旅游行为模式进行回顾，根据以往的研究和本次中国游客行为调查的结果，对比分析中国游客过去和现在的旅游行为模式差异。

本研究使用了一手数据和二手数据，前者来自问卷调查，后者来自文件、研究成果、统计数据和相关网站。问卷中包含的问题有：人口统计学基本信息、到访次数、旅行目的、旅行模式、旅行同伴、旅行准备、固有的旅行偏好、中国游客想要到访的泰国省份、旅行花费、中国游客选择停留的地方、最喜欢的食物和纪念品的类型、旅行期间最喜欢的交通工具类型、最喜欢的目的地、在清迈旅行期间的活动和最喜欢的事物、与他人分享旅行经历的意愿、重游意向、旅行中最担心的或发生的问题。

4　概念/理论：游客行为

游客行为是指旅游业中与商品和服务使用直接相关的每个个体的表现。它还包括影响这种表现的决策过程。因此，简而言之，行为受激励或动机的影响，反过来，受影响的行为旨在对这些激励或动机做出响应。

游客行为由7个重要部分组成：①目的，每个游客的行为都有目的；②准备，根据其需求开展活动的成熟度和能力；③情景，促进为响应其需求而选择活动的事件或机会；④阐释，在不同情形下实现最大满意度的相应的思维方式；⑤响应，根据一个人想要达到的结果来做决策——这可能是预期的结果，也可能是意外的结果；⑥对失望的反应，做了之后没有达到预期结果的感觉；⑦行为倾向，个体需要重新阐释和思考，以便寻找一种新的方法来满足自己的需求，或者因为它超出了自己的能力而放弃它。

对旅游者背景和行为的研究对于服务业尤其是旅游和酒店业而言至关重要。了解不同背景的游客的不同行为有助于旅游行业工作人员更好地回应游客的需求。简而言之，具备游客背景和行为知识的服务人员会发现做他们的工作很容易。此外，对旅游者行为的研究能够进一步加深我们对旅游者决策模式的认识：他们购买的服务种类、购买原因、购买时间和地点，以及购买频率。在了解了这些游客的特征之后，我们将能够找到可满足游客需求的商品或者服务。因此，服务提供商必须了解游客的一切，如他们的需求、想法、旅行方式和花费的时间等。这些知识将有助于我们清楚地了解那些影响游客决策的因素。

5 研究结果：清迈中国游客旅游行为调查结果

如表1所示，到访清迈的300名中国游客样本中女性几乎是男性的两倍：男性游客约占38%，女性游客约占62%。然而，大多数游客的教育水平并不高，只有21.6%的人具有大学及以上教育水平。在游客的职业方面，调查显示，他们中约有一半在私营公司工作（45.3%），其次是销售代表和学生。在这些样本游客中，大约1/3的人的工资为5 001～10 000元，27.5%的人的工资为2 002～5 000元。就来源地而言，大多数游客来自那些在泰国已经非常有名的中国大城市，尤其是北京和上海。来自这两个大城市的游客样本数量较多，其他游客来自深圳、广州、成都和昆明等大城市。

表1 游客样本群体概况（2017年）

题项	数量/人	百分比
性别	300	100.0
男性	114	38.0
女性	186	62.0
婚姻状态	300	100.0
单身	149	49.6
已婚	147	49.0
丧偶/离婚/分居	4	1.4
教育程度	300	100.0
初中及以下	20	6.7
高中/职业学校	215	71.7
大学（学士学位或更高）	65	21.6
职业	300	100.0
政府官员和私营公司员工	136	45.3
销售代表或销售员	20	6.7
学生	36	12.0
自营职业者	22	7.3
家庭主妇/退休人员	25	8.3

续上表

题项	数量/人	百分比
农民	5	1.7
其他人	56	18.7
平均月薪	300	100.0
2 001～5 000元	83	27.5
5 001～10 000元	105	35.1
超过1万元	112	37.4

如图1所示，70%的游客是第一次到访清迈。到访清迈的主要目的是休闲游憩（87%），少数人是来度蜜月（8%）和观光（4%）（如图2所示）。图3表明，中国游客大多喜欢结伴出行（90%以上），和家人、朋友或恋人，而不是独自旅行（仅占4%）。此外，超过90%的中国游客自己规划旅游行程，只有少数人（不到5%）依赖旅游团（如图4所示）。

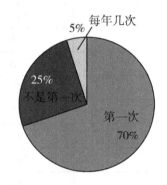

图1　中国游客访问清迈的次数

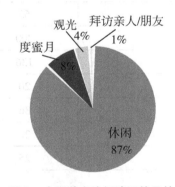

图2　中国游客访问清迈的目的

图3 访问清迈的中国游客的旅行同伴

图4 访问清迈的中国游客的旅行准备（2017年）

值得注意的是，样本中中国游客的旅游行为模式与清迈的特征高度一致。从表2中可以看出，超过60%的中国游客偏好历史文化旅游，其次是自然旅游（约40%），紧随其后的分别是探险旅游和医疗旅游。

表2 游客的旅游偏好

旅游偏好	排名（百分比）								排名总计
	1	2	3	4	5	6	7	8	
历史文化旅游	64.9	19.4	7.7	0.8	2.0	—	—	—	1
自然旅游	20.2	39.1	13.7	7.3	6.0	2.8	1.2	0.4	2
探险旅游	4.4	14.9	26.6	13.3	14.1	10.9	4.0	2.0	3
医疗旅游	1.2	9.7	17.3	27.0	14.9	8.1	8.1	4.0	4
购物	2.7	5.8	16.1	18.3	19.2	21.9	11.2	4.9	5,6

续上表

旅游偏好	排名（百分比）								排名总计
	1	2	3	4	5	6	7	8	
参观电影/戏剧场所	2.0	1.2	4.0	6.9	8.5	16.9	21.8	23.8	7
体育旅游	—	0.4	1.2	4.4	10.5	14.5	21.4	33.1	8
夜生活	2.3	5.1	8.8	14.8	16.2	12.5	20.8	19.4	—

资料来源：2017年的调查

除了游客本来就喜欢清迈这一可能的事实之外，在清迈进行的问卷调查也可能导致清迈是样本游客最希望到访的泰国地方这一结果（见表3）。除清迈之外，游客最想去的地方分别是曼谷和芭堤雅，这两个地方在中国游客中早负盛名。然而，普吉岛在这次调查中排名第16的结果并不意味着它不如许多其他排名较靠前的地方受欢迎。事实上，通过对排名1到4的目的地的详细分析，普吉岛也获得了很高的分数（除了它的分数低于前三名）。除了这4个著名的目的地外，其他受欢迎的省份还包括大城府、Prachobkirikhun和素叻他尼。对于清莱、南奔和南邦这3个北方省份，游客可能认为它们是清迈附近的地方，可能会考虑到访这些地方。

表3 中国游客想去的泰国旅游目的地

目的地	排名（比例）															排名总计
	1	2	3	4	5	6	7	8	9	10	11	12	13	14	15	
清迈府	48.4	23.8	7.3	3.6	0.4	—	—	0.8	0.8	0.4	—	—	—	—	—	1, 2
曼谷	19.8	18.1	21.8	11.3	6.5	4.4	0.4	—	0.4	—	0.4	—	—	0.4	—	3
芭提雅	1.6	7.3	16.1	14.5	11.3	5.6	6.0	1.6	0.4	—	0.4	0.8	0.8	1.6	0.8	4
大城	1.2	6.0	9.7	13.3	12.9	6.0	2.4	0.8	0.4	0.4	0.4	—	0.8	2.0	0.4	5
Prachobkirikhun	0.4	—	1.2	1.2	2.4	9.3	6.0	6.0	4.8	1.6	1.6	0.8	2.4	1.2	—	6
苏拉塔尼	—	—	0.8	1.2	0.8	3.6	10.1	6.5	4.8	0.8	2.4	1.6	1.6	3.6	—	7, 8
清莱	1.6	2.4	2.0	2.4	4.0	4.4	2.0	3.6	7.7	6.0	0.4	1.2	1.2	0.4	—	9
南奔	—	—	0.4	0.4	0.4	0.8	0.8	1.6	1.2	8.9	8.5	4.4	0.8	1.2	—	10
南邦	0.4	—	0.8	0.4	0.4	0.8	—	1.2	2.8	2.8	9.7	7.3	3.2	—	—	11
素可泰	2.0	4.4	4.0	3.2	4.4	4.8	4.8	0.8	1.2	2.0	0.8	7.3	1.6	1.2	—	12
乌汶	—	0.2	0.4	0.8	—	1.2	0.4	3.2	2.0	4.4	2.4	2.8	10.5	2.0	—	13
乌隆	—	0.4	0.4	—	0.8	0.4	2.0	0.8	4.4	2.0	1.2	2.4	2.8	11.3	1.2	14
其他	0.8	1.6	1.6	0.8	—	—	—	2.0	—	—	—	—	0.4	—	2.0	15
普吉岛	16.1	21.0	19.0	12.9	7.3	3.2	1.2	—	0.8	0.4	—	—	0.4	2.0	—	16
甲米岛	5.6	8.1	4.4	6.9	7.3	3.6	4.8	5.6	1.6	—	0.4	0.4	1.2	2.0	—	17

资料来源：2017年的调查

与之前提到的平均工资水平相比,中国游客的旅游花费相当高。近一半的人(约46%)花费了5 001～10 000元,而只有1/4的人花费不到5 000元。

调查还询问了中国游客在清迈旅游期间最喜欢的食物和纪念品,如表4和表5所示。就食物而言,泰国菜非常受欢迎,大约64%的人选择吃泰国菜;他们最喜欢的菜式是冬阴功汤(约50%)。其次是本地食物和中餐(分别占36%和28%)。令人印象深刻的是,大约有50%的中国游客喜欢杧果糯米饭——清迈当地的热门菜肴。在纪念品方面,超过50%的中国游客喜欢衣服或手提包产品,其次是干果、木制和银制产品。

表4 中国游客选择的清迈食物种类

食物类型	回答"喜欢"的百分比
泰国菜	64.1
冬阴功汤	49.0
本地食物	35.9
杧果糯米饭	49.8
水果	47.7
泰式炒粉	25.0
海鲜	24.5
中餐	27.8
Kow Soi	26.2
炒饭	24.2
面条	20.6
Khanom Chin	17.3
西餐	12.9
其他	3.2

资料来源:2017年的调查

表5 中国游客在清迈购买的纪念品类型

纪念品的类型	回答"会购买"的百分比
干果	44.1
衣服/手提包	54.8

续上表

纪念品的类型	回答"会购买"的百分比
木制产品	37.1
银器	27.4
品牌产品	17.3
竹/藤产品	14.9
其他	14.1

资料来源：2017年的调查

关于中国游客访问清迈所使用的交通工具类型的数据显示，大多数人（90%）选择飞机。然而在逗留期间，他们更喜欢乘坐突突车、双条车（red cab）、出租车（分别约为57%、50%和48%）。还有大约1/3的人租了摩托车在城市里闲逛。就活动而言（见表6），游客最喜欢的活动是传统泰式按摩（约70%）和骑大象（60%），其次是丛林索道（约29%）和皮划艇（约18%）。其他受到关注的活动（每项约10%）包括观看当地文化表演、学习泰国菜或水疗。

表6　中国游客在清迈的旅游活动

活动	回答"是"的人数（百分比）
体验传统按摩	182（73.4）
骑大象	154（62.1）
坐丛林索道	73（29.4）
划皮划艇	45（18.1）
观看当地文化表演	28（11.3）
学习泰国菜	27（10.9）
SPA	26（10.5）
学习泰语	22（8.9）
看人妖秀	20（8.1）
观看泰拳	18（7.3）
射击	11（4.4）

续上表

活动	回答"是"的人数（百分比）
骑沙滩车	10（4.0）
学习冥想	6（2.4）
学习瑜伽	2（0.8）
学习泰拳	0（0）
玩彩弹游戏	1（0.4）
其他	12（4.8）

资料来源：2017年的调查

对表7所示的中国游客最喜欢的清迈景区景点，我们大致可以分为以下4类。第一类是游客最喜爱的地方，得分超过50%；它们是塔佩门、素贴寺、夜市和清迈大学。具体来说，旅游景点集中的塔佩门最受欢迎，得分比例超过70%。第二类受游客喜爱的地方，得分在30%～50%，包括帕辛寺、周日步行街（塔佩门）和清曼寺。第三类游客喜爱的地方，得分在20%～30%，包括美莎大象营、周六步行街（瓦来路）、契迪龙寺和宁曼路。最后一类得分低于20%。然而，在这类地方中，仍有一些景点受到中国游客的关注，如瓦洛洛市场（18%）、丛林索道（17%）、蒲屏皇宫（16%）。总之，中国游客选择参观的大多数地方都是清迈的文化景点景区，自然景点景区则不太受欢迎。

表7 中国游客选择参观的清迈旅游目的地

旅游目的地	回答"是"的人数（百分比）
塔佩门	182（73.4）
素贴寺	145（58.5）
夜市	145（58.5）
清迈大学	133（53.6）
帕辛寺	123（49.6）
周日步行街（塔佩门）	101（40.7）
清曼寺	79（31.9）
美莎大象营	71（28.6）
周六步行街（瓦来路）	68（27.4）

续上表

旅游目的地	回答"是"的人数（百分比）
契迪龙寺	62（25.0）
宁曼路	58（23.4）
瓦洛洛市场	44（17.7）
丛林索道	43（17.3）
清迈夜间狩猎	41（16.5）
蒲屏皇宫	39（15.7）
悟孟寺	34（13.7）
Wat Jed Yord	29（11.7）
松德寺	29（11.7）
湄登大象营地	25（10.1）
清迈国家博物馆	25（10.1）
湄萨大象营地	23（9.3）
Rachapruek Royal Garden	22（8.9）
清迈动物园	22（8.9）
Ban Bor Sang（制伞村）	15（6.0）
茵他侬国家公园	13（5.2）
Vieang Kumkam	11（4.4）
Ban Tawai（木雕村）	9（3.6）
San Kampang Hot Spring	8（3.2）
Ban Mae Kampong（民宿村）	5（2.0）
培山苗族村	5（2.0）
诗丽吉皇后植物园	5（2.0）
Doi Ang Khang	3（1.2）

资料来源：2017年的调查

最后，样本中国游客被问及他们最喜欢清迈哪些方面。表8显示，最受欢迎的是"友好/人"（约79%），其次是美丽的风景（约67%）。美味的食物和美丽的风景也分别获得了50%以上的高人气。有了这些好印象，几乎所有的中国游客都提到会重游并会向他人推荐清迈（见表9、表10）。尽管如此，如

表 11 所示，游客仍然遇到语言障碍（约 57%），因为他们不熟悉英语，而大多数泰国人的汉语水平仍然很低。约 18% 的游客遇到了行程问题，遇到安全和欺诈问题的概率相对较低，只有 5%～6%。

表 8 中国游客最喜欢清迈的地方

题项	回答"是"的人数（百分比）
友好/人	195（78.6）
美丽的风景	165（66.5）
美味的食物	148（59.7）
美丽的旅游景点	117（47.2）
好天气	114（46.0）

资料来源：2017 年的调查

表 9 中国游客推荐他人参观清迈的意向

意向	人数	百分率
"是的，我会推荐的。"	246	99.2
"不，我不推荐。"	2	0.8
总数	248	100.0

资料来源：2017 年的调查

表 10 中国游客回访清迈的意向

意向	人数	百分率
"是的，我会回来的。"	243	98.0
"不，我不会回来了。"	3	1.2
N/A	2	0.8
总数	248	100.0

资料来源：2017 年的调查

表 11 中国游客在泰国旅游时遇到的问题（2013 年）

问题的类型	回答"是"的人数（百分比）
语言	140（56.5）
旅行	45（18.1）

续上表

问题的类型	回答"是"的人数（百分比）
安全	16（6.5）
欺骗	14（5.6）
其他	33（13.3）

6 讨论

中国游客数量和结构的动态变化主要受3个因素驱动：①中国经济格局的巨大变化导致需求增加，中国消费者的购买力增强；②城市化速度加快，影响了中国新一代的价值观和生活方式；③中国政府放松了对中国人出国旅游的限制（Jakkree等，2013）。起初，中国人只可以去亚洲的几个少数国家，但现在中国人几乎可以去全球任何地方。就中国游客赴泰旅游而言，最重要的驱动因素是第一个和第二个，因为泰国是中国政府允许其人民到访的第一批海外目的地国家之一。然而，前期到访泰国的中国游客基本集中在3个目的地，即曼谷、芭堤雅和普吉岛（Korawan，2008）。因此，泰国旅游业的利益相关者一直不断尝试将中国游客"分散"到除这3个热门目的地以外的其他地方。最近的一次尝试是，中国电影制作集团获准在泰国北部（主要是清迈）的几个地方拍摄电影《泰囧》。这部电影大受欢迎，吸引了更多中国游客来到清迈。接下来我们将总结本文的发现。为了更好地捕捉到访清迈的中国游客的变化，我们也将把Orrachorn等（2008）在2005年对中国游客到清迈旅游的行为和态度的研究结果与我们的研究结果进行一些对比。

首先，就出游目的而言，大多数中国游客（约80%）来清迈主要是为了休闲游憩。他们之所以选择清迈，是因为清迈是一座文化名城，拥有美丽的山地景观。然而，2005年来清迈的中国游客和2013年的中国游客的明显区别在于出行方式。2005年，几乎一半的中国游客依靠旅行社安排他们的旅行，而只有19%的人自由行。相反，2013年超过90%的中国游客选择自己安排行程，而不到5%的人更喜欢参加旅行团。就旅行伴侣而言，超过80%的中国游客仍然更喜欢和他们的爱人、家人或朋友一起去。

在2005年的研究中，中国游客访问清迈时喜欢的地方和活动按喜爱度排序依次是素贴山、骑大象、参观因他农山和手工艺木雕Ban Tawai。此外，这项研究还提到了那些旅游行程中没有的，但游客希望参观的地方有温泉、城市景观和帕辛寺。2013年的研究中，除了素贴山和骑大象，清迈其他不少地方也颇受中国游客欢迎。最近受到中国游客关注的地方包括塔佩门地区、步行街等。有趣的是,像清迈大学这样的学术机构也在中国游客的参观名单上。清迈大学是泰国的第一所国立大学,位置偏僻,可能是因为它坐落在通往素贴山的路上,而且它有着令人称赞的风景——绿树成荫的柚木和其他植物(因而受到了游客的关注)。大学里以素贴山为背景的静心湖也是拍照的好地方。除此之外,2005年中国游客甚至泰国游客都不知道的一个目的地是宁曼路,因为它还处于旅游的初始开发阶段。2013年,这条路上的许多商店和景点迎来了众多的中国游客,当然还有世界各地的游客到此闲逛、拍照和购物。值得注意的是,2005年的研究发现,中国游客购买的纪念品主要是珠宝(约28%)、干果(约19%)和成品衣服(约19%);但根据我们2013年的研究,他们最喜欢的纪念品是衣服或手提包(约55%),其次是干果(约44%)、木制产品(约37%)和银器(约27%)。

2005年的研究和我们2013年的研究都询问了中国游客是否有可能重游清迈。2005年的研究发现,只有37.5%的中国游客肯定会回来,43.2%的人表示他们可能会回来。在2013年的研究中,几乎100%的中国游客确认他们会再来旅游。当详细考虑他们2005年旅行满意度背后可能导致他们重游的原因时,发现主要因素是"便宜且物有所值的商品、良好的感觉、放松的氛围、美丽的风景、好天气、非常有趣以及看古迹的好地方之一"。然而,在2013年的研究中,我们发现最让中国游客满意的是友好的态度、美丽的风景、美味的食物和美丽的旅游景点。从最近的研究可以推断,中国游客可能获得了更多与当地人交流的机会,也更多地了解他们来旅游的城市。与过去相比,这可能意味着一个更好的信号,毕竟以前他们只是抱着"去过那里,见过那里(和买了一些)"的态度。

本研究发现了中国游客将推动全球旅游业发展的7个原因:①中国便利开放的金融体系;②愿意花钱;③有足够的支付能力;④更方便的签证政策;⑤对旅游业的大量投资;⑥更好的航班连接;⑦更开放的心态。

本研究还发现到访清迈的中国游客有以下特征:①偏好自由行;②长假期间扎堆出行;③热爱当地食物;④喜欢干果;⑤喜欢精品酒店;⑥偏爱传统泰式按摩。

Chiang Mai University Tourism Research

Korawan Sangkakorn, Ph. D.
Center of Tourism Research and Development,
Social Research Institute, Chiang Mai University, Thailand

Chiang Mai is the largest city in the northern part of Thailand. Chiang Mai city's strategic location on the Ping River and its proximity to major trading routes contributed to its historic importance. Chiang Mai has a lot of things to see and do. The beauty of the nature, the mountains, cultural, Lanna Style, and hill tribe villages, attracts more than 10 million of Thai and international tourists to Chiang Mai every year.

Chiang Mai literally means 'new city' and has retained the name despite celebrating its 700th anniversary in 1996. King Meng Rai and his friends the Great founded the city as the capital of the Lanna Kingdom around the same time as the establishment of the Sukhothai Kingdom. Chiang Mai not only became the capital and cultural core of the Lanna Kingdom, but also was the center of Buddhism in northern Thailand. King Meng Rai himself was a very religious leader who even founded many of the city's temples that remain important to this day. Strangely, for many years, tourists had mistaken Chiang Mai simply as the base from which they could plan trekking and rafting trips to hill tribe villages and explore other provinces. Tourists are surprised by the fact that there are so many things to discover other than its beautiful and historic temples. Intriguing diversity among ethnic tribes, a number of elephant camps, many cooking and massage schools, numerous outdoor activities, a variety of handicrafts workshops, various cultural performances, and breathtaking scenery make Chiang Mai one of Asia's most attractive tourist destinations. The phrase 'a day in Chiang Mai is enough to see things around town' was once a common expression.

1 Chiang Mai University

Chiang Mai University (CMU) is one in seven universities in Chiang Mai.

There are 21 faculties, 3 colleges, 1 graduate school, and 5 research institutes. The vision of Chiang Mai University is: A world class university committed to social responsibility and create a development for sustainable excellence. The five-fold mission addresses the challenges the nation faces amidst a globalizing world. CMU's mission is to:

a) Provide higher education and professional level training, while combine academic excellence with high moral and ethical standards under the Sufficiency Economy Philosophy.

b) Conduct research in various fields to support standards of teaching, learning and technology transfer for the social and economic development of the region and the country.

c) Provide academic services to the national community in line with the Sufficiency Economy Philosophy, particularly for Northern Thailand.

d) Preserve and nurture our religious and cultural heritage, and continuously develop the resources of the unique natural environment of northern Thailand.

e) Develop the university's administration systems and management under the Sufficiency Economy Philosophy while maintaining at sustainable development.

CMU is a place for knowledge collection, studies, research, and knowledge transfer according to academic freedom based on morality and academic excellence, application and transfer, and arts and culture development.

CMU is a beautiful university with Angkaew Reservoir, a large artificial lake with a backdrop of Suthept mountain. Here is a destination for tourists especially for Chinese tourists. CMU green campus offers tours namely 'Visit CMU' around the large campus on electric buses. The main entrance to the university is on Huey Kaew Road and this is the only entrance that tourists can enter. It is a popular place to pose for pictures. The electric buses run tours of CMU every half hour (or more during busy times). The tour costs 60 Baht for adults and 30 Bath for children. The tour takes around 40 minutes and offers a detailed description of buildings, departments, and the history of the university while customers can take pictures and see the beauty of the university. There is one stop allowing customers to get off the bus and take pictures around CMU. It might sound strange that a university is a tourist attraction, but with large gardens, a reservoir and CMU.

For learning about tourism in CMU, there are subjects offered in Department of Tourism, Faculty of Humanities, which is nationally and regionally recognized as a centre for teaching and training in tourism and hospitality in northern Thailand. This department is focusing to teach on introduction of tourism, Thai heritage, cultural tourism, tourism behavior, ecotourism, tour guide principles, tourism and hotel marketing, tour management, tourism impact management, Airline ticketing, intro to hotel management (front office, housekeeping operation, restaurants management, food and beverage, hotel fitness management, HR management, BAR, Beverage & Wine, MICE, accommodation management, Event Planning & catering Service, and service quality). The department provide academic services as tour guide training courses (annually), series of training courses on current issues in tourism (depending on the budget granted every year), and on-demand services.

The College of Art, Media and Technology teach undergraduate program in E-tourism, Introduction to E-tourism, and Event Management in Department of Modern Management and Information Technology in bilingual program. This college open 2 master degrees in software engineering and knowledge innovation management program, and 1 doctoral degree in innovation management program.

There are many faculties and institute in CMU do the research on tourism area. Especially, Center of Tourism Research and Development (CTRD) in the Social Research Institute. CTRD's researches focused on tourism management, tourism strategies, community based tourism, CTRD also develop manuscript, provide academic services, and disseminate knowledge. The area base of research is on CMU surrounding, Chiang Mai and the northern Thailand, and neighboring countries in ASEAN and Asia. The topic research is about the cultural tourism, health and wellness tourism, Community based tourism (CBT), tourism behavior, Long stay, smart city, E-tourism, etc.

The examples of completed research are as Chinese tourists satisfaction after 'The Lost in Thailand', Green tourism services, Tourism development and promotion for Chinese tourists in northern Thailand, Chiang Mai-Luang Prabang tourism development network in Lan Na Civilization route, The lesson learn from World Heritage Town of Luang Prabang to Chiang Mai's tentative list of future World Heritage: Case study of land use zoning and renovation of tourist accommodation, Development of market competitiveness of cultural tourism in northern Thailand route, Green tourism services, Homestay standard evaluation, Slow tourism for senior tourists, and Senior tourism management in upper north of Thailand.

CTRD's academic services provide the workshop, seminar for local people, the tourists entrepreneur, the government officer on tourism topic. CTRD organize the academic tourism event to share the tourism knowledge in each research area in norther part of Thailand.

The example of CTRD's research result which related to Chinese travelers is as follows.

2 Chinese Tourists Behavior in Chiang Mai

Thailand has witnessed the increasing number of Chinese tourists in recent years. Chinese tourists have become the largest group of tourists visiting Thailand. It even became a common scene to spot Chinese tourists here and there particularly after the launch of a movie '*Lost in Thailand*' that filming in many cities in Thailand (mostly in Bangkok, Ayutthaya, and Chiang Mai) around the end of 2012. Chiang Mai, once unpopular among Chinese tourists, has been rapidly explored by this new group of visitors as well. These latest phenomena, both in number and choice of destination, interestingly suggest a new trend in Chinese tourists' behavior. This study thus aimed to survey, to compare and to reconsider this change by using Chiang Mai as a case study area. We employed the questionnaires to ask 300 Chinese tourists visiting Chiang Mai between June and November in 2017. The derived data were then analyzed and also compared to the past data. The result of this study revealed that the majority of the respondents were female, half-half between single and married, the most were the company's staff, chiefly got income around 5,001 – 10,000 Yuan per month, and mostly came from the eastern part of China (e.g. Beijing and Shanghai). Most of these respondents visited Thailand for their first time with the main purpose for relaxing. The people accompanying them were mainly their family and friends. They mostly managed their trip by themselves and relied on information from website, word of mouth, and guidebook. The major interesting spot for them was the historical and cultural tourism, and the next were the natural tourism and the soft adventure. The top three cities they loved to visit were Chiang Mai, Bangkok and Pattaya respectively. Most of them spent around 5,001 – 10,000 Yuan per trip. While travelling, nearly all of them used smartphone or tablet to take pictures, post pictures and information on social network, search for travelling information and map, and also translate the languages. For place to stay, they mainly stayed at the guesthouse, hotel, and boutique hotel located in the city or nearby the shopping center. For the souvenir, most of them loved product made by cotton, wood, and silver. They also enjoyed Thai food, especially mango with sticky rice, Tom yam Kung, local food, and Chinese food. Most of them visited Chiang Mai by airplane. There are many direct flight from Chiang Mai to the important city in China, such as Beijing, Shanghai, Wuhan, Guangzhou, Kunming, Chongqing, Hangzhou, Chengdu, etc. They used TukTuk and/or motorcycle to travel around Chiang Mai city. The most attractive tourism activities for them were traditional Thai massage, SPA, soft adventure, etc. Finally, the top five tourist attractions were Tapae Gate, Wat Prathat Doi Suthep, Night Bazaar, Chiang Mai University, and Wat Pra Singh. This survey found that modern Chinese tourist behavior changed from the past which they were travelling with big group tour and mostly around the central part of Thailand.

In 1988, Thailand was among the very first countries that the Chinese government granted permission for its people to be able to visit. As a result, Thailand has since then witnessed the increasing number of Chinese tourist's year after year. From around ten thousand at the very initial period, the number of Chinese tourists has impressively climbed up to hundred thousand in the following years and finally it went beyond one million in 2006. Unsurprisingly, in 2012, Chinese tourists have set a new record with the number of 2.78 million and became number one in terms of number of tourist visiting Thailand (Department of Tourism, 2013). But in 2018, there are more than 10 million of Chinese tourists visiting Thailand (Ministry of Tourism and Sport, 2019). Impressively, this leapfrog growth has occurred only within two decades. From now on, the landscape of Thailand's tourism industry will rapidly change, not only in terms of number but also in terms of structure of tourists and travelling pattern. It is highly possible that these changes have been significantly driven by Chinese tourists and thus imperative for us to intensively study and follow the growth of Chinese tourists in order to prepare for the possible change in this near future. After all, if we just barely wait for their visit without any plans and preparation, the dramatic inflow of Chinese tourists could possibly bring more threat than opportunity and negatively affect tourism image of Thailand.

According to Kasikorn Bank Research Center, the factor that fundamentally enhances the growth of Chinese tourists to Thailand was the expanding of direct flights from many cities of China to the main tourist destinations in Thailand. This factor had greatly facilitated the travelling of Chinese tourists. In addition to this, the image of tourism in Thailand also has been promoted via movie production that used Thailand as a location. This same research center also forecast that the free independent travelers (FIT) will become the most interesting group because of their fast growing in number. The characters of this group are new generation with high purchasing power, more than 30 years old, familiar with utilizing information technology in searching for all information relating to travelling (package tour, place to stay etc.)

3 Research Methodology

Recently, Chiang Mai has witnessed the increasing number of Chinese tourists. The majority of them came in group following the popular movie '*The Lost in Thailand*' and many Thai dramas broadcasted in China. This trend has led to the study of the behavior of the new generation of Chinese tourists in Chiang Mai. The data derived from this study will be used to support the capacity development for cultural community as part of 'Chiang Mai the Creative City' project.

The study of Chinese tourist behavior in the past few years has gained a momentous and continuous interests such as the case of Kasikorn Bank Research Center mentioned above or the study of competitive strategy on tourism of Thai and countries within the Greater Mekong sub-region with respect to the expansion of Chinese tourist market by Korawan (2008). In addition to these, the study by Jakkree (2013) on Thailand's Tourism Image also contributed one section focusing on Chinese tourists' opinion on image of Thailand. According to this study, it was found that Chinese tourists emphasized on safety, value of money, and cleanliness. However, the most outstanding image of Thailand in their view is sand and sea, follows with night life, spa and traditional Thai massage.

The objective of this research was to study the travelling patter of Chinese tourists in Thailand, to investigate the present travelling behavior of Chinese tourists coming to visit Chiang Mai, and to analyze and compare the travelling pattern of Chinese tourists in the past and in the present day.

The scope of this research included reviewing the literature on travelling pattern of the Chinese tourists in Thailand from the past studies, statistic data, websites and various related data source, analyzing and comparing the travelling pattern of Chinese tourists in the past and in the present from the previous researches and the result from our recent Chinese tourists' behavior survey.

This research employed both primary and secondary data; while the latter ones were collected from documents, research studies, statistic data and related websites, the former ones were derived from the questionnaires. The questions in the questionnaires were the general information about the sample group, number of visit, purpose of travelling, travelling pattern, travelling companions, travelling preparation, travelling style affected their decision making before coming to Thailand, provinces in Thailand where Chinese tourist want to visit, travelling expenses, places where Chinese tourists choose to stay, type of favorite food and souvenir, type of favorite transportation during their stay, favorite destination, activities done during their stay in Chiang Mai, the most favorite thing or aspect about Chiang Mai, the willingness to tell other about their travelling experience, the intention of the tourists to come back, and what tourist most worry about or problem occurred during their trips.

4 Concept/Theory: Concept about Tourist Behavior

Tourist behavior means the expression of each individual directly related to the utilization of commodities and services in tourism industry. It also includes the decision making process that affects this expression. Thus, in a nutshell, the behavior is influenced by incentive or motivation and vice versa the influenced behavior is meant to response to those incentives or motivation.

The tourist behavior consists of 7 significant components: (1) the purpose, each tourist behavior must have a purpose; (2) the readiness, the maturity and ability in doing activity in response to their need; (3) the situation, the event or opportunity that facilitates the activity selecting in response to their need; (4) the interpretation, different kinds of thinking method in response to the most satisfaction in each situation; (5) the response, the decision making in doing activity according to what one has selected to achieve the result—this could be both expected or unexpected results; (6) the reaction to the disappointment, the feeling after what have done is not achieved the expected result; (7) The following result, one then has to reinterpret and reconsider in order to search for a new method to satisfy one's need or abandon it since it is beyond one's potential.

The study of tourist's background and behavior is very crucial for working in service industry especially tourism and hotel. Understanding the different behavior of tourists from different sources enable the workers in this industry adjust themselves well in response to the need of each tourist. In short, service staff equipped with tourist's background and behavior knowledge will find it easy to do their job. Moreover, the study on tourist behavior further enhance our knowledge about decision making pattern of the tourist: the kind of service they buy, the reason they buy it, the time and the venue where they buy it, and also the frequency they buy it. Upon learning about these tourist's characters, we will then search for the best way to provide goods/service that could win the heart of the tourists. Basically, the service providers must learn everything about tourists such as their need, idea, working style and time spending etc. This knowledge will help us to clearly understand, both as an individual and as a group, those factors affected the tourists' decision making.

5 Study Result: Result from Survey on Travelling Behavior of Chinese Tourists in Chiang Mai

From the general information of sample group of 300 Chinese tourists visiting Chiang Mai in Table 1 below, it was found that women were almost twice of men: while male tourists were approximately 38 percent, female tourists were 62 percent. However, the education background of most tourists was not high: only 21.6 percent graduated from university. When consider the occupation of these tourists, it revealed that about two-fourth of them worked in private companies (45.3 percent), the next are sales representatives and students. About one-third of these sample tourists were those having salary of about 5,001 – 10,000 Yuan, the next 27.5 percent were those with 2,002 – 5,000 Yuan salary. In term of their place of origin, the majority of tourists came from those major cities that already have been well known among Thai people especially Beijing and Shanghai. The numbers of sample tourists from these two large cities were big. The rest of the sample tourists were also coming from those main cities such as Shenzhen, Guangzhou, Chengdu and Kunming.

Table 1 General information of tourists' sample group

Items	Number	Percentage
Gender	300	100.0
Male	114	38.0

(To be continued)

Items	Number	Percentage
Female	186	62.0
Marital Status	300	100.0
Single	149	49.6
Married	147	49.0
Widowed/Divorced/Separated	4	1.4
Education	300	100.0
Junior High School and lower	20	6.7
Senior High School/ Vocational School	215	71.7
University (Bachelor's degree or higher)	65	21.6
Occupation	300	100.0
Government officer and Private Company Staff	136	45.3
Sales Representatives or Salesman	20	6.7
Student	36	12
Self-employed	22	7.3
Housewife/ Retired	25	8.3
Farmer	5	1.7
Others	56	18.7
Averaged Monthly Salary	300	100.0
2,001 ~ 5,000 Yuan	83	27.5
5,001 ~ 10,000 Yuan	105	35.1
More than 10,001 Yuan	112	37.4

Source: From the survey in 2017

Considering the travelling behavior of sample Chinese tourists visiting Chiang Mai, it was shown that 70 percent of them were first time visitors (Figure 1). The purpose of their visit is mainly for recreation (87 percent) whereas only a few of them came for honeymoon (8 percent) and sightseeing (4 percent) (Figure 2). When examining the travelling companions in Figure 3, it was clearly seen that Chinese tourists mostly still preferred travelling in group (more than 90 percent) with family, friend or boyfriend/girlfriend than travelling alone (only 4 percent). It was also evident in Figure 4 that more than 90 percent of sample Chinese tourists managed to prepare the trip by themselves, only a few (less than 5 percent) relied on buying package tour.

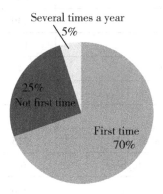

Figure 1　Number of visiting Chiang Mai by Chinese tourists

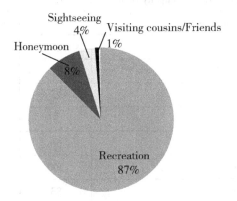

Figure 2　Purpose of visiting Chiang Mai by Chinese tourists

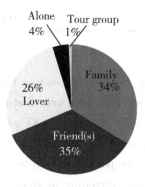

Figure 3　Travelling companion(s) of Chinese tourists visiting Chiang Mai

Source: From the survey in 2017

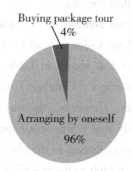

Figure 4   Travelling preparation of Chinese tourists visiting Chiang Mai
Source: From the survey in 2017

It is worth to note that the travelling pattern of the sample Chinese tourists was highly consistent with the character of Chiang Mai. From Table 2 below, more than 60 percent of tourists' travelling style was historical and cultural tour, the next choice (about 40 percent) was focused on natural travelling. The third and fourth choices were adventurous and medical tour respectively.

Table 2   Travelling style affected tourists' decision before coming to Thailand

Travelling Style	Rank (Percentage)								Rank in Total
	1	2	3	4	5	6	7	8	
Visiting historical and cultural sites	64.9	19.4	7.7	0.8	2.0	–	–	–	1
Natural travelling	20.2	39.1	13.7	7.3	6.0	2.8	1.2	0.4	2
Adventurous travelling	4.4	14.9	26.6	13.3	14.1	10.9	4.0	2.0	3
Medical tourism	1.2	9.7	17.3	27.0	14.9	8.1	8.1	4.0	4
Shopping	2.7	5.8	16.1	18.3	19.2	21.9	11.2	4.9	5 & 6
Visiting movie/drama locations	2.0	1.2	4.0	6.9	8.5	16.9	21.8	23.8	7
Sport tourism	–	0.4	1.2	4.4	10.5	14.5	21.4	33.1	8
Night life	2.3	5.1	8.8	14.8	16.2	12.5	20.8	19.4	–

Source: From the survey in 2017

Besides the possible fact that the tourists themselves previously loved Chiang Mai, the factor that the survey had conducted in Chiang Mai could also contribute to result that revealed the place where Chinese tourists most wanted to visit was Chiang Mai (ranked both number 1 and 2 as shown in Table 3). The next most-wanted-to-visit places were Bangkok and Pattaya (Chonburi) that have already long been the favorite places of Chinese tourists. However, the way that Phuket ranked number 16 in this case did not directly imply that it was less popular than many other provinces with higher rank. In fact, by investigating in details for rank number 1 to number 4, Phuket was nonetheless got a very high score as well (except that its scores were less than those top three destinations). Apart from these four well known destinations, other popular provinces also included Ayutthaya, Prachobkirikhun and Suratthani. For the other three Northern provinces including Chiang Rai, Lamphun and Lampang, it was possible that the tourist considered them as nearby locations. Thus, to visit these provinces could be what they might consider.

By comparing to their average salary previously mentioned, travelling expense of Chinese tourists was considered rather high. About 46 percent or almost half of them spent 5 001～10 000 Yuan whereas only one-fourth of them spent less than 5,000 Yuan.

Table 3 Provinces in Thailand that Chinese tourists want to visit

Provinces	Rank (Percentage)															Rank in Total
	1	2	3	4	5	6	7	8	9	10	11	12	13	14	15	
Chiang Mai	48.4	23.8	7.3	3.6	0.4	–	–	0.8	0.8	0.4	–	–	–	0.4	–	1 & 2
Bangkok	19.8	18.1	21.8	11.3	6.5	4.4	0.4	–	0.4	–	0.4	–	0.8	1.6	–	3
Pattaya (Chonburi)	1.6	7.3	16.1	14.5	11.3	5.6	6.0	1.6	0.4	–	0.4	0.8	0.8	2.0	0.8	4
Ayuthaya	1.2	6.0	9.7	13.3	12.9	6.0	2.4	0.8	0.4	0.4	0.4	–	–	0.4	0.4	5
Prachobkirikhun	0.4	–	1.2	1.2	2.4	9.3	6.0	6.0	4.8	1.6	1.6	0.8	2.4	1.2	–	6
Suratthani	–	–	0.8	1.2	0.8	3.6	10.1	6.5	4.8	0.8	2.4	1.6	1.6	3.6	–	7, 8
Chiang Rai	1.6	2.4	2.0	2.4	4.0	4.4	2.0	3.6	7.7	6.0	0.4	1.2	1.2	0.4	–	9
Lamphun	–	–	0.4	0.4	0.4	0.8	0.8	1.6	1.2	8.9	8.5	4.4	0.8	1.2	–	10
Lampang	0.4	–	0.8	0.4	0.4	0.8	–	1.2	2.8	2.8	9.7	7.3	3.2	–	–	11
Sukhothai	2.0	4.4	4.0	3.2	4.4	4.8	4.8	0.8	1.2	2.0	0.8	7.3	1.6	1.2	–	12
Ubolratchathani	–	0.2	0.4	0.8	–	1.2	0.4	3.2	2.0	4.4	2.4	2.8	10.5	2.0	–	13
Udonthani	–	0.4	0.4	–	0.8	0.4	2.0	0.8	4.4	2.0	1.2	2.4	2.8	11.3	1.2	14
Others	0.8	1.6	1.6	0.8	–	–	–	2.0	–	–	–	–	0.4	–	2.0	15
Phuket	16.1	21.0	19.0	12.9	7.3	3.2	1.2	–	0.8	0.4	–	–	0.4	–	–	16
Krabi	5.6	8.1	4.4	6.9	7.3	3.6	4.8	5.6	1.6	–	0.4	0.4	1.2	2.0	–	17

Source: From the survey in 2017

The survey also inquire the sample Chinese tourists about their favorite food and souvenir during their travelling in Chiang Mai as illustrated in Table 4 and Table 5. In case of food, Thai food was very popular since about 64 percent of them chose to consume Thai food; their favorite dish was Tom Yam Kung (about 50 percent). The next favorite dishes were local food and Chinese food (about 36 percent and 28 percent respectively). Impressively, about one-fourth of Chinese tourists chose to try Mango with sticky rice, Kow Soi — local of Chiang Mai's popular dishes. However, Western food was the least popular among them. For souvenir, more than 40 percent of sample Chinese tourists preferred dried fruit, clothes or handbag products, following with those products made of wood and silverware.

Table 4 Type of food selected by Chinese tourists visiting Chiang Mai

Type of Food	Answering 'Like' (Percentage)
Thai Food	64.1
Tom Yam Kung	49.0
Local Food	35.9
Mango with sticky rice	49.8
Fruit	47.7
Pad Thai	25.0
Sea Food	24.5
Kow Soi	26.2
Fried Rice	24.2
Noodle	20.6
Khanom Chin	17.3
Western Food	12.9
Others	3.2

Source: From the survey in 2017

Table 5 Type of souvenir bought by Chinese tourists visiting Chiang Mai

Type of Souvenir	Anseering 'Buy' (Percentage)
Clothes/Handbag	54.8
Dried Fruit	44.1
Wood Products	37.1
Silverware	27.4
Brand Name Products	17.3
Bamboo/Rattan Products	14.9
Others	14.1

Source: From the survey in 2017

Data about type of transportation used by Chinese tourists visiting Chiang Mai showed that the majority (almost 90 percent) chose air plane. However, during their stay they preferred to use Tuk Tuk, and/or red cab, and/or taxi (about 57, 50 and 48 percent respectively). Still, approximately one-third of them rented motorcycles to wandering around the city. In terms of activities (Table 6), the main activity of sample Chinese tourists was traditional massage (about 70 percent) and elephant riding (60 percent), followed with zip-lining (about 29 percent), rafting (about 18 percent). Other activities receiving fair interest (about 10 percent each) included watching local cultural show, learning Thai cooking, or spa.

Table 6 Chinese tourists' activities during their travelling in Chiang Mai

Activities	Number of Answering 'Yes' (Percentage)
Traditional Massage	182 (73.4)
Elephant Riding	154 (62.1)
Zip-lining	73 (29.4)
Rafting	45 (18.1)
Watching Local Cultural Show	28 (11.3)
Learning Thai Cooking	27 (10.9)
Spa	26 (10.5)
Learning Thai Language	22 (8.9)

(To be continued)

Activities	Number of Answering 'Yes' (Percentage)
Watching Lady Boy Show	20 (8.1)
Watching Thai Boxing	18 (7.3)
Gun Shooting	11 (4.4)
ATV Riding	10 (4.0)
Learning Meditation	6 (2.4)
Learning Yoka	2 (0.8)
Learning Thai Boxing	0 (0)
Paint ball	1 (0.4)
Others	12 (4.8)

Source: From the survey in 2017

For sample Chinese tourists' favorite destination in Chiang Mai as shown in Table 7, we might be able to roughly categorize into four groups as follows. The first group, dubbed the exceptionally most favorite destinies, was those places scored more than 50 percent; these were Tha Pae Gate, Wat Prathat Doi Suthep, Night Bazaar and Chiang Mai University. Specifically, Tha Pae Gate where tourist attractions concentrated was the most favorite one with the highest score of more than 70 percent. The next, dubbed the most favorite destinies, was the group with score around 30% – 50%. Places fell into this second category were Wat Pra Singh, Sunday Walking Street (Tha Pae Road) and Wat Chiang Man. The third, dubbed the favorite destinies, group was those receive fair interest with the score around 20% – 30%: Mae Sa Elephant Camp, Saturday Walking Street (Woa lai Road), Wat Chedi Luang and Nimmanhaemin Road. The last group, dubbed the least favorite destinies, was those scored less than 20 percent. Within this group, however, those that still received good attention from Chinese tourists were quite many, such as Warorot Market (18 percent), line-zipping (17 percent), Phuping Palace (16 percent). In sum, most places Chinese tourists chose to visit were cultural destinations where as those natural ones were still not popular.

Table 7 Tourist destinations in Chiang Mai where Chinese tourists chose to visit

Tourist Destinations	Number of Answering 'Yes' (Percentage)
Tha Pae Gate	182 (73.4)
Wat Prathat Doi Suthep	145 (58.5)
Night Bazaar	145 (58.5)
Chiang Mai University	133 (53.6)
Wat Pra Singh	123 (49.6)
Sunday Walking Street (Tha Pae Road)	101 (40.7)
Wat Chiang Man	79 (31.9)
Mae Sa Elephant Camp	71 (28.6)
Saturday Walking Street (Woa Lai Road)	68 (27.4)
Wat Chedi Luang	62 (25.0)
Nimmanhaemin Road	58 (23.4)
Warorot Market	44 (17.7)
ATV Riding /Zip-lining	43 (17.3)
Chiang Mai Night Safari	41 (16.5)
Phuping Palace	39 (15.7)
Wat U-mong	34 (13.7)
Wat Jed Yord	29 (11.7)
Wat Suandok	29 (11.7)
Mae Taman Elephant Camp	25 (10.1)
Chiang Mai National Museum	25 (10.1)
Mae Sa Elephant Camp	23 (9.3)
Rachapruek Royal Garden	22 (8.9)
Chiang Mai Zoo	22 (8.9)
Ban Bor Sang (Umbrella Making Village)	15 (6.0)
Doi Inthanont National Park	13 (5.2)
Vieang Kumkam	11 (4.4)

(To be continued)

Tourist Destinations	Number of Answering 'Yes' (Percentage)
Ban Tawai (Wood Crafting Village)	9 (3.6)
San Kampang Hot Spring	8 (3.2)
Ban Mae Kampong (Homestay village)	5 (2.0)
Doi Pui Hmong Village	5 (2.0)
Queen Sirikit Botanical Garden	5 (2.0)
Doi Ang Khang	3 (1.2)

Source: From the survey in 2017

Finally, sample Chinese tourists were asked about their favorite in Chiang Mai. The result shown in Table 8 revealed that the most favorite one was the friendliness and the people (about 79 percent), the next favorite was the beautiful scenery (about 67 percent). The delicious food and the beautiful tourist attractions, however, also received a high score with more than 50 percent each. With this good impression, it was not surprised that almost all sample Chinese tourists mentioned that they intended to come back as well as tell other about their good experience and recommend them to visit Chiang Mai (Tables 9 and 10). In spite of this satisfaction, as shown in Table 11, sample Chinese tourists still encountered on language barrier (about 57 percent) since they were not familiar with English communication whereas the level of Chinese proficiency among Thai people was still low. The next problem for them was about travelling (about 18 percent). However, safety and cheating problems were quite low with only 5% – 6%.

Table 8 Chinese tourists' favorite about Chiang Mai

Items	Number of Answering 'Yes' (Percentage)
Friendliness/People	195 (78.6)
Beautiful Scenery	165 (66.5)
Delicious Food	148 (59.7)
Beautiful Tourist Attractions	117 (47.2)
Nice Weather	114 (46.0)

Source: From the survey in 2017

Table 9 Chinese tourists' intention to recommend others to visit Chiang Mai

Intention	Number	Percentage
'Yes, I will recommend.'	246	99.2
'No, I will not recommend.'	2	0.8
Total	248	100.0

Source: From the survey in 2017

Table 10 Chinese tourists' intention to come back to visit Chiang Mai

Intention	Number	Percentage
'Yes, I will come back.'	243	98.8
'No, I will not come back.'	3	1.2
N/A	2	0.8
Total	248	100.0

Source: From the survey in 2017

Table 11 Problem(s) that Chinese tourists meet during their travelling in Thailand

Type of Worriment/Problem	Number of Answering 'Yes' (Percentage)
Language	140 (56.5)
Travelling	45 (18.1)
Safety	16 (6.5)
Cheating	14 (5.6)
Others	33 (13.3)

Source: From the survey in 2013

6 Discussion

Basically, the dynamic change within Chinese tourists in both quantity and structure was driven by three main factors: (1) the dramatic change in economic landscape of China that resulted in increasing demand with greater purchasing power of Chinese consumers, (2) the higher rate of urbanization that affected the value and life style of new Chinese generation, and (3) the relaxation of restriction for Chinese people to travel abroad by Chinese government (Jakkree et. al, 2013). Initially, only a few countries in Asia could Chinese people visit, but now it does not too exaggerate to claim that they can go anywhere around the globe. However, in terms of Chinese tourists visiting Thailand, the most significant driving factors were only the first and the second one since Thailand was already among the first group that the Chinese government allowed its people to visit. However, since their first visit, the Chinese tourists concentrated within only three destinations namely Bangkok, Pataya and Phuket (Korawan, 2008). Thus there was an impressive effort from those stake holders in Thai tourism industry to 'decentralize' the number of Chinese tourists to other destinations besides those popular three. The latest attempt was the permission granted to the Chinese cinema production group to employ several locations especially in the northern part of Thailand (mostly Chiang Mai) for shooting the movie '*Lost in Thailand*'. With a landslide welcome, this movie was expected to potentially draw more tourists from China to visit Chiang Mai. Following this paragraph, we will summarize our study. However, in order to better capture the change of Chinese tourists visiting Chiang Mai, we will also bring the result from the previous research on Chinese tourists' behavior and attitude toward tourism in Chiang Mai in 2005 by Orrachorn et al (2008) to compare with some comparable aspects of our study.

First of all, considering their intention, most Chinese tourists (about 80 percent) came to Chiang Mai mainly for recreation. They chose Chiang Mai based on its well known recognition as a cultural city with a beautiful mountainous landscape. However, the clear different between those Chinese tourists visiting Chiang Mai in 2005 and those coming in 2013 were the trip arrangement method. In 2005, almost half of Chinese tourists relied on tour agency to arrange their trips while only 19 percent of them manage the trip by themselves. On the contrary, more than 90 percent of the Chinese tourists in 2013 chose to arrange the trips by themselves whereas less than 5 percent preferred buying package tours. Still, in terms of the trip companions, more than 80 percent of Chinese tourists still preferred coming with their lovers, or family members, or friends.

In 2005 study, the most favorite to least favorite place and/or activity of Chinese tourists visiting Chiang Mai were Doi Suthep, elephant riding, Doi Inthanont and Ban Tawai. Furthermore, this study also mentioned those places not shown in the tour program but tourists wish to visit: Hot Spring, city viewing and Wat Prasingh. Comparing with the 2013 study, besides Doi Suthep and elephant riding, other tourist destinations also gained popularity. These recently focused destinations included Tha Pae Gate area, Walking Street or even Wat Prasingh. Interestingly, academic institution like Chiang Mai University was also on Chinese tourists' visiting list. This Thailand's first National University located in the upcountry received a notable attention possibly due to its location that situated on the way to Doi Suthep and also its admirable landscape with greenery tall teak tree and other plants especially in front of the university. Besides, the university's Ang Kaew reservoir with a impressive backdrop of Doi Suthep was also another good location for taking pictures. In addition to this, a destination which in 2005 was still unknown among Chinese tourists or even Thai tourists since it was still in the initial stage of its popularity was Nimmanhaemin Road. In 2013, many shops and tourist destinations along this road had an opportunity to welcome many Chinese tourists and of course tourists from around the globe: wandering, taking photos, and shopping. It is worth to note that, the study in 2005 found that the souvenirs bought by Chinese tourists were jewelry (about 28 percent), processed fruited(about 19 percent) and ready-to-wear clothes (about 19 percent), but according to our study in 2013, the favorite souvenir bought by them were clothes or handbag(about 55 percent), the next were products made of doy fiuits(44%), wood(about 37 percent) and silverware(about 27 percent).

The study in 2005 and our study in 2013 also inquired the Chinese tourists about their possibility to come back to visit Chiang Mai. On one hand, the study in 2005 found that only 37.5 percent of Chinese tourists surely intended to be back and 43.2 percent stated that they might come back. On the other hand, in 2013 study almost 100 percent of Chinese tourist confirmed that they will certainly be back to visit. When consider in details about the reasons behind their trip's satisfaction in 2005 that possibly lead to their revisit, it was found that the main factors were 'cheap and worth-of-money commodity, good feeling, relax atmosphere, beautiful scenery, good weather, very fun and one of good places to see antique'. In 2013 study, however, it was found that what most satisfied those Chinese tourists visiting Chiang Mai were friendliness, beautiful scenery, delicious food and beautiful tourist destination. It could assume from this recent study that the Chinese tourists possibly obtained more opportunity to have more communication with local people and also learned more about the city that they came to visit. This might imply a better sign comparing to the past when they just came with only 'been there, seen that (and shop some)' attitude.

From the study, we found 7 reasons why the Chinese will boost the global tourism industry:

a) China's latest financial events,
b) Willing to spend,
c) They have cash/ e-payment,
d) Visa requirements,
e) Large investment in tourism,
f) Better flight connections,
g) Different mindset.

From the study, we also found things to know about Chinese tourists in Chiang Mai as follows:

a) Free independent (FIT),
b) Peak in long vacation,
c) Love local food,
d) Love dried fruit,
e) Boutique Hotel,
f) Thai massage in Lanna Style.

References

[1] JAKKREE T, SUMETH P, MINGSARN K. Tourism image of Thailand: The case of tourists from the east [M]. Chiang Mai: Public Policy Study Institute, Chiang Mai University, 2013.

[2] KORAWAN S. The study of competitive strategy on tourism of Thai and countries within the greater Mekong sub-region with respect to the expansion of Chinese tourist market [M]. Chiang Mai: Nopburi Co. Ltd., 2008.

[3] ZHIQIANG H. Tourism perception to Thailand of the Chinese mainland tourists [C]. Bangkok, Thailand: First Thai–Chinese Strategic Research Seminar, 2012.

泰国旅游教育的单一化发展

Ploysri Porananond　泰国清迈大学

1　引言

泰国的旅游教育是随着国家旅游业发展而兴起的。在专制的沙利特政权（1959—1963 年）期间，政府通过发展旅游业来促进地方和国家增收（TAT，1985），开启了泰国现代旅游业的序幕。1960 年，泰国旅游组织（TOT）成立，作为一家国有企业，其主要目标是吸引和招揽国际游客（Jaruwat，1996）。

在 1976 年泰国游客人数和收入下降后，政府立即聘请顾问为泰国制订旅游总体规划（TAT，1985）。该规划随后被纳入泰国的第四个经济社会发展五年计划（1977—1981 年）。该规划提出在泰国各地建立分散的旅游中心：曼谷和芭堤雅作为泰国中部的旅游中心，合艾（Hat Yai）作为南部的旅游中心，清迈作为北部的旅游中心。尽管当时泰国东北地区有着丰富的地方文化，但是没有一个省份被指定为旅游中心。清迈和合从这一规划中获益，得以发展成现代大都市。

国家旅游规划的出台进一步提升了泰国旅游组织（TOT）的地位。1979年，泰国旅游局（TAT）在泰国旅游组织的基础上成立，专注于旅游营销和规划。然而，一项旨在建立一套法律体系来控制私营旅游企业的法案被否决了（TAT，1985）。这反映了泰国民间旅游资本的力量，也表明政府在试图为整个旅游业制定标准时面临的挑战。

2　泰国旅游教育开端

鉴于泰国旅游业的快速发展，在联合国开发计划署（UNDP）和国际劳工组织（ILO）的支持下，1979 年酒店和旅游培训学院（HTTI）在泰国旅游局的指导下成立（时任局长为 Somchai Hiranyakit 上校），这是泰国第一家酒店和旅游教育机构。学院位于当时颇受欢迎的海滨度假胜地 Bang Sean 海滩。酒店和旅游培训学院（HTTI）的目标是培训泰国当地人成为泰国酒店和旅游业所需的熟练人才。该机构的师资队伍由西方国家的专业人员以及训练有素的泰国讲师组成。1981 年，学院开启了酒店和旅游业的培训课程。这些课程包括为期一年的前台、厨房、餐厅和酒吧、家政、旅游和贸易项目的证书培训课程，以及为期两年的旅游管理和导游、客房管理、食品和餐饮管理的文凭课程。此外，还提供短期培训课程，例如，为酒店员工、旅行社、餐馆提供的酒店和旅游培训课程，以及为大学讲师提供的培训项目。此外，还设立了针对柬埔寨和中国学员的国际酒店管理、旅游管理和餐饮管理教育项目（Department of Tourism Investment Promotion，TAT，2019）。

2002 年，为提高政府效率，旅游和体育部成立，旅游相关的管理工作被分配到不同的机构。泰国旅游局作为国有企业只负责旅游推广和营销，其他旅游相关的工作都交由旅游和体育部这一政府机构来负责。在这一背景下，泰国旅游局指导下的酒店和旅游培训学院的任务转变为泰国旅游局的工作人员提供培训。

3　泰国旅游教育现状

泰国旅游业的发展推动了酒店和旅游业相关学科和教育项目的发展，尤其是在职业和本科教育层面上。然而，这些项目仅仅是为了满足国家旅游业对熟练劳动力的需求。尽管有一些硕士和博士学位项目，但这种高等教育项目似乎只是为政府机关和私营旅游企业的员工提供学历升级的机会。

3.1　本科教育层面

目前，泰国各地的高校有大量与酒店和旅游业相关的本科课程。旅游业对劳动力日益增长的需求是泰国教育机构开设酒店和旅游项目的主要动力。

随着清迈、曼谷和合艾等区域旅游中心的建立，以及普吉岛作为南部主要海滨度假胜地的发展，这些旅游城市也成了旅游教育中心。

泰国高校旅游教育项目的增长显而易见。目前，泰国共有 18 所公立大学、37 所皇家大学（Rajabhat Universities，以前在泰国许多省开设的师范学院）、5 所皇家技术大学（Rajamangala Universities，以前是在泰国许多省设立的技术学院）和 20 所私立大学提供旅游教育。这 18 所公立大学包括清迈大学（Chiang Mai University）、皇太后大学（Mae Fah Luang University）、东方大学（Burapha University）、梅州大学（Maejo University）、瓦莱腊大学（Walailak University）、玛哈沙拉坎大学（Mahasarakham University）、西纳克林威洛大学（Srinakharin University）、佛统皇家大学（Nakhon Phanom University）、碧瑶大学（University of Phayao)、孔敬大学（Khon Kaen University）、艺术大学（Silpakorn University）、那黎宣大学（Naresuan University）、农业大学（Kasetsart University）、宋卡王子大学（Prince of Songkla University）、乌朋拉其尼大学（Ubon Ratchthani University）、国王理工大学（King Mongkuts University of Technology）、皇家技术大学（Rajamangala Universities）、皇家大学（Rajabhat Universities）等。提供旅游教育项目的私立大学大多在曼谷。上述的教育机构基本都开设了旅游管理、旅游和酒店管理等教育项目，但仅部分高校开设了航空公司商务管理、厨房管理、烹饪艺术、餐饮管理等课程。这些教育机构每年为泰国旅游业输送约10 000名毕业生。

在泰北的旅游城市清迈，清迈大学（1964年创立的曼谷以外地区的第一所公立大学）人文学院在20世纪80年代首次开设了"旅游学概论"这一旅游课程。1993年成立了旅游教育小组，为主修语言的学生提供辅修课程。2006年开设了四年制"旅游和酒店管理"专业项目，每年招收约50名学生，这些学生大多来自泰国北部地区。在最后一年的第二学期，所有的学生必须在酒店、航空公司和旅行社实习。清迈大学旅游系的学生大多在清迈、曼谷和普吉岛的酒店以及航空公司工作。少数学生在旅行社工作或成为自由执业导游。

随着清迈旅游业的发展，2005年，前公立农业学院梅州大学创建了旅游管理学院，首先开设了旅游发展学士学位课程，随后又分别开设了硕士和博士学位课程。梅州大学每年招收约100名学生攻读旅游发展学士学位。与其他大学不同的是，梅州大学的毕业生主要接受旅游开发理论和实践方面的培训，他们大多在国家公园管理处或景点以及皇家项目地工作。许多毕业生是探险导游，少数会在酒店业工作。

西北大学（Payap University）是位于清迈的一所私立大学，由泰国基督教会资助，本科开设了酒店和旅游管理项目，以及酒店业管理的国际项目，每年招收约80名学生。绝大部分学生来自泰国北部地区，只有约10%的学生来自泰国其他地区。西北大学（Payap University）的大多数毕业生在泰国的酒店业工作，只有少数人在航空公司和旅行社工作。很少有学生继续攻读硕士学位。

曾是师范学院的清迈皇家大学（Rajabhat Chiang Mai University）也开设了一个旅游管理教育项目，为旅游业培养熟练劳动力。泰国还有其他36所皇家大学也开设了类似的旅游项目，每所皇家大学的旅游专业项目每年招收约120名学生。这意味着每年有大约4 440名来自所有皇家大学的旅游毕业生。这些毕业生有20%～30%的人在酒店业工作，30%的人是探险导游，5%～10%在航空公司工作，其余的人在旅行社或自己的企业工作。

泰国首都曼谷是泰国中部的旅游中心，许多高校，包括公立大学、私立大学和私立学院,都在此开设了酒店和旅游教育项目。例如,川喜登大学(Suan Dusit University),其前身是在烘焙和烹饪艺术领域享有盛名的川喜登皇家大学(Suan Dusit Rajabhat University),在1975年成立了旅游和酒店学院,开设了关于旅游管理和酒店管理的学士学位项目,2007年又开设了航空公司商务课程和管理服务国际课程。旅游管理和酒店管理项目每年各招收近100名学生,航空商务项目则招收50名学生。川喜登大学的大多数毕业生在曼谷的酒店和旅行社以及其他旅游企业工作,如泰国旅游局和泰国航空。

公立的蓝康恒大学(Ramkhamhaeng University)不仅在工商管理学院旅游系开设旅游课程,还在人文学院开设旅游历史这一特别教育项目。该项目可能是泰国第一个也是唯一一个旨在鼓励学生了解泰国历史、保护和传承文化遗产的大学教育项目。

私立的兰吉特大学(Rangsit University),由众议院前议长、科技部前部长、公共卫生部前部长和外交部部长 Arthit Ourairat 博士所有,设立了旅游和接待业学院。学院开设了旅游和酒店管理、酒店和餐厅管理、烹饪艺术和技术、航空商务管理、国际酒店和旅游等教育项目,以帮助感兴趣的学生获得相关知识,为其投身泰国旅游业打下基础。

都喜天丽学院(Dusit Thani College)是曼谷的一所私立学院,1993年由豪华连锁酒店和度假村都喜天丽酒店(Dusit Thani Hotel)的所有者成立。该学院开设了酒店管理、厨房和餐厅管理、旅游管理、度假村与水疗中心管理、会议和活动管理等教育项目,同时开设了酒店管理、厨房和餐厅管理等国际教育项目。学院的大多数学生来自泰国的主要旅游城市。与其他开设类似教育项目的高校相比,都喜天丽学院的学费更为高昂。但是,都喜天丽酒店的良好声誉和优质服务可以确保教育项目的质量。该学院的毕业生大多在自己的旅游相关企业工作,一些在国内外的其他酒店工作,不到10%的人在都喜天丽连锁酒店和度假村工作。

宋卡王子大学酒店和旅游学院成立于1993年,前身是泰国第一所社区学院——普吉岛社区学院(PCC)。它是泰国第一个酒店和旅游学院,旨在服务于旅游业的快速发展,特别是普吉岛和安达曼海沿岸的发展。学院最初开设了酒店管理、旅游管理和服务创新管理等教育项目,之后增设了餐饮服务管理、会议和活动管理、水疗管理等教育项目。为了满足南方旅游业的需求,该学院的毕业生主要在普吉岛及安达曼海沿岸的其他海滨度假地的酒店和旅行社工作。

3.2 职业教育层面

职业学院和私立学院也开展了旅游教育。泰国各地约有 20 所职业学院开设了旅游和酒店商业与服务教育项目,以满足希望获得旅游教育证书和文凭的学生的需求。这些职业院校开设了两年制证书课程和三年制文凭课程。每个学院每个教育项目每年招收约 120 名新生。值得一提的是,职业教育也为泰国的少数民族群体提供了接受培训的机会,以便他们从事旅游业。据了解,清迈职业学院近 20%~30% 的学生是少数民族学生,如山区部落和来自缅甸的傣族移民。在获得证书或文凭后,50% 的职业院校学生从事导游工作,其余的学生在酒店和旅行社工作,许多人之后会去泰国其他高校攻读学士学位。

国际酒店和旅游业管理学院(I-TIM)是曼谷的一所私立旅游学院,于 1988 年由泰国旅游局原局长和世界旅游组织(WTO)原副主席 Somchai Hiranyakit 上校成立,开设了一年制的酒店和旅游管理课程和两年制的酒店和旅游管理证书课程。每年有近百名学生注册这些课程。该学院 60% 以上的毕业生在泰国主要旅游地的酒店工作,约 20% 的毕业生会继续深造,10% 的毕业生在国外工作。

3.3 硕士和博士学位

泰国少数大学开设了硕士学位和博士学位项目。然而,这些高等教育项目的培养目标与学士学位教育项目的培养目标并无差异,即培训更高技能的劳动力以满足行业需求。

例如,泰国国立发展管理学院(NIDA)的旅游管理学院只开设旅游和酒店综合管理的管理硕士学位项目和旅游和酒店综合管理的哲学博士项目。此外,学院也在曼谷和普吉岛开设了额外的硕士学位课程,为有兴趣从事旅游的学生和工作人员提供提升学历水平的机会。

2003 年,宋卡王子大学酒店与旅游学院推出了酒店和旅游工商管理硕士项目,旨在为泰国培养国际酒店和旅游业管理人员,希望吸引"有志于成为泰国酒店和旅游业实践和学术研究精英"的学生。该项目希望通过将学术洞察力与行业实践结合起来,通过 2 年的学习来提升学生的职业生涯。

2005 年,梅州大学开设了旅游发展硕士项目;2007 年又推出了旅游发展哲学博士项目。目前约有 35 名硕士生是旅行社的老板或雇员,还有一些硕士生是皇家大学的讲师;博士生则主要是皇家大学的讲师。这些学生希望通过提升教育水平以获得更好的职业发展机会。

4 问题与挑战

通过审视泰国各地高校旅游教育的发展情况，我们发现泰国的旅游教育没有实现真正意义上的发展，更多是在重复酒店与旅游培训学院大约40年前（1981年）开启的旅游培训项目。

许多大学都设立了旅游和酒店管理学院，这反映出泰国旅游教育项目数量的增长以及旅游业的需求。虽然有一些高校引入了航空公司业务、餐厅和烹饪艺术等新的旅游教育项目，但大多数高校的旅游教育还是聚焦旅游和酒店管理。通过对这些项目的培养理念和内容的分析，可以发现，这些教育项目仅仅是为泰国旅游业提供熟练劳动力。当然，职业教育和本科教育培养这方面的人才无可非议。

然而，即便是泰国大学的硕士和博士学位项目，也强调是为了满足行业对高技能人才的需求，这与传统高等教育理念存在明显反差。此外，许多已取得硕士和博士学位的学生已经在旅游机构或教育机构工作，更高的教育水平能够为他们现有的职业生涯提供更好的机会。在这种情况下，高等教育培养思想家或旅游学者的理念就不受尊重。这直接反映了泰国旅游研究的质量（有待提升）。

此外，与发达国家相比，在泰国由不同学科或理论背景的学者开展旅游研究非常罕见。现有的研究大多聚焦如何利用旅游规划和开发以及营销和推广理念或理论，打造新的旅游目的地或产品。此外，政府研究资助机构的管理条例旨在将泰国的旅游研究转变为服务于政府规划的应用研究，而非学术研究。例如，泰国国家研究委员会发出了只对专注于旅游发展的管理领域的旅游研究项目进行资助的公告，而且只接受与"泰国20年国家发展战略"相一致的研究计划。

尽管旅游是一个跨学科研究领域，但与亚洲其他国家（如中国、日本和韩国）相比，泰国很少有其他社会科学背景的学者从事旅游研究。跨学科的旅游研究的缺乏恰恰反映了泰国旅游研究的不足。值得一提的是，泰国的旅游研究不应仅仅关注旅游开发、营销和推广，因为旅游发展会产生诸多影响，如对经济和社会文化的影响。泰国旅游在这些方面所面临的问题与挑战急需不同学科背景的学者从不同角度开展研究。

5 结论

随着泰国旅游业的快速发展，泰国各地的高等院校开设了大量旅游职业教育和本科教育课程，满足了泰国旅游业对熟练劳动力的需求。然而，目前的旅游教育项目的设计或理念并没有跳出 1981 年成立的泰国第一家旅游教育机构——酒店与旅游培训学院的培训项目范畴。这意味着泰国旅游教育的理念在 40 年间并未变化。即便是高层次的旅游教育项目，即硕士和博士学位课程，多数仍以为旅游行业培养更高技能劳动力或提升行业劳力资本为导向，而不是以培养合格的旅游研究者为导向。

此外，在泰国从事旅游研究的具有跨学科背景的学者非常少，这与中国、日本和韩国等国形成了鲜明的反差。在这些国家，受过社会学、人类学、历史学、地理学、心理学和文学训练的学者利用他们多元的思想和理论来开展旅游研究。综上，泰国旅游发展对经济和社会文化产生了诸多影响，跨学科的旅游研究不仅有助于政府部门制定战略和规划，也有利于旅游产业的进一步发展。

The Unvaried Growth of Tourism Education in Thailand

Ploysri Porananond
Chiang Mai University, Thailand

1 Introduction

Tourism education in Thailand was established following the tourism development of the country. It was the government policy during the authoritarian Sarit regime (1959 – 1963) to use tourism as a tool to encourage income both at the local and national level (TAT, 1985). Thus, it prompted the start of modern tourism in Thailand. The Tourism Organization of Thailand (TOT) was subsequently established in 1960 as a State enterprise with a principal objective to encourage international tourists to visit Thailand (Jaruwat, 1996).

Following the decrease in tourist numbers and income in 1976, the government promptly hires consultants to devise a tourism master plan for Thailand (TAT, 1985). This plan was then included in the Fourth National Social and Economic Development Plan (1977 – 1981). As part of this plan, decentralized tourist centers are created across Thailand: Bangkok and Pattaya were promoted as tourist centres in central Thailand, Hat Yai as a tourist centre in the south, and Chiang Mai as a tourist centre in the north. None of the provinces in the northeast part of the country were nominated as tourist centre at that time even though this region is rich in local culture. Chiang Mai and Hat Yai profited from this plan which contributed to their development into large modern cities.

The emergence of the National Tourism Plan further upgraded the Tourist Organisation of Thailand (TOT) to become the Tourism Authority of Thailand (TAT) in 1979 with a mandate to focus on tourism marketing and planning. However, a bill to create a proper legal framework to control private tourism businesses was defeated (TAT, 1985). This reflects the power of the commercial tourism sector and the difficulty that the government faces in trying to set standards for the industry as a whole.

2 The Initiative of Tourism Education in Thailand

Due to the rapid tourism development in Thailand and the support of United Nation Development Program (UNDP) and International Labor Organization (ILO), in 1979 the Hotel and Tourism Training Institute (HTTI) was approved to establish under the supervision of the Tourism Authority of Thailand (TAT), when Colonel Somchai Hiranyakit was a governor. The institute was located at Bang Sean Beach, a popular beach resort at the time. The aim of the HTTI was to train local Thais to become skilled personnel for the Thai hotel and tourism industry. It was the first institution for hotel and tourism education in Thailand. Instructors of the institute were professionals from the western countries, as well as the well-trained Thai instructors. In 1981, pioneer training courses in hotel and tourism were launched. They were one-year certificate training courses on Front Office, Kitchen, Restaurant & Bar, Housekeeping, Travel and Trade programs, and two-year diploma programs on Tourism Management, and Tour Guide, Room Division Management, Food and Beverage Management. Furthermore, short-term training courses were also available, for instance, short-term training courses on Hotel and Tourism for interested persons, employees of hotels, tour companies, restaurants, as well as training programs for college lecturers. Moreover, international programs on Hotel Management, Tourism Management and Food & Beverage Management were also created targeting trainees from Cambodia and China (Department of Tourism Investment Promotion, TAT, 2019).

In 2002, along with the government policy to improve the government's efficiency, the Ministry of Tourism and Sports was established, and the tourism mandate was divided among different agencies. As a result, the TAT as a state enterprise was only in charge of tourism promotion and marketing and leaving all other tourism-related tasks to the Ministry, a governmental body. In this way, the HTTI, under the supervision of the TAT was stripped of its original mandate and was turned into the training center exclusively for the TAT staffs until the present.

3 The Current Situation of the Thai Tourism Education

The growth of tourism development in Thailand leads to the creation of subjects and programs related to the hotel and tourism industry especially at the vocational and bachelor level. However, it is seen that these programs only aim to train students to satisfy the demand for skilled labor in the tourism industry in the country. Although there are some programs at the master and doctoral level, these higher education tourism programs seem to provide an opportunity for the staff or employees in government offices and private tourism business companies to upgrade their degrees.

3.1 Bachelor Level

At present, there are a large number of courses related to hotel and tourism industry taught at a bachelor's degree in colleges and universities across Thailand. The growing demand for labor in the tourism industry can be seen as the major stimulation to create hotel and tourism programs in those educational institutions in Thailand.

Following the establishment of regional tourist centers, including Chiang Mai, Bangkok, and Hat Yai, and the development of Phuket as a major beach resort in the south, these tourist cities also became centers for tourism education.

The growth of tourism education programs in colleges and universities across Thailand is obvious. Currently, there are 18 public universities, 37 campuses of Rajabhat Universities (formerly teacher colleges which used to open in many provinces throughout Thailand), 5 campuses of Rajamangala Universities (formerly technical colleges which were established in many provinces in Thailand), and 20 private universities offering tourism education. The public universities include Chiang Mai University, Mae Fah Luang University, Burapha University, Maejo University, Walailak University, Mahasarakham University, Srinakharin University, Nakhon Phanom University, University of Phayao, Khon Kaen University, Silpakorn University, Naresuan University, Kasetsart University, Prince of Songkla University, Ubon Ratchathani University, King Mongkuts University of Technology, Rajamangala Universities, and Rajabhat Universities. The private universities offering tourism programs are mostly located in Bangkok. Programs on Tourism Management and Tourism and Hotel Management are designed and taught in almost all of these educational institutions. Courses on Airlines Business Management, Kitchen Management and Culinary Arts, and Food and Beverage Management only appear in some colleges and universities. As a result, approximately 10,000 graduates from these educational institutions enter the tourism industry in Thailand each year.

In the case of Chiang Mai, a major tourist city in the north, a subject related to tourism study, Introduction to Tourism, first appeared in the beginning of 1980s in the Faculty of Humanity, Chiang Mai University, which was the first regional public university outside Bangkok and was found in 1964. In 1993, the Division of Tourism was created, offering minor courses for students who took languages as their major courses. In 2006, the program on 'Tourism and Hotel Management' was started as a four-year major program accepting each year around fifty students, who finished high school mostly from the north. During the second semester of the final year, all students have to intern mainly in hotels, airline companies, and tour companies. Students who were awarded bachelor degree from the Department of Tourism, Chiang Mai University, mostly work in hotels in Chiang Mai, Bangkok, and Phuket, as well as in airline companies. A few students work in tour companies or as an independent tour guides.

Tourism growth in Chiang Mai also inspired Maejo University, former public agricultural college, to create the School of Tourism Management in 2005, offering 'Tourism Development' programs first at the bachelor level, and then at the master level and eventually the doctoral level. Each year, approximately a hundred students are accepted to study at the bachelor's degree. Different from other universities, graduates from Maejo University, who are mainly trained in tourism development theories and practices, are mostly employed in the national park offices or sites and the Royal Project sites. Many of them work as adventure tour guides, and limited numbers of them work in the hotel industry.

Payap University, a private university located in Chiang Mai and funded by the Church of Christ in Thailand, opened a program on 'Hotel and Tourism Management', as well as an international program on 'Hospitality Industry Management', at bachelor level and accepts around 80 students to study each year. Almost all of the students are from the northern region, with only around 10 percent of them are from other parts of the country. Most of the graduates from Payap University work in the hotel industry in Thailand and only a small number of them work in airline and tour companies. Very few of these students further their study at the master level.

Rajabhat Chiang Mai University, a former teacher college, also created a program on 'Tourism Management' to train skilled labor for the industry. In addition, the other 36 Rajabhat Universities across Thailand, also opened similar tourism programs. Around 120 students are accepted to study in the tourism program in each Rajabhat University. That means each year, there are around 4,440 graduated students from all Rajabhat Universities. Approximately 20 – 30 percent of the graduates work in the hotel industry, 30 percent of them work as adventure tour guides, around 5 – 10 percent work in airline companies, and the rest of them work in tour companies or in their own businesses.

Hotel and tourism programs are opened in many colleges and universities in Bangkok, the capital of Thailand and the tourist center of the central part. These colleges and universities include public universities, private universities, and private colleges. For instance, Suan Dusit University, formerly Suan Dusit Rajabhat University which used to have a good reputation for its bakery and culinary arts course, established the School of Tourism and Hospitality offering a bachelor program on 'Tourism Management' and 'Hotel Management' in 1975 and later developed Airline Business course and international course on Management Services in 2007. The programs on 'Tourism Management' and 'Hotel Management' each accepts nearly 100 students, and about 50 students are accepted in the program of 'Airline Business'. Most graduates from Suan Dusit University work in hotels and tour companies in Bangkok, as well as other tourism agencies, for instance, TAT, and Thai Airways.

Ramkhamhaeng University, an open public university in Thailand, not only launched a program on tourism in the Division of Tourism, Faculty of Business Administration but also opened a special program on 'History for Tourism' in the Faculty of Humanities. It may be the first and only university program that aims to encourage students' knowledge on Thai history, and to conserve and translate cultural heritage.

Rangsit University, a private university which is owned by Dr. Arthit Ourairat, the former Speaker of the House of Representatives, former ministers of the Ministry of Technology, the Ministry of Public Health, and the Ministry of Foreign Affairs, established the College of Tourism and Hospitality. Thus, programs on 'Tourism and Hospitality Management' 'Hotel and Restaurant Management' 'Culinary Arts and Technology' 'Aviation Business Management' 'International Hospitality and Tourism' were created for interested students to gain their knowledge and to be trained for the tourism industry of Thailand, for instance, airline companies, tour companies, hotel industry, and restaurants.

Dusit Thani College, a private college in Bangkok, was established in 1993 by the owner of Dusit Thani Hotel, a luxurious chain hotel, and resort. Programs on 'Hotel Management' 'Kitchen and Restaurant Management' 'Tourism Management' 'Resort and Spa Management' 'Convention and Event Management', alongside international programs on 'Hotel Management' and 'Kitchen and Restaurant Management' are provided in this college. The majority of students come mainly from major tourist cities of Thailand. The tuition fees of this college are more costly comparing to similar programs in other colleges and universities. However, the good reputation and excellent services of the Dusit Thani Hotel may guarantee the quality of the programs. Graduates of this college mostly work in their own tourism-related businesses, some of them work in other hotels both domestic and abroad, and less than 10 percent works in hotels and resorts of the Dusit Thani chain.

The Faculty of Hospitality and Tourism of the Prince of Songkla University was found in 1993, having grown from the Phuket Community College(PCC) — the first community college in Thailand. It was formed as the first Faculty of Hospitality and Tourism in Thailand in order to serve the rapid growth of tourism development, especially in Phuket and along the Andaman Sea. Programs on 'Hospitality Management' 'Tourism Management' and 'Service Innovation Management' were introduced. Later, courses on 'Food and Beverage Services Management' 'Convention and Event Management' and 'Spa Management' were added. To respond to the demand of the tourism industry in the south, graduates from this faculty mainly work in hotels and tour companies in Phuket, and other beach resorts along the Andaman Sea.

3.2 Vocational and Certificate Level

Tourism education is also introduced in vocational colleges and private colleges. In this regard, around twenty vocational colleges across Thailand opened programs on 'Tourism and Hotel Business and Services' to satisfy students, wishing to obtain certificates and diplomas in tourism education. As a result, a two-year certificate program and a three-year diploma program are opened in these vocational colleges. Each year, roughly 120 new students register for each program in each college. Moreover, education at the vocational level also provides an opportunity for the minority groups in Thailand to be trained for their future careers in the tourism industry. It is seen that nearly 20 – 30 percent of students in the Chiang Mai Vocational College are minority groups, such as the hill-tribe groups, and the Tai migration people from Burma. After accomplishing their certificates or diplomas, 50 percent of the students from vocational colleges work as tour guides, the rest of them work in hotels, tour companies, and many of them further their education at the bachelor level in other colleges and universities in Thailand.

The International Hotel and Tourism Industry Management School (I-TIM), a private tourism college in Bangkok, was established in 1988 by the former Governor of the Tourism Authority of Thailand (TAT) and former Vice-Chairman of the World Tourism Organization (WTO), Colonel Somchai Hiranyakit, introduced a one-year program and a two-year certificate program on 'Hotel and Tourism Management'. Nearly a hundred students register in the programs each year. Over 60 percent of these graduates work in hotels in major tourist destinations, around 20 percent of them further their studies at a higher level, and 10 percent work abroad.

3.3 Master and Doctoral Level

A limited number of universities in Thailand launched programs at master and doctoral levels. However, the aims of these higher education programs are still connected to the same philosophy as the bachelor programs, which is to train higher-skilled labor to feed the industry.

For instance, the School of Tourism Management of the National Institute of Development Administration (NIDA), a public university, which only provides graduate programs, offers a master of management program on 'Integrated Tourism and Hospitality Management' and a doctor of philosophy program on 'Integrated Tourism and Hospitality Management'. Further, the extra classes for master program, are also opened in Bangkok and Phuket. This can provide an opportunity to interested students and staff in the tourism industry to upgrade their education.

In 2003, the Faculty of Hospitality and Tourism of the Prince of Songkla University, introduced a Master of Business Administration program on 'Hospitality and Tourism'. The philosophy of this program was then launched with the aims 'to prepare students for leadership positions in the hospitality and tourism industry in both Thailand and the broader global marketplace'. Interestingly, the program wishes to attract students 'striving to be the best practice and academic excellence in Thai hospitality and tourism'. The program aims to enhance students' career 'with a 2-year journey of transformation, an interface between academic insight and the real-life priorities of the business world in hospitality and tourism management'.

In 2005, the master program on 'Tourism Development' was found at Maejo University, and in 2007, a 'Doctor of Philosophy Program on Tourism Development' was launched. Mainly of about 35 master students are owners or employees of tourism companies, as well as lecturers from Rajabhat Universities, and principally of doctoral students, are lecturers of Rajabhat Universities. To upgrade their education for their career opportunity can be seen as their main inspirations to further the study.

4 Issues and Dilemmas

Through the growth in the numbers of tourism programs in colleges and universities across Thailand, it is found that tourism education in Thailand has not truly developed but has constantly repeated the same pioneer training courses of the HTTI, which was started in 1981, around 40 years ago.

Many universities established a school or a faculty of tourism and hospitality, which reflects the growth in numbers of tourism programs, as well as demand of the tourism industry in Thailand. However, most of these programs are based on tourism and hospitality management, although some programs on airline business, and restaurant and culinary arts are introduced in some colleges and universities. Through the aims or philosophy and contents of the programs, it can be viewed that those programs aim to prepare only skilled labor to supply the tourism industry of the country. In this regard, programs at vocational certificates and at bachelor levels can be recognized as the sources of the supply for the demand of the industry.

It is obvious that even programs at the master and doctoral levels in Thai universities are still aimed to support the demand of high-skilled staff of the industry, which is in contrast to the older philosophy of the higher education. Further, many students in the master and doctoral levels are already working as staff in tourism organizations or educational institutes. Studying at a higher educational level may provide better opportunities for their existing careers. In this way, the philosophy of the higher education programs to create thinkers or tourism researchers are not respected. This directly reflects the quality of tourism research in Thailand.

Additionally, in comparison to developed countries, tourism research, which is conducted by scholars in different disciplines or theories, is very limited in Thailand. Most of them typically aim to create new tourist destinations or products, using the ideas or theories of tourism planning and development as well as marketing and promotion. Moreover, the regulations by governmental research funding institution contribute to the transformation of tourism research in Thailand into a part of a government plan rather than academic research. For example, the National Research Council of Thailand made a call for application announcement for tourism research grant only on the theme 'Tourism Management', which focused on tourism development. The announcement mentioned only accepts research proposals that are in accordance with the 20 Year National Strategy.

Although tourism is an interdisciplinary study, there are very limited number of scholars in other philosophies or theories in Thailand conducting tourism research, comparing to the scholars in other societies in Asia, for instance, in China, Japan, and Korea. The lack of interdisciplinary tourism research in Thailand reflects the shortage of tourism research that is based on different academic ideas or theories. In fact, tourism research in Thailand should not focus only on tourism development or marketing and promotion because there are many effects from tourism development, such as, economic and socio-cultural impacts. To solve these tourism issues and challenges in Thailand, different lenses from different academic theoretical backgrounds are required.

5 Conclusion

The growth of tourism education in Thailand is in line with its rapid tourism development with the creation of a large number of programs at the vocational level and bachelor level in colleges and universities across the country. This reflects the success of tourism education to supply the demand of skilled labor of the Thai tourism industry. However, it can be observed that the present programs' design or philosophy of tourism education does not advance beyond the starting training programs of the first tourism educational institution in Thailand, the HTTI, which was founded in 1981. It signifies that the attitude of tourism education in Thailand has never changed from its beginning, which was established around 40 years ago.

Moreover, tourism programs at the higher educational level — the master and doctoral level — are mostly still attached to the vocation of creating higher skilled labor for the industry or upgrading existing industry labor. None of these educational institutions aims to train qualified tourism researchers in the country where tourism is the principal source of income and also the foundation of many socio-cultural impacts.

Additionally, there is very limited number of scholars with interdisciplinary background conducting tourism research. Compare to China, Japan, and Korea, where scholars with the training in sociology, anthropology, history, geography, psychology, and literature use their diverse ideas and theories to conduct tourism research. As mentioned, the growth of tourism in Thailand contributes to many economic and socio-cultural impacts. Thus, the ideas from interdisciplinary theories can be advantageous not only for the government sector for its strategies and planning, but also for the tourism business sector.

References

[1] CHIANG MAI UNIVERSITY. Department of tourism [EB/OL]. [2019-12-01]. http://www.human.cmu.ac.th/?page=organize.php&org_id=182be0c5cdcd5072bb1864cdee4d3d6e.

[2] CHIANG MAI VOCATIONAL COLLEGE. Course [EB/OL]. [2019-12-01]. https://www.cmvc.ac.th/2016/course/.

[3] FACULTY OF HOSPITALITY AND TOURISM, PRINCE OF SONGKLA UNIVERSITY, PHUKET CAMPUS. Master degree program [EB/OL]. [2019-12-01]. http://www.fht.psu.ac.th/fht/index.php/en/mba/program-highlights.

[4] JARUWAT C. The old story of the tourist organization of Thailand (TOT). The 36th anniversary of the tourism authority of Thailand [M]. Bangkok: Dok Bia Publishing, 1996.

[5] MAEJO UNIVERSITY. Master program in tourism development [EB/OL]. [2019-12-01]. http://www.tourism.mju.ac.th/master.html.

[6] MAEJO UNIVERSITY. School of tourism development [EB/OL]. [2019-12-01]. http://www.tourism.mju.ac.th/.

[7] PAYAP UNIVERSITY. Bachelor of business administration program in hotel and tourism management [EB/OL]. (2017-5-17) [2019-12-01]. https://programs.payap.ac.th/site/?p=306.

[8] RANGSIT UNIVERSITY. College of tourism, hospitality and sports [EB/OL]. [2019-12-01]. https://www.rsu.ac.th/hospita/.

[9] RAJABHAT CHIANG MAI UNIVERSITY. Department of tourism and hotel, faculty of humanities and social sciences [EB/OL]. [2019-12-01]. https://tourhotelcmru.wixsite.com/thcmru.

[10] RAMKHAMHAENG UNIVERSITY. Division of tourism, faculty of business administration [EB/OL]. [2019-12-01]. https://tourhotelcmru.wixsite.com/thcmru.

[11] SUAN DUSIT UNIVERSITY. School of tourism and hospitality [EB/OL]. [2019-12-01]. https://thmdusit.dusit.ac.th/.

旅游研究转变及其对泰国旅游教育的影响

Therdchai (Ted) Choibamroong　泰国国立发展管理学院

1　前言

泰国正处于政权交接的过渡时期,政局新变化也对旅游研究和教育产生了巨大影响。泰国目前有接近 130 所大学提供旅游和接待业课程。因此,在新时期,重新审视旅游研究和旅游教育之间的内在关系,分析新动向对旅游研究和教育的影响具有必要性。

泰国皇家政府的组织结构自 2002 年实施《重组法案》以来就再未变动。只有当新政府建立时,才会选举组建新的内阁。内阁由 19 个政府部门和总理府(OPM)组成。2019 年 6 月,内阁增设了高等教育、科研和创新部门。时任内阁总理是普赖努(Prayut Chan-o-cha)将军,他曾担任泰国皇家陆军将军和国家和平与秩序委员会的负责人。自组建新内阁以来,他在泰国实行了多项改革措施,这些新政策对旅游研究和旅游教育产生了巨大影响。

泰国的经济发展经历了 4 个阶段:1960 年前,泰国处于 1.0 发展阶段,国家专注农业发展;1960 年至 1987 年,泰国 2.0 战略发展的重心是轻工业;1987 年以来,泰国 3.0 战略发展重心转移到重工业领域。泰国 4.0 战略是泰国政府自 2016 年以来实施的国家发展政策,也是与旅游业发展紧密相关的战略计划。自此,泰国开始转向发展价值经济,国家致力于培育"智慧的企业、智慧的城市和智慧的人民"。基于价值经济的发展理念,泰国发展的关键是为强调内在体验的产品创造附加值。

新发展战略中也包括旅游业的转型。在当前的旅游业中,传统的旅游产品缺乏市场竞争力,新的旅游产品需要通过创意来打造体验,从而实现旅游产品的增值。通过设计产品体验来创造更多的价值已经成为泰国人的一句流行语,但是在为产品赋值之前,旅游业首先需要有行业标准,如果没有具体的标准,那么增值将毫无价值。

2 泰国旅游的发展现状

2018 年的数据显示,服务业占泰国 GDP 的比重达 56.1%。其中,旅游业是国家经济结构中的重要组成部分,为泰国创造了可观的收入,政府也将旅游业视作促进经济增长的重要产业。因此,旅游研究倾向于关注如何利用旅游业来为国家创造更多收入。当然,旅游业还有许多其他功能,如环境保护、文化传承、提高国际地位等。

根据 2016—2017 年的统计数据,在全球旅游人次上,泰国在世界中排名第 9～10 位,目前最大的游客群体来自中国,其次是马来西亚、俄罗斯、韩国、日本和印度;在全球旅游收入方面,泰国在世界排名第 4 位。这些数据表明,当前泰国在旅游人次和旅游收入方面做得非常成功。但近来,泰国宣布了"人数少,收入高"的国家旅游发展新观念。这意味着泰国将不再密切关注游客人数,而是会更多关注如何提高游客人均消费以及如何吸引更高质量的游客。

根据世界经济论坛 2017 年发布的旅游竞争力指数,泰国在 136 个国家中仅排名第 34 位。在过去,泰国拥有良好的旅游资源和营销战略,但是在旅游管理方面却不尽人意。管理不善造成的不良问题已经被政府注意到并给予重视。例如,从泰国旅游业整体表现来看,未来影响泰国旅游业的重大问题之一是环境的可持续发展(仅排名 122 位)。泰国政府对此十分重视,呼吁并资助更多有关这方面的研究。与此同时,旅游安全(136 个国家中排名第 118 位)也是一个严峻的现实问题,因此在旅游研究基金资助上,泰国政府对安全话题尤为关注。此外,健康和卫生(136 个国家中排名第 19 位)以及地面和港口基础设施(136 个国家中排名第 72 位)也都是关键性问题,是未来旅游研究基金资助的重点议题。

总的来说,上述问题都出现在旅游管理的供给侧一方,而不在于营销方面。泰国每年大约有 4 000 万游客到访,从游客人数上来看,泰国旅游业发展非常成功。即使出现政治动荡,游客仍然会在一两个月后继续回到泰国旅游。基于以上原因,政府在研究基金上会更多地侧重于旅游供应方面的研究问题。

3 旅游研究热点转变

在过去,泰国将旅游业当作刺激经济发展的工具。如今,泰国政府提出了新的旅游发展观。泰国旅游发展总体规划、可持续旅游规划或社区旅游规划等都是基于提高旅游竞争力来编制的。泰国过去认为，出色的市场营销策略就能保证旅游业的成功；但事实证明，旅游产品和旅游资源同样要纳入考虑范围。可持续性是目前旅游发展的关键词，甚至有人将它视作一种时尚趋势。过去的泰国人将关注重点放在需求侧上的旅游营销，但是忽视了谁来推动旅游发展并对其负责的问题。

泰国当前的学术研究重点发生了很大改变。泰国的研究者们认为有必要通过为旅游利益相关者和旅游机构增权，以及创造高质量的旅游产业网络来促进旅游业的进一步发展。目前泰国尚未形成强有力的旅游机构，因此，泰国政府将在未来的旅游研究经费中重点支持那些有关旅游利益相关者、旅游机构增权的研究，以促使他们更好地管理旅游资源。因为只有当旅游资源得到更完善的管理时，泰国的旅游产品才会有广阔的发展前景，旅游业本身才可以实现可持续发展，最终高质量的旅游服务才能吸引更多游客来泰国。因此，旅游行业必须从依赖市场和游客需求管理转向关注旅游资源供给端的开发与管理。

4 国家研究架构转变对旅游研究的影响

泰国皇家政府下属的高等教育、科研和创新部门自成立后随即制定并发布了一个新的国家研究架构，该架构由4个平台构成。第一个平台是关于人力资本和知识机构发展的科研创新平台；第二个平台是关于社会事务的科研创新平台；第三个是关于提高国家竞争力的科研创新平台；最后一个平台是关于泰国地区间均衡发展的科研创新平台。一直以来，旅游和接待业研究被视为整合国家发展和经济发展的工具，在平台基础上，该部门还将对大学和研究机构进行改革。

除了上述泰国研究架构中的4个平台，该部门还同时建立了3个新的教育委员会。第一个委员会的职责是推进泰国大学管理体制改革。政府认为泰国大学的行政管理需要以培养更多专业人士和研究生为目标。第二个委员会负责重新制定泰国大学的课程质量标准。过去实施的旅游和接待业课程标准是在澳大利亚政府和其他国家的帮助下制定的。因此，泰国将重新制定课程标准，新标准将更加注重实际工作中的综合学习。该委员会还将根据实际情况分配财政预算用来开发旅游和接待业课程。最后一个委员会负责重新制定学术职称申请流程。由于学术职称申请非常复杂和困难，泰国大学中拥有教授职称甚至助理教授职称的人数非常少。泰国目前大约有130所大学提供旅游和接待业课程，但该研究领域中没有人获得过教授职称，只有五六位副教授。

5 研究基金机构转变对旅游研究的影响

泰国政府会根据新成立的政府部门制定新的研究经费预算计划，如内阁批准了教育部 120 亿泰铢发展泰国一流研究机构的计划。然而，只有研究型大学才有机会获得额外的研究基金。2008 年，泰国有 7 所大学进入了泰晤士高等教育世界大学排名前 500 名，分别是朱拉隆功大学（Chulalongkorn University）、玛希隆大学（Mahidol University）、泰国农业大学（Kasetsart University）、泰国国立法政大学（Thammasat University）、清迈大学（Chiang Mai University）、孔敬大学（Khon Kaen University）和泰国宋卡王子大学（Prince of Songkla University）。这些学校作为国家研究型大学拥有获取额外研究基金的资格。而泰国国立发展管理学院（NIDA）只能授予硕士和博士学位，并且无法进入世界排名，因此不具有研究型大学的资格。

国家研究基金管理机构的重塑对泰国来说是一个具有冲击力和有些令人困惑的改变。在过去，国家政策研究和预算制定都由泰国国家研究委员会负责，如设立大学研究预算的分配方案；此外，泰国国家研究基金会主要负责研究项目的管理。现在新成立的高等教育、科研和创新部门取代了原来的泰国国家研究委员会，继续发挥国家政策研究和预算制定的职能。泰国国家研究委员会改组了原来的泰国国家研究基金会并承担起研究项目管理的职能。在新的研究基金管理机构的管理下，泰国将推进 4 个平台的研究工作。政府宣称在接下来的 3 年中，所有这些基金管理机构都将变成脱离政府管控的公共组织。而由于所有的部门都转换了工作职能，研究基金管理机构的未来发展依然充满不确定性。

泰国研究基金机构带来的改变可以总结为以下 6 个方面。第一，旅游研究者们的研究问题关注点将更加聚焦供给侧。第二，通过大学财政年度预算控制，用于直接研究的经费额度会有所减少。第三，政府将增加各地区的整体研究预算。政府曾经将专款分配给特定的大学，但是现在这种分配额度将减少。第四，研究基金管理机构的职能在国家层面发生了变化。第五，大学讲师需承担更多科研工作并发表更多的论文（发表 1 篇论文才能够成为课程助教和硕士学位论文的助教/在国家级刊物上发表 10 篇论文可以成为硕士学位授予主席/在 ISI 或 Scopus 上的国际期刊发表 5 篇论文能够成为博士学位授予主席）。第六，案例研究将在旅游和接待业的教学中得到进一步推广。

所有这些研究基金机构带来的变化都要求旅游和接待业的研究者发表更多论文。此外，这种趋势还要求研究者将他们的关注点从基础研究转移到应用研究和实验研究中来。创造新知识的基础研究将不再被大力推崇，因为政府认为创造知识并教授学生是一所大学的本职责任。更重要的是，大学还需要让学生将掌握的知识应用到解决国家旅游业发展的实际问题。这种应用型研究也叫问题导向型研究或者解决方案导向型研究，其研究成果必须可用于实践，应用于解决旅游业发展中的现实问题。

在研究方法论上，研究者过去重点关注量化研究，但高等教育、科研和创新部门表示旅游和接待业研究应该重视参与性研究。如果研究者在研究过程中只是单纯地外出发放问卷，并不会推动事情发生实质性的改变。研究者们必须采取实际行动，集思广益，进行如焦点小组访谈之类的参与性研究。人们对研究过程中能够带来的改变抱有积极的期望，因此，我们不能等到获得最终研究成果后再开始改变。

6 结论

建立新的高等教育、科研和创新部门对旅游研究和旅游教育产生了重大影响。泰国已经进入了国家发展4.0时代，更加重视价值经济的发展。目前，泰国在旅游收入和游客人数方面都非常成功，但旅游业竞争力仍然很弱，面临着诸多发展瓶颈。研究重点的转向以及新的国家研究架构和平台的转变都将极大地改变泰国旅游研究以及旅游和接待业研究者的生活。

Dynamic Movements of Tourism Research and Its Impacts to Tourism Education in Thailand

Therdchai (Ted) Choibamroong
National Institute of Development Administration, Thailand

1 Introduction

Thailand is now experiencing a period of political transition, which has a great impact on tourism research and tourism education. When talking about tourism curriculum in Thailand at present, there are approximately one hundred and thirty universities offering tourism and hospitality curriculum. Therefore, it is important to rethink how tourism research and tourism education are interrelated and how they are influenced by these new dynamic movements.

The present structure of the Royal Thai Government is unchanged since *the Administrative Re-organisation Act*, BE 2545 (2002). Once the Thai has a new government, a new cabinet subsequently forms. The cabinet includes 19 ministries plus the Office of the Prime Minister (OPM). This year, A new ministry, the 'Ministry of Higher Education, Science, Research and Innovation', was established in June 2019. General Prayut Chan-o-cha serves as new Prime Minister of Thailand now, who was the retired Royal Thai Army general officer and former head of the National Council for Peace and Order. He has changed a lot of things in Thailand and has implemented many new policies that have a great impact on tourism research and tourism education.

The Thai government has launched a policy to move the country, which is tightly related to tourism industry. They call it the philosophy of the country development Thailand 4.0. From Thailand 1.0 to Thailand 4.0, it summarized the four phases of evolution of Thai economies. On Thailand 1.0, the country focused on agriculture before 1960, and then turned to Thailand 2.0, which focused on light industries from 1960 to 1987. The focus area of Thailand 3.0 was in heavy industries since

1987. But from now on, the country has changed its focus on value-based economy, which was called Thailand 4.0. It means smart industry, smart city and smart people. By following that value-based economy, the point is that Thailand needs to create value adding to the products, which lay emphasis on experience insides.

Tourism industry is included in this philosophy as well. Nowadays in tourism industry, products can not be sold as before, because the key at present is to think about how to use creativity to add up more value to tourism products by selling experiences instead. One of the big words in Thailand at the moment is about experience design to create more value. But before value-adding, the tourism industry needs to have the standard first. If there is no specific standard, value adding will be worthless.

2　Current Development of Tourism in Thailand

The Tourism industry is very important to economic structure in terms of GDP composition, according to the data in 2018, with the part of the services accounting for 56.91%. Tourism has created considerable income for Thailand, so the government positions it as an important tool for economic development. Therefore, the tourism research tends to focus on how to employ tourism industry to create more income to the countries. However, tourism can be used for other things as well, for example, environmental conservation, culture conservation, uplifting the stages and so on.

According to the statistics 2016 – 2017, in terms of the number of global tourism visitors, Thailand was ranked Number 9 – 10 in the world. At present, the largest number of international tourists are from China, followed by Malaysia, Russia, South Korea, Japan, and India. For the global tourism income, Thailand was ranked Number 4 of the world ranking. This demonstrates that at present Thailand is very successful in terms of incomes and the numbers of visitors. The country has just announced the philosophy for tourism development in the countries using the word 'low volume high income'. This illustrates that Thailand won't pay close attention to the number of visitors, but pay more attention on how to increase the spending opportunity for tourists and how to attract visitors of higher-quality to Thailand.

However, according to the travel and tourism competitiveness index released from the world economic forum in 2017, Thailand was ranked No. 34 out of 136 countries. In the past, Thailand had good resources and attracting marketing strategies, but was not successful in terms of tourism management. These bad performances in management have already been noticed and taken seriously by the government. For example, the performance overview data showed that the critical issues for Thailand tourism in the future were about environmental sustainability (ranked No. 122), so the Thai government would take this into consideration calling for the research proposal for funding in the future. Besides, safety and security issues are serious at the same time (ranked No. 118), so that's why Thai government pays attention on safety and security topics for tourism research funding now. Health and hygiene (ranked No. 19) and ground and port infrastructure (ranked No. 72) are also critical issues that tend to be the focus for research funding in the future.

In summary, all of these are the supply side of the tourism management, not from the marketing side. That is because Thailand is very successful regarding the number of visitors, with approximately nearly forty million visitors coming to Thailand. Even there is political turbulence, tourists will still come back to the country in one or two months. So, the government concerns and focuses more on the supply side of tourism issues management for research funding.

3 Dynamic Research Focus Movement

In the past, Thailand has employed tourism industries as a tool for economic development. Nowadays, the government has come up with new philosophy for Thailand tourism development. Master plans in Thailand for tourism development, sustainable tourism development or community tourism are all based on tourism competence. Thailand used to believe that the best marketing can guarantee the success. But it has been proved that tourism product and tourism resources are also necessary to be taken care of. Sustainability is the key word at the moment, some also see it as a fashion word. In the past, Thai people focused on tourism marketing, the demand side, but ignored who should be responsible for it and who could make it forward.

At the moment in Thailand, there is a dynamic research focus change movement. Thai researchers believe that there is a need to empower the tourism stakeholders and the tourism mechanism, and create a high-quality network to move the tourism industry forward. Thailand's tourism doesn't have a strong mechanism now, so in the future, for tourism research funding, the Thai government will focus on empowering the tourism stakeholders to enable them to better manage tourism resources. And then with more perfect resources, the Thai tourism products are expected to have a promising future. The tourism itself will also achieve sustainability, and finally, the high-quality tourism service will bring more visitors back to the country. Therefore, the tourism industry will shift their concerns to relying more on tourism resources development instead of marketing and demand management.

4　The Impact of a New National Research Framework on Tourism Research

The Royal Thai Government by the 'Ministry of Higher Education, Science, Research and Innovation' has launched a new national research framework for Thailand Development immediately after its establishment. The research framework of Thailand is divided into four platforms. First of all, it is about research on human capital development and knowledge institution development. Secondly, it is the platform on research and innovation for challenging social issues. Thirdly, it's about research and innovation for creating national competitiveness. And the last one is the research and innovation for area-based development and inequality reduction in the country. As for 'Tourism and hospitality research', it has been seen as a tool integrated for national development and economic development. In addition to that, the new ministry announced to reinvent the university and research institutes as well.

Along with four platforms of Thailand research framework, the minister also sets up three new committees simultaneously. The first one is the committee to reform the administrative system of all Thai universities. The government believes that the administration of Thai universities needs improvements to produce the professionals and graduate students.

The second one is the committee to re-standard Thailand qualification standards of the curriculums in Thai universities. The qualification standards for tourism and hospitality were built with the help of Australian government and other countries previously. So, Thailand will make new standards which pay more attention on real work integrated learning. The new ministry will also allocate some budgets to develop tourism and hospitality curriculum based on a real approach.

And the last one is the committee to reconsider the process to apply for academic titles in Thailand. At the moment there are approximately one hundred and thirty universities in Thailand offering tourism and hospitality curriculum. The number of professorships or even assistant professors is quite small, which is very complicated and challenging to apply for. In tourism and hospitality research, there are only five or six associate professors in Thailand, and there is no professor at all.

5 The Impact of Dynamic Research Funding on Tourism Research

Once Thailand has the new ministry, the government provides new budgets for research. The scheme for developing Thailand's leading institutions has been approved by the cabinet, and the Education Ministry will spend 12 billion Bhat on it.

However, only research universities in Thailand have the chance to get extra research fund. Up to now, there are seven Thai universities that appear in the Top 500 of the Times Higher Education — QS World University Rankings in 2008 qualified to become national research universities. They are the universities of Chulalongkorn, Mahidol, Kasetsart, Thammasat, Chiang Mai, Khon Kaen and Prince of Songkla. NIDA cannot be research university because it has only Master and PhD programs and they cannot enter to the world ranking.

As for reinventing the national research funding agencies, it is a big bang and a little bit confusing in Thailand. Previously there was National Research Council of Thailand responsible for country research policies and budgeting. They set up the framework that allocated the budget to the university. Besides, Thailand Research Fund was used to do the research management. But now, the National Research Council of Thailand was changed by Thailand Science Research and Innovation, which is now in charge of country research policies and budgeting. Thailand Research Fund was reformed by National Research Council of Thailand, which is now responsible for research management. Thailand is going to have four platforms with a new research funding agency responsible for them. In the next three years, the government says that all these four funding agencies will turn to be the public organizations out of government control. Since they all changed the responsibility, what will happen in research management and research funding is still uncertain in the future.

The dynamic research funding in Thailand can be summarized into six aspects. Firstly, Thai researchers have changed the focus on tourism research issues to focus more on the supply side. Secondly, there has been a reduction of direct research fund through the Fiscal Year Budget of the Universities. Thirdly, the government will increase the overall research budgets of the countries. It used to allocate the money special to particular universities, but that money will be reduced. The fourth one is the change in functions of the research funding agencies at the National level. The fifth one is the requirements of university lecturers to undertake research and publish more papers (1 paper for being able to be in the curriculum and a thesis advisors for the master degree/ 10 national journal publications to be a chair for master thesis examination/ 5 international journal publications in ISI or Scopus to be a chair for PhD thesis examination). Finally, the case studies are promoted for tourism and hospitality teaching in Thailand.

All of these dynamic research fundings require the tourism and hospitality lecturers to undertake and publish more papers. Furthermore, this trend also asks the lecturers to shift their concern from basic research to applied research or experimental development research. Basic research that creating new knowledge will be less promoted because the government believes that it is the duty of the university to create knowledge and teach the students. Moreover, the university needs to make that knowledge to be able to solve the problems for tourism developments in this country as well. Once the research is done, the output must be applicable for the practice. So, the applied research also has a nickname called problem-based research and another one called solution-targeted research, because in Thailand, knowledge must be applied to overcome the problems created by the tourism industry.

In terms of research methodology, lecturers used to see importance on quantitative research, but the ministry said tourism and hospitality research should emphasize on participatory action research. The new ministry doesn't recommend the lecturers just go out and deliver questionnaires. Nothing happened along the way of research undertaking. Lecturers have to take real actions calling for participation like brainstorming, focus group and so on. Because positive changes are highly expected along the ways of research undertaking, we can't wait until we have the research output finally.

6　Conclusion

The establishment of new ministry of Higher Education, Science, Research, and Innovation has great influence on tourism research and tourism education. Thailand has come into the era of new philosophy of the country development named Thailand 4.0, which emphasizes on value-based economy. Currently, Thailand is very successful in terms of incomes and the numbers of visitors, but still has weakness in tourism competitiveness and faces many critical issues in the tourism industry. The dynamic research focuses movement, and the new framework and platforms will change Thailand a lot on tourism research as well as the lives of tourism and hospitality lecturers in Thailand.

手工艺对旅游扶贫的直接和间接影响：对越南承天顺化省案例的研究

Le Minh Tuan　越南顺化大学

1　旅游扶贫

近十年来，评估旅游业对当地经济的影响，尤其是旅游业对贫困的影响，一直是学术界和旅游咨询界关注的话题（Asley 和 Mitchel，2007）。作为经济和社会的重要议程，在许多国家尤其是越南等发展中国家，旅游业已被用作减轻贫困的有效战略工具。在 2000 年纽约千年首脑会议上，联合国将"消除极端贫困和饥饿"确定为八项全球千年发展目标中的首要任务，"扶贫旅游"是有助实现这一目标的工具之一，并被公认为是减贫和可持续发展的关键因素（UNWTO，2007）。

"旅游扶贫"（pro-poor tourism，PPT）一词于 1999 年提出，目的是将"贫困置于旅游议程的核心"，并"增加贫困者的净福利，确保旅游增长有助于减贫"（Ashley，2001）。在大众理解中，它是一种旨在利用旅游业减贫的发展方法（Gascón，2014）。自那时起，为实现这一目标已采取了许多举措。世界旅游组织的"旅游与扶贫"报告认为旅游业是贫困者为数不多的发展机会之一，呼吁采取行动发展旅游（WTO，2002；Goodwin，2006）。

旅游业似乎在以不同的方式影响着社区居民。Mitchell 和 Ashley（2007b）指出，事实上存在 3 种不同的影响途径：直接影响、间接影响和动态影响。这 3 种影响途径共同反映了一个综合的图景，回答了"旅游业如何影响贫困者"的问题。直接影响是指直接参与提供旅游产品和服务的过程中所产生的收入和非财务影响。间接（或次要）影响反映了非旅游部门通过为旅游业提供商品（如为酒店装修所需提供的食品或手工艺品），或旅游收入再投资所获得的间接收益。通常情况下，当贫困者居住在旅游目的地或附近时，他们参与旅游业相对容易，旅游减贫的直接影响显著。相反，当贫困者住在离旅游目的地较远的地方时，间接影响可能更为显著（Mitchell，Ashley，2007b）。动态影响是指旅游业增长下的更为广泛的影响，如基础设施、自然环境、私营部门发展、出口部门、工资变化和土地价格变化。

根据 Mitchell 和 Ashley（2007b），旅游业可以通过 3 种不同的途径——直接影响、间接影响和动态影响——影响贫困者（如图 1 所示）。下图改编自 Mitchell 和 Ashley（2007b）。

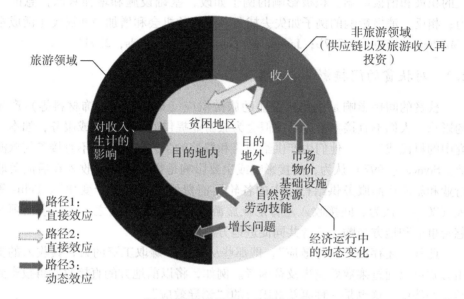

图 1　扶贫旅游的三种影响途径

2　扶贫的影响

2.1　对扶贫的直接影响

扶贫的直接影响是当贫困人口直接参与或提供旅游产品时，旅游业对贫困人口的影响。这种影响包括通过旅游工作向市场提供旅游商品和服务所获得的劳动收入，如旅行社、酒店、旅游公司、餐馆、纪念品销售等；此外，它也包括非劳动收入以及目的地内部积极和消极的非金融生计变化。

劳动收入：劳动收入是通过直接参与为旅游业提供产品和服务的非管理就业收入，它是旅游业向穷人提供资源的主要途径，特别是在非技术性工资较高、创业环境较差的发展中国家（Mitchell，Ashley，2007b）。

非劳动收入：通常情况下，它是由社区获得的收入而非个人或家庭的收入。它有多种存在形式，如游客或旅游公司的捐赠、商业社区与私营部门的企业合资、社区旅游或公园管理局的收入分成（Mitchell，Ashley，2007b）。这一收入十分重要，能使缺乏直接经济参与能力的人受益，这对当地居民（特别是偏远农村地区居民）来说尤为重要。

生计影响：旅游业可以通过现金流动的方式对贫困者的生计生活带来更广泛的积极和消极影响。积极影响的例子如改善基础设施和增强获取信息的能力；相反，消极影响的例子如失去捕鱼、放牧的机会和增加当地居民生活成本（Mitchell，Ashley，2007b；Jamieson，Goodwin，Edmunds，2004）。

2.2 对扶贫的间接影响

扶贫的间接影响是由非旅游业的旅游供应（如食品、装饰材料等）产生的影响。人们不直接参与旅游，但会为旅游业提供商品、材料或服务，如本研究中的村民或工匠，他们生产供给酒店和餐馆的工艺装饰品，不直接参与旅游业。Stynes（1997）认为，间接影响或次要影响是指"旅游业收入在后向关联行业和旅游产品服务供给行业中的各轮再消费所导致的生产变化"。Pellis等人（2014）认为，间接收入是肯尼亚旅游业三大间接影响之一，其余两项是慈善事业和地方采购，三者共同促进地方经济的发展。

此外，还存在"诱导效应"，即那些从旅游中赚取工资的人，其收入的支出方式可以通过乘数效应惠及贫困者。例如，将以前地方的直接收益再投资到地方经济中，这也是一种惠及贫困者的"诱导效应"。

这些间接影响不易衡量，因为它们并非由旅游业本身直接造成的，而是与旅游关联产业的发展相关（Pellis等，2014）。Mitchell和Ashley（2007b）认为，由于旅游业需要一系列根植于国民经济的供应链支持，因此，旅游业和非旅游业之间的联系十分重要。供应链之所以重要，是因为它们可以"在地理上分散旅游业的利益，使之不局限于目的地"。贫困现象多集中于农村地区，大多数贫困者从事农业和手工业，可能无法遇见游客，进而无法从旅游业受益。这些间接影响对减贫的影响是明显的，但在生活中相对被忽视，这是由间接影响的复杂性和地理范围的不确定性导致的，因此需要在所研究的目的地网络中进行长期、广泛和深入的观察。

2.3 对扶贫的动态影响

扶贫的动态影响是对自然资源、企业家精神、要素市场等的影响。旅游业的发展可能需要在更广泛的层面上发展其他因素，如基础设施和公共服务体系、市场生产结构、人力资源等。例如，农民可能会受到来自政府境外旅游投资的重大影响，这些投资可能增加经济、文化、社会或环境成本，但它也能在基础设施、地方通信/网络、人力资源等方面带来积极效益（Pellis，2014）。

以旅游为导向的基础设施改善也可以使非旅游业受益，进而使当地居民也从中受益（Mitchell，Ashley，2007b）。此外，旅游业也能通过给予当地企业与国际接轨的机会，来促进企业发展（Pellis 等，2014）。

长期来看，积极与消极影响的类型是多样的，包括旅游业税收的再利用，将其用于可造福贫困者的公共产品；出口产业的变化，入境旅游带来的国际接轨刺激了出口产业，而汇率升值也导致农业出口衰退；地方创业经济的发展；自然资源的退化与保护；旅游业引起的劳动力市场或土地价格的变化等。

尽管动态影响也有助于减少贫困，但动态影响还未得到充分研究（Mitchell，Ashley，2007b）。动态影响的复杂性、多样性和长期性使对它的评估与对间接影响的评估一样困难。因此，许多旅游经济影响研究都关注相对容易测量的直接影响、指示性间接影响和部分动态影响。

综上所述，很少有关于旅游目的地的研究能够成功地对这 3 种类型的旅游扶贫影响进行评估。此外，我们还需要更多的证据来支持旅游扶贫在发展战略中的作用，同时也需要数据和系统的文件来证明旅游业的扶贫影响（WTO，2004；Goodwin，2006；Ashley，Mitchell，2007）。间接影响的程度取决于每个目的地的情况，本研究把重点放在传统的手工业村落上，它们的位置离省内的旅游景点很远，不利于其直接参与旅游业的发展。他们的手工艺产品主要以间接的形式而非直接的方式为旅游需求服务。

3 宝拉村概述——承天顺化省最大的传统手工艺村之一

宝拉村位于承天顺化省广田县，距顺化市 15 千米，处博河（Bo river）北中段。它是越南著名的传统手工艺村，有竹藤编织手工艺品。据广田县人民委员会副主席介绍，宝拉村有着非常悠久的发展历史。这个村庄形成于 600 多年前，在过去，人们利用农闲时间，通过生产竹藤制成的家庭用品（如篮子、鱼缸、托盘等）来赚取额外的收入。所有工艺品都是由越南特产的竹子制作而成。随着时间的推移，为了满足人民日益增长的需求，宝拉村的竹藤编织产业也在迅猛发展。目前，它已成为村民的重要收入来源。除了生产满足农耕需要的产品外，宝拉村还生产竹藤灯笼、竹袋、鸟笼、花瓶、扇楠等多种极具美感的手工艺品，供应宾馆、饭店、咖啡馆等场所。

4 研究方法

本研究采用深度访谈法，结合个人观察和案例研究，针对 3 个不同的群体展开研究,他们是合作社工作的工匠、不为合作社工作的家庭工匠和非手工艺人(农民或小企业主)。虽然他们都生活在宝拉村,但访谈结果显示,他们对贫困和旅游业的影响有自己的看法。此外,本研究还采访了当地领导和人民委员会副主席、党组书记等权威人士,对贫困问题、政策问题和时间演化问题等有一个全面的了解。最后,本研究与直接组织带客的导游和旅行社进行了面谈,便于收集游客的旅游需求、旅行目的和承天顺化省手工艺旅游发展概况等信息。访谈提纲包括17个关键的开放性问题,分别涉及3个主题:个人对贫困的看法、乡村旅游业的发展和手工艺对乡村旅游扶贫的影响。此外,本研究还对当地政府人员及导游进行了访谈,多维度探讨旅游扶贫问题。

5　对贫困的定义

正确理解贫困,明确界定贫困人口,清晰衡量贫困,这对当地发展来说是至关重要却又十分复杂的,特别是不同地区、国家或目的地,对贫困的依赖程度不同(Jamieson,Goodwin,Edmunds,2004;Holden,2013)。

通常,扶贫工作都是针对特定目标群体进行的,这些群体被定义为处于某一"贫困线"之下的人群,贫困线是通过家庭收入或消费支出计算的。

但这可能是不够的,因为贫困可以被解释为一个更广泛、更动态的概念,即更多维的概念。不同的维度包括收入、资产、环境、教育、健康、歧视和脆弱性(Baulch,Bob,Neil McCulloch,2002)。它们反映了构成人类生活质量的不同方面。Mayoux和Chambers(2005)认为,贫困或贫穷的定义已经从一个经济概念发展到一个更广泛的概念,其中包括文化、社会和环境因素,这也是衡量扶贫旅游影响的相关挑战之一(Hummel,2015)。

多维贫困指数(MPI)是联合国开发计划署(UNDP)和牛津贫困与人类发展倡议(OPHI)在其2010年《人类发展报告》中首次发布的一项新的贫困指标(Alkire,Conconi,Roche,2012)。MPI认为,贫困是一个多层面的问题,表现为缺乏能力,无法满足人类生活的基本需求。除了收入贫困线,它还增加了3个维度:健康、教育和生活水平,这3个方面被认为是人类生活的三大基本需要(如图2所示)。

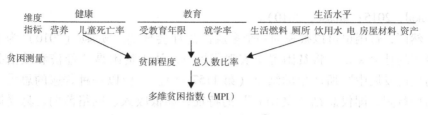

图2 多维贫困指数①

6 贫穷的多维视角和关系方法

若将贫困视为一个多维问题，它往往与越南宏观背景下的收入分配问题相关联。本研究表明，贫困在实际中常被定义为缺乏收入，即那些没有钱来满足最低生活需求的人被定义为贫困者。但在不同的受访者群体中也发现了对贫困的不同理解，他们认为贫困也与缺乏食物或生活水平低下有关。前人研究中也有相似的发现。Truong（2014）发现，Sapa（越南北部的一个农村城镇）的贫困者也将贫困定义为缺乏大米；Holden、Sonne 和 Novelli（2011）指出，加纳的贫困者可能认为贫穷不仅指缺乏金钱，也指缺乏参与开发过程的机会。总的来说，依据这些观点，贫困不应被视为一个单一的经济层面，而应在不同的地点/国家/地区做出不同的解释，即贫困取决于情境。

本研究结果表明，当地社区对贫困的感知主要还是基于收入指数。由于人们对贫困的认识仍然局限于一个政府贫困框架下的单一维度，因此，他们认为的贫困成因主要反映在收入方面。宝拉村的案例表明，对农耕的严重依赖和老龄化是贫困重现的结构性条件。因为严重依赖农耕，所以大多数村民的收入很低，极不稳定，并存在风险。而年龄是限制他们获得工作机会的另一个因素。因此，这两个原因都直接影响他们的收入能力。

此外，在越南，贫困也常被定义为不同的类别（绝对贫困和相对贫困），并被视作一个社会问题，而非一个宏观社会现象。"绝对贫困"是指无法满足生活最低需求，如食物、衣服和住所等。"相对贫困"是指无法达到可接受的合理生活水平（Dhakal，2015），这一概念取决于社会生活水平的变化，并会随着时间的推移而变化。此外，人们的阶级、种族、年龄、地区或宗教也会影响其对"可接受的合理生活水平"的判断（Dhakal，2015）。贫困者不是一个同质群体，不同社会对贫困的认识不同，因此，对贫困的理解十分复杂

---

① 资料来源：http://hdr.undp.org/en/content/multidimensional-poverty-index-mpi

(Dhakal，2015；Mosse，2010)。

然而，贫困也可以被视为一个多层面的社会现实。Mosse（2010）为了解释贫困的社会关系，将贫困置于宏观背景下，认为贫困是"经济和政治关系在历史的发展中"所产生的结果（第1157页）。不应以一种普遍的思维方式去考虑贫困，即仅总结"贫困者"的特征，如低收入、网络薄弱、易受风险影响等，而应在更广泛的经济社会体系中思考，在这个体系中，贫困者在关系影响下递归地产生（Mosse，2010；Tilly，2007）。此外，Mosse（2010）认为，贫困与资本主义经济体的"正常"发展进程密不可分。他还指出，融入市场的过程给贫困者带来了一些好处（如流动性），但也加深了社会不平等，尤其是农村地区。事实上，贫困在越南是一个长期的挑战。贫困、经济增长和社会不平等之间的关系也是近年来共同研究的课题之一（Dao，1994）。Nguyen（2016）认为，减贫、社会不平等和经济增长之间存在密切的关系。如果社会能持续高速发展而收入不平等现象能持续减少，那么贫困率在规模和水平上都将降低（Nguyen，2016）。越南以前的研究表明，减贫成功主要反映在与社会平行的发展政策的结果上。

此外，贫困的相对性也表明，长期来看，造成贫穷和不平等的社会进程的另一后果是社会排斥。宝拉村的案例展示了贫困与社会排斥之间的相互关系。首先，贫困主要集中在农村地区。贫困者的收入可能很低，但他们的日常开支和储蓄机会也会减少。然而，当他们遇到健康问题或生命危险时，他们往往需要借钱或抵押资产来克服。经济困难直接影响贫困者获得健康服务和教育的能力。总体而言，贫困者往往技能较低，获得生产资源（资本、技术等）和信息的机会较少，因此，他们在找工作时会面临许多困难。此外，在政治方面，宝拉村的贫困者大多是老年人或丧失劳动能力的工人，因为贫穷，他们失去了在社区中的政治角色。他们往往在村庄或合作社的管理中不担任任何职务，甚至对他们是否贫困的判断也取决于其他更有劳动能力的人。因此，贫困是工作关系中常常要面对的。此外，性别不平等也是一种社会排斥。合作社80%的雇员都是女性，其原因是男性比女性更容易获得更高收入的工作。越南农村地区男女不平等的状况仍然相当普遍，女性雇员参加合作社是因为当她们的丈夫做其他工作时，她们也可以在家务活之外工作赚钱，以此来解决贫困。女人只扮演一个次要的角色来支持家庭中的男人。这些原因对农户的收入产生了不利影响。低收入不仅影响家庭的消费能力，而且对家庭的其他决策也会产生重大影响，如子女的教育等。

因此，被视为贫困者的人在社会上会感到被"孤立"。通过对贫困相对性的审视，我们可以看到贫困嵌套于就业、社会、文化和政治关系之中。例如，宝拉村的案例表明，贫困者往往严重依赖农业，因为这是小规模的工作，收入低，容易受到风险。但这并非他们的错，他们在农村出生长大，那里的农业是主要产业，也是传统产业。此外，由于他们生活在农村地区，获得教育、卫生或通信等社会服务的条件非常有限，这些限制直接影响到他们寻找工作的能力以及他们在社会中的政治地位。

然而，尽管 Mosse（2010）反对个人主义，强调"贫穷和不平等是社会分工和身份认同的结果"（第 1156 页），但本研究结果表明，贫困并不总是在"更广泛的背景"下运作，不能忽视个人属性。即使在政治、经济和地理环境相同的情况下，人们在不同程度上可能是穷人或非穷人。宝拉村的情况说明了这一点。该村的贫困家庭往往不参与手工业的生产或服务，而是主要依赖农业。

国家政府和地方当局也在界定贫困方面发挥了作用。自 2015 年以来，国家政府首次将贫困视为一个多层面的问题，并应用 MPI 来衡量贫困。根据越南的 MPI 框架调整的当地指标也反映了政府对贫困问题认识的进步。除了用收入指数来划分贫困线之外，与越南社会经济特征相符的基本社会服务水平不足的指标也被纳入贫困衡量的范围。

但这一应用无意中硬性地将贫困衡量标准强加给了人们。贫困者的衡量标准是严格的指标，政府认为这些指标准确地反映了贫穷问题。此外，地方当局和当地人民被迫接受使用 MPI，而目前 MPI 在本质上只是衡量和反映贫困的指标，而非具体说明或解释贫困原因的指标，没有把贫困纳入社会关系中。贫困被定义为一种状态，这是国家政府在地方界定贫困和如何有力地衡量贫困水平的一部分。因此，MPI 框架的话语权制约着扶贫的效果。此外，宝拉村村民目前主要通过收入标准来界定贫困，这也显示出他们在从地方政府获取 MPI 方面的局限性。

根据以上讨论，通过用关系方法补充多维视角，可以形成对贫困更全面的认识。贫困被认为是产生社会性的结果，并与社会不平等和社会排斥联系在一起。另外，多维视角间接地反映了这些情况，其指标是获得基本社会服务的机会不足，包括保健服务、教育、住房、清洁水/卫生和信息的水平，以及按收入标准划分的贫困线。

7　旅游的间接影响及其对减贫的贡献

宝拉村是一个典型的受旅游的间接影响远大于直接影响的例子，特别是在经济方面。虽然旅游业的参与和直接影响微小，但间接影响的扶贫作用，特别是通过合作社的作用，得到了相当大的体现。本研究表明，宝拉村的地理距离和旅游吸引力的缺乏是限制游客数量、限制旅游对村落产生直接影响的两个主要原因。Lee 和 Kim（2011）认为，地理距离和旅游吸引力是决定游客目的地选择的重要因素。直接影响涉及对旅游就业收入的直接分析，宝拉村与这两个因素相关的局限会影响游客数量，同时也限制了旅游扶贫的直接影响。然而，通过像生产手工艺品的途径为旅游业服务，旅游业以间接的方式对村民的生活产生了巨大影响。这些间接影响对经济等层面的减贫目标具有积极作用。

最明显的扶贫影响是为当地提供就业机会。宝拉村相当一部分人从事旅游手工艺品的生产。因为手工艺品生产对年龄、性别、创业资金要求不高，因此被村民，特别是贫困人口认为是理想的就业选择。参与手工业生产不仅有助于村民利用农闲时间，还为中年妇女、老年人/丧失劳动能力的人提供了就业机会。通过参与手工艺品生产，人们可以在缺乏机会和缺乏权力的情况下改善贫困。由于工艺生产能为当地提供就业机会，使村民可以赚取额外收入，因此拥有传统工艺村的地区在执行减贫任务方面比其他地区更有优势。此外，特别是对于老年人和丧失工作能力的人来说，找到工作可以用工资收入养家，并建立社会关系，尤其是还可以加入合作社，这有助于他们减少自身的无用感。

农村地区的就业机会在越南农村地区实施减贫中发挥着重要作用（Nguyen，2014；Truong，2014）。虽然越南的贫困主要集中在农村地区，但拥有手工艺村庄或手工艺人的地区摆脱贫困的概率更大（Ngo，2005）。此外，在越南国家总理关于 2016—2020 年国家可持续减贫计划的第 100/2015/QH13 号决定中，越南政府还决定，减贫必须与创造就业同步进行，"授人以鱼不如授人以渔"。目前如果仅从单一维度（收入贫困）来认识贫困，宝拉村村民正在通过参与手工艺品生产、服务旅游需求来增加收入，有效地利用这一优势来减少贫困。但如果从多维角度考虑贫困，这个问题将会截然不同。尽管他们的平均收入高于贫困线，但他们仍然缺乏获得基本社会服务的机会，特别是在医疗保险/服务、信息获取和教育等方面。

另一个值得考虑的明显发现是，旅游业间接对妇女福利和权利产生了积极的影响。虽然农村地区的性别不平等是与贫困密切相关的社会排斥的原因之一，但如前所述，增加妇女的收入（HBT 为她们提供了金钱收入和工作机会），直接影响了这一问题。此外，合作社以妇女为主体，作为一个集体组织，发挥着平台的作用，不仅有助于妇女交流经验、解决生活问题，而且有助于妇女接受培训和教育。经济影响和非经济影响之间的关系也是重要发现。经济间接影响有助于影响与贫困相关的其他因素，如获得教育、信息或住房质量的能力。利用间接影响，转而生产更高端的产品以满足旅游需求的适当方向，这也给宝拉村社区带来了一些互惠互利的机会，如参加节日活动、接受来自国家政府和地方当局的支持政策（设计手工艺培训、机械、资本等）。

此外，宝拉村传统竹编合作社这一集体组织的建立也是旅游业间接影响的结果，对宝拉村的发展也起着重要的作用。

8　合作社——一种受旅游间接影响的产物，在农村地区发挥了重要作用

本研究结果表明，合作社不仅在执行减贫任务中发挥了重要作用，而且对生产流程的重新定向、手工艺村与旅游业的联系以及发展传统工艺村旅游方面也做出了重要贡献。

Amin 和 Berstein（1996）强调了农业合作社在农村发展中的代表性作用，Tran 等人（2012）指出了农业合作社在连接生产消费和提供市场产出方面的重要作用。首先，宝拉村合作社发挥着生产者代表的作用，获取和收集市场信息，然后向村里的生产者提供关于时间、数量、价格和方向等订单信息，以便向不同的市场生产和供应产品。此外，由于生产点和消费点之间的地理距离较远，合作社在产品收集和市场运输方面起着协调作用，从而节省了流通成本，为生产者带来更高的利润率。此外，合作社也是政府惠民政策的中介。来自政府的支持是多种多样的，如投资、政策机制、区域或村庄发展战略。

合作社的重要作用还体现在它是为旅游需求生产手工艺品的"先锋"，为宝拉村带来了更高的经济效益。在越南，合作社被认为是支持农村地区发展的最重要组织（Dung，2011）。合作社有助于创造就业机会、发展市场、提高农村地区的收入以及帮助人们获得社会服务（Chambo，2009）。

在此必须指出合作社并非由政府初创，它是"一个通过共同拥有和民主控制的企业，成员们自愿联合起来满足其共同的经济、社会和文化需求和愿望的自治协会"（国际合作社联盟，1995 年）。但合作社自成为村里合法认可和具有代表性的组织以来，与当地政府有着密切的关系。大多数发展旅游手工艺品的投资政策，如提供机械或培训，都集中在合作社。这个问题无形中造成了合作社和其他一些有手工艺品生产传统的家庭之间的隔阂。合作社手工艺产品的复杂程度和生产数量远高于家庭，这是使手工艺品价格、收入以及合作工匠收入提高的主要原因。事实上，也有一些家庭整体或合作参与合作社，为旅游业生产手工艺品。但其他一些家庭生产手工艺品以满足农业需求，因为他们想保持家庭传统及原有的商业关系。同时，尽管手工艺品生产主要是用于旅游业，但合作社也接收农业需求品或家庭用品的产品订单，无形中减少了该村一

些生产家庭的利益和机会。因此，政府在支持和投资合作社政策中的优先次序也在一定程度上造成了社会不平等，并使宝拉村的贫困人口再度出现。

此外，从本研究的结果来看，要维持和发展合作社，仍存在一些局限性和困难。

首先，合作社管理委员会的管理能力仍然有限。合作社管理委员会由合作社社员选举产生，设理事1人、副理事2人、会计1人。大多数合作社经理在担任管理职务之前没有受过管理技能和专业知识的教育和培训。作为合作社的代表，他们在收集订单、与地方当局合作、接受政策和实施规划方面的作用仍然有限。在向顾客提供产品时，由于订单运营经常处于被动状态，因此经常出现延误。其次，资金限制是合作社发展的另一个问题。营运资本通常只占平均资本的一小部分。据了解，由于缺乏资本，许多发展生产和投资方面的合作受到限制，无法使基础设施和商业运作现代化。合作社往往是被动的，期待着政府的投资，开办展览馆就是一个例子。最后，动员和支持村民参与合作社也是一个挑战。尽管与越南农村地区的平均收入水平相比，合作社的平均收入相对较高，特别是对于老年人和丧失劳动能力的人来说。但正如合作社主任所提及的，劳动力短缺和订单延迟交货的情况仍然频繁发生。由于技术要求或工作时间的限制等原因，村民参与合作社的积极性受到限制。这个问题还涉及该村面临的世世代代维持传统手工艺村的挑战。在手工艺术品生产给宝拉村村民带来有利影响的情形下，如何维护和发展传统村落是一个具有挑战性的问题，也是需要解决的问题。

总之，尽管存在局限性，但像宝拉村竹藤编织合作社这样的集体组织在越南农村地区显示了其独特的重要性。它不仅是一个重要的合法的中介，为适应不断变化的社会需求而调整工艺的生产方向，而且为当地人提供就业机会和额外收入，因而为减贫做出了重要贡献。

9 结论

旅游业已被确定为越南和顺化省发展地方经济和实现减贫任务的关键产业。传统手工艺村具有多样化的体系，它在当地人民的社会经济生活中发挥着重要作用，特别是在农村地区。因此，在利用手工艺进行减贫方面，承天顺化省被认为具有直接优势。本研究以传统的竹藤编织村宝拉村为研究对象，系统梳理了贫困的理论基础和方法，揭示了当地居民对贫困的认知，并通过对扶贫直接和间接影响的理解探讨了手工艺与扶贫之间的相互关系。

在全球范围内，对贫困的认识和衡量从单一层面转向多维层面。人们不再仅仅从收入贫困的角度来理解贫困。除了缺乏收入，贫困的多维视角将健康、教育和生活水平不足等基本社会服务水平不足的几个指标结合起来，克服了单一维度在衡量贫穷方面的缺陷。

越南政府自2016年起对新MPI进行调整和应用，越南的扶贫随之进入新的发展阶段。然而，本研究表明，越南的扶贫仍处于早期阶段，并受到诸多限制。虽然越南政府认为贫困是一个多层面的问题，包括基本社会服务的各个方面，但收入指数仍然是当地人普遍用来界定贫穷的主要指标。应用新的MPI中的非收入指标来定义和衡量贫困，将显著改变贫困率，但也给实施和衡量过程带来许多挑战。此外，改变地方人民和地方政府对贫困的看法，从传统方式转变为各级地区和地方层面的多维方式，是最具挑战性的步骤之一。

此外，通过对贫困相关的因素进行梳理，贫困也可以被认为在社会关系中发挥多层面影响。减贫、社会不平等和经济增长之间有着密切的关系。这项研究还表明，社会排斥是社会进程的另一个结果，从长期来看，社会进程继续产生各种形式的贫困和不平等。找工作的能力受教育程度、收入性别、收入年龄、应对卫生服务风险的能力和生活水平等因素的限制。

界定贫困的方式对于衡量和解决贫困问题具有重要意义。由于人们仍然将贫困视作"缺乏收入"，而金钱被视为满足贫困人口基本需求的工具，因此，执行减贫任务的首要关键行动应是增收。

旅游业对扶贫的影响因素主要包括地方因素和渠道因素。宝拉村的案例表明，虽然地理区位限制和旅游联系不足，是阻碍村民直接参与旅游业的关键因素，进而限制了旅游业的直接影响，但当地人通过参与手工艺品生产间接满足旅游需求，仍然能从旅游业中获益。

严重依赖农业和个体老龄化是贫困的主要原因和共同特点，旅游对宝拉村在提供工作机会和增加收入方面的间接贡献特别高，特别是对妇女和中老年群体来说，这表明手工艺对旅游扶贫的潜在影响非常大。此外，虽然越南农村地区的性别不平等是造成与贫困密切相关的社会排斥的原因之一，但宝拉村的案例表明，旅游业通过为妇女提供机会、增加福利待遇和权利，间接地促进了减贫。此外，合作社等集体组织在手工艺品生产的定位和转型过程中是必要的，也发挥了重要作用，满足了旅游业发展对手工艺村的需求。尽管政府支持下的合作社因与非合作社成员的传统生产家庭之间存在一定的生产竞争关系而导致新的贫困现象，但它在发挥村庄代表性组织的作用、提供更高收入的工作、市场拓展等方面产生了更大的扶贫效应，将这个村庄和旅游业联系了起来。

虽然拥有极具发展潜力的多样化传统工艺村体系，但总体而言，宝拉村和承天顺化省等地的手工艺服务仍处于起步阶段，其对扶贫产生的影响仍主要体现在经济方面。宝拉村的案例表明，手工艺村只是在为满足旅游业的直接和间接需求而在手工艺品生产中发挥作用，它仍然不是真正的工艺旅游村，也不能提供真正的旅游体验。

　　加强当地社区和旅游业之间的联系是加强旅游扶贫的有效途径，因为这直接涉及建立旅游业和贫困者之间的联系。但目前宝拉村和旅游业之间的联系还很薄弱。合作社是目前旅游价值链中唯一有贫困者参与的环节。因此，有必要增进合作社管理委员会在联系旅行社和村庄方面的关键作用，提高当地人特别是贫困者在旅游价值链中的参与度，开发潜在的当地服务供应商，以增强对扶贫的影响，发展手工艺生产地的旅游。

Pro-poor Direct and Indirect Impacts of Handicraft-Based Tourism: The Case of Thua Thien Hue Province, Vietnam

Le Minh Tuan, School of Hospitality and Tourism, Hue University

1 Pro-poor Tourism

Over the past decade, the assessment of tourism impacts on the local economy is the topic that has received many attentions in academia and tourism consultancy, especially the impacts of tourism on poverty (Asley, Mitchel, 2007). Being part of an economic and social agenda, tourism has been used as an effective strategic tool to alleviate poverty in many countries, especially in developing or poor nations such as Vietnam. At the Millennium Summit in 2000 in New York, the United Nations (UN) identified Eradicate, 'extreme poverty and hunger' as the first and most important task of the eight Global Millennium Development Goals and 'pro-poor tourism' is one of the tools that might contribute to achieve this goal and was recognized as one of the key agents to poverty reduction and an important contributor to sustainable development (UNWTO, 2007).

The term 'pro-poor tourism' (PPT) was coined in 1999, with the aim to put 'poverty at the heart of the tourism agenda' and 'increase net benefits for the poor and ensure that tourism growth contributes to poverty reduction' (Ashley, 2001). It is understood as a development methodology that aims to use tourism for poverty reduction (Gascón, 2014). Since then, many initiatives have been carried out to pursue this goal.

Tourism and Poverty Alleviation by the World Tourism Organization argued that tourism was one of the few development opportunities for the poor and hence constituted a call for action (WTO, 2002; Goodwin, 2006). Tourism seems to affect community residents in different ways. Mitchell and Ashley (2007b) indicated that there were three different pathways in fact: direct effects, indirect effects and dynamic effects. These three kinds of effects together reflect a comprehensive picture to answer the question of 'how does tourism affect poor people?'. The direct effects describe the income and non-financial influences from direct participation in the process of providing tourism products and services. Contrast to the direct effects, the indirect (or secondary) effects reflect indirect earnings from non-tourism sectors by either supplying goods for tourism (e.g. food or handicraft products for hotel's decoration demand) or describe impacts from reinvestment of earnings from tourism in the local economy. Usually, the pro-poor direct effect is significant when the poor live inside or near the destinations where they can participate in tourism relatively easily. Conversely, when the poor live further away from tourism destinations, the indirect effects may be much more significant (Mitchell, Ashley, 2007b). Dynamic effects are about the wider impacts from tourism growth such as infrastructure, natural environment, development in private sector, export sector or changes of wages, and land prices.

According to Mitchell and Ashley (2007b), tourism can affect the poor in three different pathways: direct effects, indirect effects and dynamic effects (Figure 1). This figure was adapted from Mitchell and Ashley (2007b).

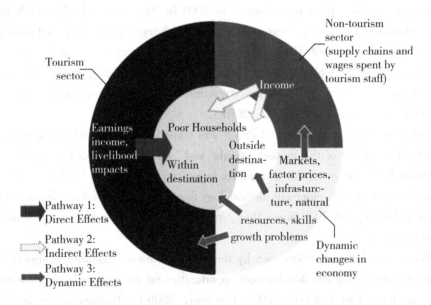

Figure 1　Three impact types of tourism on the poor

2　Pro-poor Effects

2.1　Pro-poor Direct Effects

They are impacts from tourism sectors to the poor when the poor are directly involved and supply tourism products. They are labour incomes earned from tourism jobs providing tourism goods and services to the market such as tour operators, hotels, travel companies, restaurants, selling souvenirs, etc. Besides, it also includes the non-financial livelihood changes in both positively and negatively within the destination.

● Labour income: According to Mitchell and Ashley (2007b), this is the major element of the resource flow to the poor from tourism sector through earnings of non-management employment directly involved in providing products and services for tourism, especially in developing countries where unskilled wages are high and having a weak entrepreneurial environment.

● Non-labour income: Normally, it is the income that accrues to the community instead of individuals or households. They exist in many forms, for example: donation from tourists or tourism companies, commercial community and private sector joint ventures, community tourism, or revenue shares from park authorities (Mitchell, Ashley, 2007b). This amount of income is important because people lacking the capacity for direct economic participation, which will become beneficiaries. This may be important and significant for people who become involved, especially in remote rural areas.

● Livelihood effects: Tourism can affect the wider livelihoods of the poor in many positive and negative ways through cash flows. Improvements of infrastructure and enhancements of ability to access information are positive examples, conversely, lost access for fishing or grazing, increasing living cost for local people are negative examples (Mitchell, Ashley, 2007b; Jamieson, Goodwin, Edmunds, 2004).

2.2　Pro-poor Indirect Effects

They are impacts that are occurred by supplying tourism from non-tourism sectors (e.g. food, decoration materials). People who are not directly involved but supply goods, materials, or services for tourism sectors. Villagers or craftsmen in my research are examples. They are producing and supplying handicraft products for hotels and restaurants as decorations. According to Stynes (1997), indirect impacts or secondary impacts are 'the production changes resulting from various rounds of re-spending of the tourism industry's receipts in backward-linked industries' and small industries that are supplying products and services to tourism business such as hotels or restaurants. According to Pellis et al. (2014), indirect earning is one of the three most important tourism's indirect impacts in the case of Kenya. The rest two are philanthropy and local purchasing in contributing to the local economic development.

In addition, there are 'induced effects', where those people earning salaries from tourism spend their income in ways that can benefit the poor through co-called multiplier effects. For example, the re-investment of former direct earnings in the local economy can be called an induced effect.

These indirect effects are not easy to measure because they are not directly created by the tourism sector itself, but they deal with the developments of other sectors that are affected significantly by the tourism sector (Pellis et al., 2014). According to Mitchell & Ashley (2007b), because tourism often requests a range of supply chains that can be extended deeply into the economy, the link between the tourist and non-tourist sector is important. Supply chains are important because they can 'disperse benefits of tourism geographically, well beyond the destination' (Mitchell, Ashley, 2007b). Obviously, poverty is concentrated in rural areas with the majority of people engaged in agriculture and handicraft industry but with farmers, villagers, or craftsmen — their need may never meet tourists to benefit from the sector. These indirect effects are relatively neglected despite its impacts for reducing poverty are apparent and significant (Mitchell, Ashley, 2007b). This is due to the complexity and geographic reach of indirect effects that are hard to grasp, hence demanding extensive observations over time amongst wide networks of the destination studied.

2.3 Pro-poor Dynamic Effects

They are impacts on natural resources, entrepreneurialism, factor markets, etc. Tourism development can entail the development of other factors that are in the wider levels such as infrastructure and public service system, changes in the productive structure of market, human resources, etc. For example, farmers might be significantly affected by foreign tourism investments from the government that possibly bring economic, cultural, social, or environmental costs. However, it also can bring positive benefits in infrastructure, local communication/networks, human resources, etc. (Pellis et al., 2014). The improvement of tourism-oriented infrastructure can also benefit the non-tourism sector then under which local people also benefited (Mitchell, Ashley, 2007b). In addition, by giving opportunities to interaction between local businesses and international tastes, clients, tourism can stimulate enterprise development (Pellis et al., 2014).

These positive and negative longer term impacts are very varied, and include spending of tax collected from the tourist sector on public goods that benefit the poor; stimulation of export industries from knowledge of international tastes resulting from inbound tourism; decline in agricultural exports due to appreciation of the exchange rate; development of a more entrepreneurial local economy; degradation or conservation of natural resources; changes in labour market or land prices due to tourism.

Although the dynamic effects also contribute to reduce poverty significantly, they are still under-researched (Mitchell, Ashley, 2007b). Its complexity, diversity, and also in a long term make the assessment just as difficult and time-consuming as indirect effects. As a result, many economic impact studies of tourism delimit themselves to relatively easy impact measurements of direct effects, indicative indirect and dynamic effects.

As mentioned above, there are very few tourism destinations studied to evaluate all three types of tourism pro-poor impacts successfully. Besides, we need more evidences to support the movement of PPT in development strategies and also still lack data and systematic documents to prove the pro-poor impacts of tourism (WTO, 2004; Goodwin, 2006; Ashley, Mitchell, 2007). The magnitude of the indirect effects is different depending on each destination. In my research, I focus on traditional handicraft villages, where their locations are quite far from tourism sites of province and unfavorable for developing tourism directly. Their handicraft products serve mainly for tourism demands and more in indirect ways than direct ways.

3 Overview of Bao La—One of the Biggest Traditional Handicraft Villages of Thua Thien Hue Province

Bao La is one village belonging to Quang Phu ward, Quang Dien district, Thua Thien Hue province. It is 15km far from Hue city and along to the northern middle section of Bo river. It is a famous traditional handicraft village of Vietnam with handicrafts of bamboo and rattan weaving. According to the Vice Chairman of People's Committee of Quang Dien district, Bao La has a very long development history. This village was formed more than 600 years ago. In the past, from the starting point as extra jobs-leveraging, the off-farm time to earn extra income by producing household items made by bamboo and rattan, such as some kinds of baskets, fish containers, pallet, etc. All of them are made by special Vietnamese bamboo. Over time, bamboo-rattan weaving in Bao La village has a strong development to ensure the increasing demands of the people. Currently, It has become a significant income source of villagers. Besides producing products to serve the needs of agriculture and farming, Bao La village is also producing many kinds of high aesthetic handicraft products such as bamboo-rattan lanterns, bags, bird cages, vases, fans nan, and other furniture items to supply hotels, restaurants, and cafes.

4 Research Methodology

This research used in-depth interview methodology, combined with personal observations and case study for three different groups: (1) craftsmen who working for the Co-operative, (2) household craftsmen who are not working for the Co-operative and (3) non-craftsmen (farmers or small businesses). Although all of them are living in Bao La village, the interview results show that they have their own interesting perceptions about poverty and tourism's impacts. Besides, this research also conducted interviews with local leaders and authorities such as the Vice Chairman of People's Committee and the Party Secretary to have a comprehensive view concerning issues of poverty, policy, and local changes over time. Finally, interviews with tour guide and tour operator that directly organize and take the tourists to the village will help to collect information of the demand of the tourist, purposes of trips, and general status of the development of handicraft-based tourism in Thua Thien Hue province. The interview guides included 17 key open questions that respectively related to three main topics: (1) personal perception of poverty, (2) development of Tourism in the village and (3) pro-poor impacts of HBT in the village. Besides, this research also conducted interviews with local authorities and tour guides to have a multi-dimensional perspective for research issues.

5 Defining Poverty

It is essential but complicated to properly understand poverty, define who counts as poor and how we can measure poverty, especially if we consider its dependency on different regions, countries, or destinations (Jamieson, Goodwin, Edmunds, 2004; Holden, 2013).

Very often, the effort of poverty alleviation is made for targeted groups, defined as being under a certain 'poverty line', which is calculated through either income or consumption expenditure of a household.

However, it may not be sufficient because poverty can be interpreted as a broader and dynamic concept, that is rather more multidimensional. Different dimensions can be income, assets, environment, education, health, discrimination and vulnerability (Baulch, Bob, Neil McCulloch, 2002). They reflect different aspects that make up the quality of human life. According to Mayoux and Chambers (2005), the definition of poverty or poor has been considered from an economic concept to a wider one that includes cultural, social, and environmental factors. This is also one of related challenges for measuring the pro-poor tourism impacts (Hummel, 2015).

Multidimensional Poverty Index (MPI) is a quite new poverty measure that was developed by the United Nations Development Programme (UNDP) and the Oxford Poverty and Human Development Initiative (OPHI) published the first time in their 2010 *Human Development Report* (Alkire, Conconi, Roche, 2012). MPI considers poverty as a multidimensional issue that is shown by deficiencies, inability to meet the basic needs of human life. Besides income poverty line, it adds three dimensions including health, education, and standard of living, which are recognized as 3 main basic needs of human life (Figure 2).

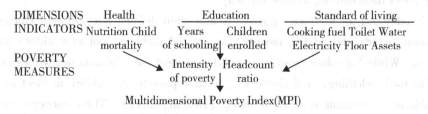

Figure 2 Multidimensional poverty index

6　Multidimensional Perspective and Relational Approach to Poverty

In terms of considering poverty as a multidimensional problem, it often associates with the income distribution issues in the wider context of Vietnam. This study demonstrates that poverty is indeed typically defined in practice as lack of income. In other words, those, who do not have enough money to meet the minimum needs in life, are formally defined as the poor. However, other poverty views are also found among the different groups of interviewees: poverty in their perspective also relates to either lacking of food or suffering in low living standards. Some previous studies underlined the similar yet differentiated findings. While Truong (2014) found that poor people in Sapa (a rural town in the north part of Vietnam) also defined poverty as lacking of rice; Holden, Sonne & Novelli (2011) showed that poor people in Ghana may perceive poverty as lacking of money and opportunities to participate in the development processes. Overall, these evidences suggest that poverty should not be considered as a single economic dimension and instead become interpreted differently in differing locations/nations/regions. In other words, poverty is highly context specific.

This study result shows that poverty still perceives based on income index by the local communities. Because people's perceptions of poverty are still limited to a single-dimensional description, which matches with governmental framing of poverty, therefore these poverty's causes that they gave still just also mainly reflect the income aspects. The case of Bao La village showed that the heavy dependence on agriculture/farming and elderly were the main (perceived) structural conditions in which poverty became reproduced as a condition. While depending heavily on agriculture/farming, most villagers' incomes are low, unstable, and risky. Furthermore, age is another factor that limits their opportunities to work. Thus, both of these causes directly affect their earning income capacity.

In addition, in Vietnam, poverty is also often defined into different categories (absolute poverty and relative poverty) as a social problem, not as a wider societal process. While 'absolute poverty' is inability to meet the minimum necessities of life such as food, clothing, and shelter; 'relative poverty' is inability to meet an acceptable and reasonable standard of living (Dhakal, 2015). These concepts change over time, depending on the changes in the living standards of the society. Besides, class of people, ethnicity, age, region or religion can also impact the judgments of 'acceptable and reasonable standards of living' (Dhakal, 2015). Therefore, the poor are not a homogenous group and poverty is perceived differently in various societies, and then, again, it is complicated to compare and fully understand poverty (Dhakal, 2015; Mosse, 2010).

However, poverty can be also considered as a multidimensional social reality. Mosse (2010), in order to explain the social relations of poverty, claimed that poverty is a consequence of historically developed economic and political relations by locating poverty into a broader context. Poverty should not be considered by a common way of thinking poverty as a condition that uses characteristics of 'the poor' such as low income, weak networks, vulnerability to risk, and so on. It should be considered on the wider economic-social systems in which the poor recursively become produced as relational effects (Mosse, 2010; Tilly, 2007). In addition, Mosse (2010) argued that poverty is inseparable from 'normal' development processes of capitalist economies. He also indicated that the integration process into markets gave the poor some benefits (e.g. mobility) but also deepened the social inequality, especially in rural areas. Indeed, poverty has been a long-term challenge in Vietnam. The relationship among poverty, economic growth and social inequality is also one of the common research topics in recent years (Dao, 1994). According to Nguyen (2016), there is a strong relationship among poverty reduction, social inequality, and economic growth. The poverty rate will be reduced in both size and level if society has a high and sustainable growth together with decreasing inequalities of income (Nguyen, 2016). Previous research in Vietnam showed that the successes in poverty reduction primarily reflected the results of development policies parallel with social equality.

In addition, the relational approach of poverty also indicates that social exclusion is a consequence of social processes that make poverty and inequality in the long term. The case of Bao La shows a remarkable relationship between experiencing poverty and social exclusion. Firstly, poverty is mostly concentrated in rural areas. Poor people may indeed have a low income, but also experience lower daily expenses as well as saving opportunities. Yet, when they get health problems or life risks, they often have to borrow money or pledge their assets to overcome such shocks to their livelihood. Economic difficulties directly affect the ability to access health services as well as the education of poor people. Overall, the poor often have low skills, less access to production resources (capital, technology, etc.) and information. Therefore, they face many difficulties in finding jobs to earn money. Moreover, in terms of politics, poor people in Bao La are mostly old people or incapability workers. Because they are poor, they lose the political roles in their community. They usually do not hold any position in management of the village or the Cooperative. Even determining whether they are poor/not poor belongs to others who are more capable as a workforce. Poverty is hence inherent in work relationships. In addition, gender inequality is also a social exclusion. The reason that made 80 percent of employees of the Co-operative are women is that men can easier get higher income jobs than women. The status of unequal treatment between women and men in Vietnam rural areas is still quite common. Female employees participate in the Co-operative because it seems as a good solution for them to earn money beside their house/farm work when their husbands do other jobs. Women only play a minor role and support the men of their family. These causes have an adverse effect on the income of farmer households. Low income not only affects to the spending ability but also has a major impact on other decisions of households such as their children's education or household's items.

Thus, people who are considered poor, in fact, become socially isolated. By using a relational approach to poverty, we can see that poverty becomes to position in employment, social, cultural, and political relations. For example, the case of Bao La shows that poor people often depend heavily on farming/agriculture because this is a small-scale job, low income and easy to get risk. However, this is not their fault. They were born and raised in rural areas where agriculture is the main sector and also tradition. Moreover, because they live in rural areas, the access conditions to social services such as education, health or information are very limited, and these limitations affect directly on their abilities to seek jobs and also their political positions in society.

However, although Mosse (2010) rejected the individualism to emphasize on poverty and inequality as an effect of social categorization and identity, this study result shows that poverty does not always operate on broader context and disregard to the individual attributes. People can be poor/non-poor in different levels even if they share the same political, economic and geographical contexts. It is illustrated by the case of Bao La village. The village's poor households often did not participate in handicraft productions/service sector, instead, they dependence mostly on agriculture.

National government and local authorities also play roles in determining poverty. For the first time (from 2015), national government recognized poverty should be considered as a multidimensional issue and applied the multidimensional poverty index (MPI) to measure poverty. Moreover, adapting local indicators to the MPI frame in Vietnam also reflects the advancement of poverty understanding of the government. Besides lining poverty by an income index, indicators of insufficient levels of basic social services, which consistent with the socio-economic characteristics of Vietnam, are included to measure poverty.

However, this application inadvertently imposes on people about the poverty measurement standards rigidly. The poor is measured rigidly by indicators, whose government believes that they reflect poverty accurately. In addition, local authorities and local people automatically have to accept to use MPI while MPI essentially only measure the indicators reflecting poverty at the present rather than specifying or explaining the causes but not putting poverty in social relations. Poverty is continuously also reproduced as a condition that is part of how powerful national government orchestrated definitions of poverty and define poverty locally. Therefore, the relational achievements or poverty is constrained by the discursive power of MPI framework. Besides, Bao La villagers also show their limitations in the access to MPI from local authorities through mainly using income criteria to define poverty at the present.

From what discussed above, more comprehensive perspectives of poverty are given by complementing multidimensional perspectives with the relational approach. Poverty is considered as a result produced socially and associates with social inequity and exclusion. In other hand, multidimensional perspective indirectly reflects these things by its indexes of insufficient levels of access to basic social services, including health service, education, housing, clean water/hygiene, and information along with a poverty line by an income index.

7 Indirect Effects and Its Contributions for Poverty Reduction

Bao La village is a typical example where the indirect effect is much greater than the direct effects, especially in terms of the economic aspect. While the participation and the direct effects of tourism are still insignificant, pro-poor roles of the indirect effects, particularly via the Co-operative's roles, are expressed considerably. This study shows that geographical distance and the lack of tourism attractiveness/

connections of Bao La are two main reasons that limit the number of tourists, the direct participation of tourism's local, as well as the direct impact of tourism to the village. According to Lee & Kim (2011), geographical distance and tourism attractiveness are regarded as signification factors for determining the destination choices of tourists. While the direct impacts deal with straightforward analyses of direct earnings through tourism employment, these limitations/disadvantages of Bao La related to these two factors affect directly to the number of visitors as well as limit the direct impacts. However, by the transition to produce handicrafts serve tourism, tourism had a significant impact on the lives of the villagers in indirect ways. These indirect impacts are mostly positive for poverty reduction goals, particularly in terms of economic.

The most significant and obvious pro-poor impact is the ability of providing job opportunities locally. A considerable part of Bao La village is engaged the handicraft productions for tourism. Because making handicraft productions does not strictly require age, gender, or startup capital, thus it has been considered as an ideal employment option for villagers, especially the poor. Participating in handicraft production not only helps villagers take advantage of off-farm time but also provides jobs to middle-aged women and elderly/loss of working capacity people. By participating in producing handicrafts, people can improve two of three aspects of poverty: lack of opportunities and powerlessness. The rural areas that own traditional craft villages have more advantages than others in terms of implementation of poverty reduction tasks because of the ability in providing jobs and earning extra income locally by participating in craft production. In addition, especially for the elderly and incapable of working people, getting jobs helps them feel less useless by helping their family using their incomes and also building social relationships, particularly when they join the Co-operative.

Employment opportunities for rural areas play an important role in the implementation of poverty reduction in Vietnam rural areas (Nguyen, 2014; Truong, 2014). While the poverty rate in Vietnam is mainly concentrated in rural areas, those rural areas which owns craft village/occupation has a higher chance to get rid of poverty (Ngo, 2005). In addition, in Decision No. 100/2015/QH13 of National Prime Minister about national program for sustainable poverty reduction period 2016 - 2020, Vietnamese government also has identified that poverty reduction must be in parallel with job creation— 'giving a fishing rod is better than fish'. At the present, if only recognized poverty from single dimensional approaches (income poverty), Bao La villagers are taking advantage effectively to reduce poverty through ability to increase their income by participating in handicraft production serve tourism demands. However, if considering poverty under the multidimensional approach, this issue will be extremely different. Although their average income is higher than the poverty line, they still show their shortages of accesses to basic social services, especially in health insurance/service, information access and education.

Another remarkable finding that should be taken into account is that tourism indirectly impact on increasing benefits and entitlements for women. While gender inequality in rural areas is one of the reasons of social exclusion related closely to poverty as mentioned before, through increasing income for women, HBT has directly impacted this issue by providing them with sources of monetary income and working opportunities. Besides, with the majority of members are women, the Co-operative, as a collective organization, plays a role of a platform, which helps women not only exchange experiences and address their life's issues but also be trained and educated. In addition, the relations between economic impacts and non-economic impacts are also found. Economic indirect impacts contribute to affect other factors in the relation to poverty such as the ability to access education, information or housing quality. Besides, the proper orientation of switching to produce higher sophisticated products serving tourism demands as well as taking advantage of the indirect impacts also bring some mutual benefits to Bao La community such as opportunities to participate in Festivals, receiving support policies (design handicraft trainings, machinery, capital, etc.) from the national government and local authorities.

Moreover, the establishment of collective organization as the traditional Bao La bamboo-rattan weaving Co-operative, which is considered as a result of tourism's indirect impacts, also plays important roles in development of Bao La village.

8 Co-operative—a Product of Indirect Impacts and Its Important Roles in Rural Areas

This study results show that the establishment of the Co-operative not only plays an important role in the implementation of poverty reduction mission but also contributes significantly to the redirection for production process, connection between craft villages with tourism sector and development handicraft-based tourism for traditional crafts villages.

While Amin & Berstein (1996) gave prominence to the representative role of agricultural Co-operatives in rural development. Tran et al. (2012) indicated its important role in linking between production-consumption and providing market outputs. Firstly, the Bao La's Co-operative plays functions as the representative of producers, access and collect market information, then gives the producers in the village forecasts about time, quantity, price and orientation in order to produce and supply products to different markets. Besides, because of the big geographical distance between production and consumption point, the Co-operative plays a role as a focal point in charge of collecting and delivering to the markets, therefore, saving the circulation costs that may bring a higher profit margin for producers. Moreover, Co-operative is also served as an intermediate receiving the support policies for villagers. These supports from the government are diverse. It could be investments or policy mechanisms or orientations for region/village.

The important role of the Co-operative is also reflected through being the 'pioneer' of the transition into producing handicrafts for tourism demands to bring a higher economic efficiency for Bao La village. In Vietnam, co-operatives are considered as the most important organizations in supporting the development of rural areas (Dung, 2011). Co-operative contributes to creating jobs, developing markets, improving the income for rural areas as well as helping people to access social service (Chambo, 2009).

It must be claimed that the Co-operative is initially not a product of the government. It is 'an autonomous association of persons united voluntarily to meet their common economic, social, and cultural needs and aspirations through a jointly-owned and democratically controlled enterprise' (ICA, 1995). However, since the Co-operative became an accredited and representative organization with legal status for the village, it has a close relationship with the local government. Most of the investment polices developing handicraft production for tourism such as machinery or training are focused on the Cooperative. This issue inadvertently creates the gap between the Co-operative and some households that also have tradition in producing handicrafts. The differences in sophistication and in the number of handicraft products of the Co-operative are much higher than households. This is the main reason that made the higher price, revenue as well as Co-operative craftsmen's income. In fact, there were some households that entirety or cooperatively participated in the Co-operative to produce handicrafts for tourism. On the other side, some other households produce handicraft for agriculture demand because they want to maintain their family's tradition and previous business relationships. Meanwhile, although production is mainly for tourism, the Co-operative also accepts orders of products that serve agriculture demand or coincide with households. Thus, the existence of the Co-operative inadvertently reduces the benefit and opportunities of some producing households in the village. Therefore, the Co-operative and government' priorities in policies for supporting and the investment for the Co-operative also contributes to a part of negative impacts on social inequality and reproducing poverty in Bao La.

Besides, from this study's result, there are still limitations/difficulties that should be mentioned in order to maintain and develop the Co-operative.

Firstly, management capacity of the management board of the Co-operative remains limited. The Co-operative's management board including one director, two deputy directors, and one accountant were elected by Co-operative members. The majority of Co-operative managers have not be educated and trained on management skills and professional knowledge before taking the management positions. Their roles are still limited as being a representative for the Co-operative to collect order, work with local authorities, receive policies, and implement outlined plans. There are delays while supplying products to customers as their orders show they are still passive in operational activities. Secondly, the limitation on capital is another problem of the development of the Co-operative. The working capital usually just accounts for small part of the average capital. They also admit that lack of capital causes the limits to Co-operative in many development production activities and investment to modernize both infrastructure and business operations. The Co-operative is often passive and looks forward to the investment from the government, the exhibition building is an example. Finally, the issue of mobilizing and supporting villagers to participate in the Co-operative is also a challenge. Although the average income in the Co-operative is relatively high if compared to the average income level of rural areas of Vietnam, especially for elderly and incapable of working people, the shortage of labor and the late order's delivery still happens frequently as mentioned by the Co-operative director. There are some reasons given such as skill requirements or restraints of working time that suggest the limitations, which encourages the villagers to participate in the Co-operative. This problem also relates to the challenge of maintaining traditional handicraft villages through generations that the village is faced with.

With the advantaged contributions producing handicraft brings to Bao La villagers, the question of how to maintain and develop the traditional village for young generations is a challenged question and needs to be addressed.

In conclusion, despite there are limitations, a collective organization like Bao La bamboo rattan weaving Co-operative showed its importance for rural areas in Vietnam. It not only serves as an important legal represented intermediate to orient the craft's production for meeting the changing needs of society, but also shows its important roles in contributions for poverty reduction mission by its ability in providing jobs and chances to increase incomes for local people.

9 Conclusion

Tourism has been identified as a key sector to develop local economic sector, including the mission of poverty alleviation in Vietnam and Thua Thien Hue province. With a diversified system of traditional craft villages playing an important role in the socioeconomic life of local people, especially in rural and agricultural areas, Thua Thien Hue is considered to have an indirect advantage in using handicraft-based tourism for poverty reduction purpose. By using the traditional Bao La bamboo-rattan weaving village, this study has systematized the poverty rationales and approaches about poverty, then discovered the perception of local people about poverty and examined the interrelationships between handicraft-based tourism and poverty alleviation through understanding the pro-poor direct and indirect effects.

The perception and measurement of poverty shift from single-dimensional to multidimensional approach globally. Poverty is no longer understood only in terms of income poverty. Beside lack of income, multidimensional poverty approach is built up to overcome the shortcomings in measuring poverty of single-dimension approach by combining several indicators of insufficient levels of basic social services—such as health, education, and inadequate living standard.

Adaptation and application of new MPI of Vietnamese government from 2016 are considered as new development step in the struggle to reduce poverty in Vietnam. However, this study shows that it is still in the early stage and limited. While the Vietnamese government considers poverty as a multidimensional issue that includes aspects of basic social services, the income index is still the main important indicator, which is used commonly for local people to perceive poverty. The application of non-income indicators of the new MPI, which is used to define and measure poverty, will changes the poverty rate significantly and also poses many challenges to the implementation and measurement processes. Moreover, changing perceptions of local people and authorities about poverty from traditional way to multidimensional way at all levels of regions and localities is one of the most challenging steps.

In addition, with a relational approach to poverty, poverty can be also considered as a multidimensional effect that performs in social relations. There is a strong relationship among poverty reduction, social inequality, and economic growth. Moreover, this study also indicated that social exclusion was another consequence from social processes that continued to produce forms of poverty and inequality in the long term. The ability to find jobs is limited by the access level of education, income inequality between gender and age, or the ability to deal with risks of health service and living standards are examples.

The ways of defining poverty hold an important implication for measuring and giving solutions for poverty reduction. Because people still recognize poverty as 'lack of income' and money is considered as a tool to satisfy their basic needs, therefore, the first key action should be taken to perform the poverty reduction mission is to increase their income.

Tourism's pro-poor impacts are different among various locals and through variety pathways. The case of Bao La shows that although geographical limitations and lack of tourism connections are considered as factors that impede the direct participations of villagers and then limit the direct effects from tourism, local people still benefit from tourism significantly by participating in handicraft production to serve tourism demands indirectly.

While the heavy dependence on agriculture and elderly is the main cause and common characteristic of poverty, the particularly high indirect contributions in terms of providing working opportunities and increasing income in Bao La village, especially for middle-aged women and elderly suggest the potential substantial contribution of handicraft-based tourism for poverty alleviation. Besides, while gender inequality in Vietnam rural areas is one of the reasons of social exclusion related closely to poverty, the case of Bao La village showed that tourism indirectly contributed to reduce poverty by providing opportunities and increasing benefits and entitlements for women. Moreover, collective organizations such as a Co-operative is necessary and plays an important role in the process of transformation and orientation of handicraft production to serve tourism demand for craft villages. Although the Co-operative under the support from the government also indirectly reproduces poverty through creating production distance with producing households, its greater pro-poor impacts in playing the role as representative organization for the village, providing jobs with higher income, developing markets, and inking the village with tourism are undeniable.

Although there are potentials for development by owning a diverse system of traditional craft villages, handicraft-based tourism in Bao La and Thua Thien Hue in general are still in the early stages and its pro-poor impacts are still recognized mainly in terms of economic. Currently, the case of Bao La showed that craft villages just played their roles in production of handicraft products for serving the direct and indirect tourism's demands, they were still not a type of tourism or provide true tourism experiences.

Strengthening linkages between local community and tourism is an effective way to enhance pro-poor tourism because it is directly involved in building the connections between tourism and the poor. However, the current connection between Bao La and tourism is weak. The Co-operative is the only chain link that has the participation of the poor in the current tourism value chain. Moreover, there is a need of proposed suggestions to promote the key role of the management board in linking tour operators with the village, improving the participations of local people, especially the poor in the tourism value chain, and developing potential local service suppliers in order to enhance pro-poor impacts and develop handicraft-based tourism.

References

[1] ALKIRE S, CONCONI A, ROCHE J M. Multidimensional poverty index 2012: Brief methodological note and results [M]. Oxford: University of Oxford, Department of International Development, Oxford Poverty and Human Development Initiative, 2012.

[2] ASHLEY C, MITCHELL J. Assessing how tourism revenues reach the poor: Findings from the application of innovative diagnostic tools offer new ways to understand and boost revenues from tourism for the poor [J]. ODI briefing paper, 2007 (21).

[3] BAULCH B, MCCULLOCH N. Being poor and becoming poor: Poverty status and poverty transitions in rural Pakistan [J]. Journal of Asian and African studies, 2002, 37 (2): 168-185.

[4] DHAKAL S. Getting into and out of poverty: An exploration of poverty dynamics in eastern Tarai, Nepal [J]. Studies in Nepali history and society, 2015, 20 (1): 137-167.

[5] GASCÓN J. Pro-poor tourism as a strategy to fight rural poverty: A critique [J]. Journal of agrarian change, 2015, 15 (4): 499-518.

[6] HOLDEN A. Tourism, poverty and development [M]. New York: Routledge, 2013.

[7] HOLDEN A, SONNE J, NOVELLI M. Tourism and poverty reduction: An interpretation by the poor of Elmina, Ghana [J]. Tourism planning & development, 2011, 8 (3): 317-334.

[8] ICA. International cooperative alliance statement of the co-operative identity [EB/OL]. [2019-12-01]. http://www.wisc.edu/uwcc/icic/issues/prin/21-cent/identity.html.

[9] MAYOUX L, CHAMBERS R. Reversing the paradigm: Quantification, participatory methods and pro-poor impact assessment [J]. Journal of international development, 2005, 17 (2): 271-298.

[10] MITCHELL J, ASHLEY C. Can tourism offer pro-poor pathways to prosperity? Examining evidence on the impact of tourism on poverty [J]. ODI briefing paper, 2007 (22).

[11] MOSSE D. A relational approach to durable poverty, inequality and power [J]. The journal of development studies, 2010, 46 (7): 1156-1178.

[12] NGUYEN M D. Characteristics of agricultural cooperatives and its service performance in Bac Ninh province, Vietnam. [J]. Journal of ISSAAS (International society for southeast Asian agricultural sciences), 2011, 17 (1): 68-79.

[13] TRAN Q N, LE D, DO V H, et al. Analyzing benefits of agricultural cooperative. Case study of long Tuyen cooperative, Binh Thuy, can Tho city [J]. Scientific journals, 2012: 283-293.

印度尼西亚巴厘岛旅游专业人才培养

I Gusti Ayu Oka Suryawardani；Agung Suryawan Wiranatha

印度尼西亚乌达雅纳大学

1 引言

众所周知，巴厘岛是世界闻名的旅游目的地，每年吸引数百万来自世界各地的游客，但是仍然需要继续提升我们的旅游服务。20世纪70年代，巴厘岛的旅游业得到了蓬勃发展，游客们陆续来到巴厘岛观光。2005年以后，来巴厘岛旅游的人更是急剧增加，每年大约增长15%。

2 巴厘岛的旅游发展

2016—2017年，巴厘岛的十大客源国中排在第一位的是澳大利亚，其次是中国。2017年和2018年，中国取代澳大利亚，成为巴厘岛的第一大客源国。对比2004—2014年巴厘岛和印度尼西亚外国游客的停留时间及消费可以发现，外国游客通常在印度尼西亚停留7～10天，但是在巴厘岛停留的时间会更长一些，一般是9～10天。游客在巴厘岛的消费也高于在印度尼西亚的平均消费水平。由此可以发现，巴厘岛在印度尼西亚的旅游发展中发挥着非常重要的作用，所以更需要旅游专业人才来助力巴厘岛和印度尼西亚的旅游发展。

旅游业带来的经济收益不仅提高了巴厘岛的整体生产总值，也提升了当地居民的家庭收入。巴厘岛的旅游竞争力在于其独特的文化，它是一个艺术和文化遗产丰富的岛屿，其中宗教文化更是根深蒂固，巴厘岛有上千座寺庙，寺庙每天都举办文化活动。巴厘岛的沙滩也吸引了大量游客，很多人喜欢在这里享受阳光。巴厘岛的自然风光和景观也是非常重要的吸引物，当然游客在这里也可以参加很多节庆活动，这些节庆活动几乎每天都有举办。

3. 乌达雅纳大学的旅游硕博专业

乌达雅纳大学的旅游硕博专业正逐渐成为巴厘岛和印度尼西亚旅游专业人才培养的"高地",通过研究和教育来培养旅游专业人才非常重要。为了进一步促进巴厘岛旅游业发展,我们需要牢记三件事:第一,注重人才培养;第二,重视酒店服务业;第三,提高英语能力。最后,为了更好地理解游客,掌握专业的知识和技能以及友好的服务态度也是非常重要的。

乌达雅纳大学的博士项目始于2010年,现在已有39名毕业生,包括完成乌达雅纳大学和法国巴黎第一大学双博士学位课程的学生。我是第一个从该博士项目毕业的学生,在乌达雅纳大学和法国巴黎第一大学分别读了两年。乌达雅纳大学的旅游硕士专业始于2001年,目前已有700名毕业生,其中有10名毕业生完成了乌达雅纳大学与巴黎第一大学或法国昂热大学的双学位。2010—2015年,乌达雅纳大学和法国之间有双学位专业,印度尼西亚和法国政府都为这一项目提供奖学金,法国政府主要提供学费,印度尼西亚政府提供生活补贴。我们还和澳大利亚格里菲斯大学合作开设了旅游硕士和国际旅游与酒店管理硕士的双学位专业。

2010年至今,乌达雅纳大学还开设了旅游硕士联合项目。有来自法国昂热大学的学生,今年有一个,去年有两个。我相信未来会有更多的学生来这个专业就读。

另外一个已经发布的双学位是指澳大利亚格里菲斯大学旅游硕士和国际旅游与酒店管理硕士。印度尼西亚技术研究和高等教育部已经批准了这一项目。这个项目将于2020年4月启动,就读该项目的学生将在乌达雅纳大学旅游学院接受为期一年的硕士研究生教育,然后在澳大利亚格里菲斯大学再学习一年。

4 乌达雅纳大学的旅游专业

乌达雅纳大学的旅游专业是印度尼西亚旅游教育的翘楚,与其他项目相比,旅游专业的优势如下:首先,在教育方面涵盖了3个层次,即S1(本科)、S2(硕士)和S3(博士);其次,在研究方面,印度尼西亚教育文化部在我们学校出资设立了一个研究中心——卓越旅游研究中心(Centre of Excellence in Tourism);第三,旅游专业以文化为发展基础,同时吸取地方智慧,这也与乌达雅纳大学的愿景一致。最后,我们的项目借鉴了所有与旅游相关的技能资源,如经济、管理、文化、环境、健康、建筑、规划、农业和畜牧业,以整体的方式评估旅游业的发展。

旅游专业的培养目标是培养在旅游领域具有专业知识和能力并符合资格认证的硕士和博士毕业生。具体人才培养目标如下:第一,成为掌握旅游科学的专业学者;第二,有能力将旅游科学知识应用于社会实践;第三,能够向公众传播研究成果;第四,能够对旅游发展问题进行全面研究;第五,成为一名在旅游领域具有创造力并善于合作的毕业生。

乌达雅纳大学旅游教育专业的愿景和乌达雅纳大学的愿景一致,即建设一个卓越、独立和具有文化底蕴的研究生院。这具体包括4项使命。首先,我们的目标是建立一个基于地方智慧的学习系统,通过信息通信技术和质量保障系统支撑,培养独立、优秀的旅游专业硕士生和博士生。其次,我们致力于培养在旅游学领域具有学术研究能力的人才。再次,我们要为旅游业的发展提供创新型人才。最后,我们希望与地方、国家和国际的各级政府和民间机构建立伙伴关系,以提高社区发展的能力与参与度。

乌达雅纳大学的毕业生应具有《印度尼西亚国家教育资历框架》要求的能力,应当学会求知、学会做事、学会做人和学会共处(联合国教科文组织提出的未来教育的四大支柱)。我们的博士教育项目的具体课程如下:热点问题探讨、文化旅游、旅游分析方法、科学哲学、旅游研究方法、文化研究、旅游业、科学写作方法、旅游规划与开发、旅游经济、旅游消费者行为学以及旅游营销与传播。我们的硕士项目课程包括可持续旅游、文化遗产旅游、旅游营销、旅游研究方法、社区旅游、科学哲学、旅游创业、定量研究方法、旅游经济、旅游社会学,以及旅游法、数字旅游、旅游人力资源和旅游规划4个选修课。我们认为硕博旅游教育项目会成为巴厘岛及印度尼西亚旅游专业人才的主要培养途径。

5 结论

巴厘岛是世界著名的旅游目的地,拥有美丽的自然风光、温暖的气候和丰富的文化遗产。过去10年里,巴厘岛的旅游发展尤为迅速,近两年中国游客的到访数和旅游消费均排名第一。为了给游客提供更好的旅游体验,巴厘岛急需高端旅游人才。因此,旅游专业的硕士和博士培养必不可少。乌达雅纳大学是印度尼西亚旅游教育的典型代表,开设了各种实用而有趣的课程,具有远大的旅游教育愿景。当然,要实现为巴厘岛和印度尼西亚培养充足的高端旅游人才这一目标,我们还有很长的路要走。

Preparing Scientific-Based Professionals in Tourism for Bali Indonesia

I Gusti Ayu Oka Suryawardani and Agung Suryawan Wiranatha

Udayana University, Indonesia

1 Introduction

First of all, I would like to express my gratitude to Professor Xu, who has invited me to come here to this nice conference. The title of my presentation is preparing scientific-based professionals in tourism for Bali and Indonesia. As everyone knows, Bali, a really famous destination in the world, attracts several millions of tourists from all over the world every year, but we still need to improve our performance to be better next time. Tourism in Bali has developed significantly, in 1970s, there was a tourism boom in Bali, which meant tourists started to come to Bali. After 2005, the number of tourists coming to Bali has increased dramatically, about fifteen percent a year.

2 Tourism in Bali

The graph displays the best ten direct foreign tourist arrivals to Bali in 2016 – 2017, the first rank is Australian, and the second rank is Chinese. In 2017 and 2018, the Chinese stay in the first rank. We can also see the length of stay and expenditure of tourists in Bali and Indonesia from 2004 to 2014, foreign tourists usually stay 7 to 10 days in Indonesia, but for Bali, the length of stay is a little longer, which is 9 to 11 days, and the expenditure of foreign tourists in Bali is also higher than the average Indonesia level. We can conclude that Bali plays a really important role in the development of Indonesia tourism, and there is a need of professionals to manage the tourism development in Bali and Indonesia.

We can see that the economic benefits of tourism, not only making up most of the GDP of Bali, but also supporting family income in Bali. The competitiveness of

Bali tourism lies in the unique cultural-based tourism. Bali is an island abound with rich art and cultural heritage, among which religious culture is entrenched in the blood of Bali. As you can see from the picture, there are thousands of temples in Bali. Activities related to culture happen nearly every day. Beaches in Bali also appeal to tourists, lots of people come here to enjoy the beach and sun. Natural scenery and landscape in Bali are also powerful draws for tourists. You can also watch lots of festivals, which are on show almost every day.

3 Master and Doctoral Program in Tourism Udayana University

Master and Doctoral Program in Tourism Udayana University is becoming the main source of human resources preparation for tourism professionals in Bali and Indonesia. Preparing scientific-based professionals in tourism is really important, mainly through research and education. To further the development of tourism in Bali, we need to keep three things in mind. Firstly, we need to focus on human resource development. Secondly, hospitality is also really important in tourism industry. Thirdly, we need to improve English capability as well, without English capability, we can't do well in hospitality. And lastly, to understand tourists' behavior, it is really important to master knowledge, skill, and take friendly attitude. It is significant for us to understand what they need and want in destinations.

Next, I will talk about Master and Doctoral Program in my university. There are the Doctoral and Master programs. The Doctoral program was established in 2010, we already have 39 graduates, including graduates who had finished the Double Degree Program in Doctoral Degree between Udayana University and Sorbonne Universite Paris 1 in France. I am the first graduate from the Doctoral Program, and I did my Double Degree two years in Udayana University and two years in Sorbonne Universite Paris 1 in France. Meanwhile, the Master Program in Tourism Udayana University was established in 2001. We have 700 graduates already, including 10 graduates who had finished the Double Degree Program between Udayana University and Sorbonne Universite Paris 1 and Universite de Angers in France. From 2010 to 2015, there were also Double Degree Program between Udayana University and France, which just finished yet. Indonesia and France government both offered scholarship for this program, the France government mainly provided intuition fees, and the Indonesia government offered living allowance. We also have the Double Degree Program between Udayana

University and Master Degree in Tourism and Master in International Tourism and Hospitality Management of Griffith University in Australia.

We also have Joint certificate for undertaking one semester in the Master Program in Tourism Udayana University, since 2010 up to now. We have lots of students from Angers Uni France, at the moment we have one, last year we have two, in the future I believe there will be more.

Another Double Degree Program has been released between the Master Program in Tourism and Master of International Tourism and Hospitality Management of Griffith University Australia. The Ministry of Research Technology and Higher Education of Republic of Indonesia has already given the permit to undertake this program. This program will be started in April 2020. Students who take this program will undertake one year study at Master Degree in Tourism Udayana University and one year study at Griffith University Australia.

4 Tourism Program in Udayana University

Tourism program in Udayana University is a leading program in Indonesia, which is multidisciplinary. Our tourism study program is an excellent program compared with other programs. The main reasons are as follows. Firstly, in education aspects, the linear covers three strata, namely S1 (Undergraduate), S2 (Master), and S3 (Doctorate). Secondly, in the field of research, the University has the Centre of Excellence in Tourism, which is a leading center of research supported by the Ministry of Education and Culture, the Republic of Indonesia. Thirdly, the tourism program is characterized by a local wisdom that is universal characteristic, using culture as basis for development in accordance with the vision of Udayana University. And finally, the tourism program uses all skill resources related to tourism, such as economic, management, culture, environment, health, architecture, planning, agriculture, and animal husbandry, which has a mission to assess the development of tourism in a holistic manner.

Here are our program objectives and graduate profile, we aim to cultivate master and doctorate graduates who have the expertise and competence in the field of tourism with qualification standards. The concrete graduate profile are as follows. Firstly, as an accomplished scholar who masters the science of tourism. Secondly, as a researcher in the field of tourism with the ability to develop and apply science in the community. Thirdly, as a graduate who has the ability to disseminate research results to the general public. Fourthly, as a graduate who has the ability to conduct scientific studies of tourism development issues in an integral manner. And finally, as a graduate who possess creativity in the field of tourism and is able to cooperate with other parties.

Next is our vision and science mission. The vision of our tourism program is an integral part of the vision of Udayana University, which is to become a graduate school of excellence, independent and cultured. There are four concrete missions. Firstly, we aim to develop a learning system based on local wisdom that is supported by communication and information technology as well as adequate quality assurance system that is able to produce a superior tourism master and doctorate, independent and cultured. Secondly, we are devoted to produce human resources who have academic ability in the field of tourism studies. Thirdly, we want to produce human resources in innovative and creative research for the development of tourism. And finally, we wish to develop the partnership with various government and private institutions locally, nationally and internationally, which is aim to improve the capacity and participation in community development.

Our graduates are expected to have competency in accordance with the Indonesian National Qualification Framework and education in accordance with the four pillars of UNESCO, which are as follows, learning to know, learning to do, learning to be, and learning to live together. Here are the detailed curriculums of our doctoral course program, there are current issues, cultural tourism, tourism analysis methodology, philosophy of science, tourism research methodology, cultural studies, dimensions of tourism, methodology of scientific writing, tourism planning and development, tourism economy, tourism consumer behavior, and marketing and communication in tourism. Our curriculums of master course program include sustainable tourism, cultural and heritage tourism, tourism marketing, research methods in tourism, community-based tourism, philosophy of science, tourism entrepreneurship, quantitative research method, tourism economy, tourism sociology, and four electives, which are tourism law, digital tourism, tourism human resource and tourism planning. So we can finally conclude that the master and doctoral program is to become main sources of human resources preparation for tourism professionals in Bali and Indonesia.

5 Conclusion

Bali, a world-famous tourism destination, enjoying beautiful natural scenery, warm climate and rich cultural heritage, attracts several millions of tourists from all over the world every year, especially in the last decade. Among all the tourists, the Chinese ranked first in terms of tourists' arrivals and expenditures in recent two years. To offer better tourism experience for tourists, there is a need for high-end education talents. So master and doctoral program in tourism is integral. Udayana University is a typical representative in tourism education in Indonesia, which provides various kinds of useful and interesting courses, and has a very ambitious vision for tourism education. But to fully achieve the aim of training ample high-end tourism talents for Bali and Indonesia, there is still a long way to go. Udayana University has done much excellent work, and we believe that in the future, it will continue to lead the tourism education development in Bali and Indonesia.

粤港澳暨东盟旅游研究与教育论坛宣言

2019年10月31日至11月1日，粤港澳暨东盟旅游研究与教育论坛在广州顺利举办。论坛上各方认为，需要共同的观点和共同的原则，以激励和促进该区域的大学和研究所的旅游研究与教育的交流合作与提升。

宣言如下：

1. 有关各方应寻求发展学术和教育合作，促进相互理解。

2. 有关各方应寻求在平等和互惠的基础上，在共同感兴趣的学术领域开展以下合作活动：

（1）学术人员和行政人员的交流；

（2）学生交流；

（3）开展合作研究项目；

（4）举办讲座和研讨会；

（5）学术信息和资料的交流；

（6）促进共同感兴趣的领域的合作；

（7）促进双方同意的其他学术合作。

3. 基于本宣言的具体活动的开展将由负责具体项目的大学或研究所协商和商定，并以书面协议为准。经充分协商，有关各方将根据各自国家的法律法规开展这些活动。

4. 可以理解的是，第2条中规定的任何类型的合作的实施应取决于相关方的资源可用性和财政支持。

5. 有关各方同意，在任何广告或相关宣传中使用另一方的名称、徽标或其他知识产权之前，需要事先获得书面批准。

6. 如果本声明项下的合作研究活动产生任何潜在的知识产权，各方应就可能产生的所有权和其他财产利益寻求公平和公正的协议。

Declaration of the Tourism Research and Education Forum of Guangdong – Hong Kong – Macau and ASEAN

The Tourism Research and Education Forum of Guangdong – Hong Kong – Macau and ASEAN, which is held at Guangzhou from 31 October to 1 November 2019, has considered the need for a common outlook and for common principles to inspire and guide the universities and institutes of the region in the communication and enhancement of tourism research and education.

Proclaims that:

1. Relevant parties shall seek to develop academic and educational cooperation and promote mutual understanding.

2. Relevant parties shall seek to develop the following collaborative activities in the academic areas of mutual interest, on a basis of equality and reciprocity.

1) Exchange of academic and administrative staff
2) Exchange of students
3) Conducting collaborative research projects
4) Conducting lectures and organizing symposia
5) Exchange of academic information and materials
6) Promoting collaboration in fields of mutual interest
7) Promoting other academic cooperation as mutually agreed

3. The development and implementation of specific activities based on this declaration will be separately negotiated and agreed between universities or institutes which carry out the specific projects and will be subject to a separate written agreement. Relevant parties agree to carry out these activities in accordance with the laws and regulations of the respective countries after full consultation and approval.

4. It is understood that the implementation of any types of co-operation stated in Clause 2 shall depend upon the availability of resources and financial support of the parties concerned.

5. Relevant parties agree that prior written approval is required before using the other party's name, logo, or other intellectual property rights in any advertising or

associated publicity.

6. If the collaborative research activities under this declaration result in any potential for intellectual property, each party shall seek an equitable and fair agreement as to ownership and other property interests that may arise.